Ethics of Belonging

New Southeast Asia

Politics, Meaning, and Memory

Justin McDaniel and Nancy J. Smith-Hefner

Series Editors

Ethics of Belonging

Education, Religion, and Politics in Manado, Indonesia

ERICA M. LARSON

UNIVERSITY OF HAWAI'I PRESS
HONOLULU

© 2024 University of Hawaiʻi Press
All rights reserved
Paperback edition 2024

Printed in the United States of America

First printed, 2024

Library of Congress Cataloging-in-Publication Data

Names: Larson, Erica M., author.
Title: Ethics of belonging : education, religion, and politics in Manado, Indonesia / Erica M. Larson.
Other titles: New Southeast Asia.
Description: Honolulu : University of Hawaiʻi Press, [2023] | Series: New Southeast Asia: politics, meaning, and memory | Includes bibliographical references and index.
Identifiers: LCCN 2023023171 | ISBN 9780824894436 (hardback) | ISBN 9780824896256 (epub) | ISBN 9780824896263 (kindle edition) | ISBN 9780824896249 (pdf)
Subjects: LCSH: Religion and civil society—Indonesia—Manado. | Religious pluralism—Indonesia—Manado. | Belonging (Social psychology)—Indonesia—Manado. | Religion in the public schools—Indonesia—Manado. | Manado (Indonesia)—Religion—21st century.
Classification: LCC BL2120.C4 L37 2023 | DDC 201/.720959842—dc23/eng20230914
LC record available at https://lccn.loc.gov/2023023171

ISBN 9780824899134 (paperback)

Cover photo: Students at Lokon School raise the Indonesian flag during the Flag Ceremony (*Upacara Bendera*)

University of Hawaiʻi Press books are printed on acid-free paper and meet the guidelines for permanence and durability of the Council on Library Resources.

CONTENTS

Acknowledgments   vii
Note on Language   ix
Figures   xi
Abbreviations   xiii

1 Introduction: Deliberating the Ethics of Belonging   1
2 Religion, Nation, and Politics of Difference through the Lens of Education   30
3 Public High School: Influence of the Protestant Majority   65
4 Private Catholic High School: Developing Faith and Character to Develop the Nation   95
5 Public Madrasah: Islamic Discipline as the Foundation of Civic Deliberation   125
6 Interreligious Exchange: A Pedagogical Project of Ethics across Borders   155
7 Going Public: Scaling Deliberation about Belonging   179
8 Conclusion: Pluralized Ethics for a Plural Society   200

Notes   213
Works Cited   217
Index   231

ACKNOWLEDGMENTS

This research project and the resulting book would not have been possible without the students, teachers, administrators, and friends in Manado and Tomohon who let me into their schools and into their lives. A special thanks is in order for Ibu Mary and Pak Ronald, and all of the teachers, staff, and students at Lokon St. Nikolaus Catholic School, which became my home for the duration of my fieldwork. I am also very appreciative of the teachers and students at MAN Model Manado and SMANSA Manado. In addition, I am grateful for the university students who were my coparticipants in the Pertukaran Mahasiswa Lintas Agama at the STF-SP and who were willing to openly share their experience with me during the program.

I am also sincerely indebted to the many scholars, activists, *budayawan*, religious leaders, and friends in North Sulawesi who have supported my research in various ways. My research was made possible through the sponsorship and support of my local research counterpart, Professor Sjamsi Pasandaran, and the Civic Education department at Universitas Negeri Manado. Fellow scholars at other area universities, including IAIN, UKIT, and UNSRAT, have also been important conversation partners. The Mawale Movement and its enthusiastic members have also given me *semangat* for understanding the cultural dynamism of Minahasa. While I am not able to name all of these colleagues and friends here, I would like to briefly mention Muhammad Iqbal Suma, Denni Pinontoan, Rahman Mantu, Almunauwar Bin Rusli, Nono Sumampouw, Rinto Taroreh, Ruth Wangkai, Fredy Wowor, and Sofyan Jimmy Yosadi.

Terima kasih banyak to my Indonesian-language teachers at SEASSI, especially Ibu Amelia Liwe, who piqued my interest in Manado and introduced me to contacts there. Grace Nelwan and Maria Walukow have been such important guides and friends as well. Also, I am very appreciative of John Soucy and Mary Heather White for providing quiet places for me to write and think, but most of all, for sharing their friendship.

This project began during my time at Boston University, and I am honored and grateful to have had Bob Hefner as my advisor and mentor throughout the process. I also appreciate the mentorship and comments from Nancy Smith-Hefner, Kimberly Arkin, and Merav Shohet. This project has continued and evolved during my time at the Asia Research Institute, National University of Singapore. Here I have benefitted from the feedback of Kenneth Dean and my colleagues in the Religion and Globalisation Cluster on portions of the manuscript. Funding for my research was secured from multiple sources: a Wenner-Gren Foundation Dissertation Fieldwork Grant, a Boston University Graduate Research Abroad Fellowship, a Global Religion Research Initiative Fellowship, and a USINDO Society Travel Grant.

I am grateful to my series editors at the University of Hawai'i Press, Justin McDaniel and Nancy J. Smith-Hefner, and to executive editor Masako Ikeda for their guidance throughout the publication process. In addition, comments provided by the reviewers at the peer-review stage proved extremely useful in improving the manuscript. It goes without saying, however, that any and all faults that remain are my own.

I am extremely thankful that my family and friends have continued to provide motivation and moral support. Finally, I could never have completed this book without the unwavering support of my partner and colleague Michel Chambon, who has seen the project evolve over time and has been an ongoing source of inspiration and encouragement.

NOTE ON LANGUAGE

Words in Indonesian (Bahasa Indonesia) are designated by italics, except for proper nouns. Words in Manadonese (referred to as Bahasa Manado or Melayu Manado), a local form of Malay, are also italicized with the qualifier "Manado" preceding the italicized words. All translations from these languages are my own, unless otherwise specified.

FIGURES

Figure 1.1	Map of North Sulawesi (excluding Sangihe and Talaud islands)	4
Figure 1.2	Jesus Bless Monument (Monumen Yesus Memberkati) in Manado	12
Figure 3.1	Protestant students from SMA sing praise songs under a tent at a weekend retreat	66
Figure 3.2	Islamic education classroom at SMA	76
Figure 3.3	Restaurant sign claiming "1000% Non-halal"	85
Figure 4.1	Lokon students participate in the Flag Ceremony (*Upacara Bendera*)	104
Figure 4.2	Students in Catholic religious education at Lokon	121
Figure 5.1	Madrasah students perform a nationalist song	126
Figure 5.2	Newly refurbished mosque at MAN	132
Figure 5.3	MAN students take turns reciting for the Khataman Al-Qur'an event	138
Figure 6.1	Muslim and Protestant exchange program participants pose with Catholic seminarians in a chapel at the Sacred Heart Seminary	159
Figure 6.2	Exchange program participants eat in the cafeteria among seminarians	170
Figure 7.1	Governor Olly Dondokambey inducts new members into the FKUB in 2016	184

ABBREVIATIONS

Aliansi Makapetor:	Aliansi Masyarakat Kawanua yang Peduli Toleransi (Alliance of Minahasans Who Care about Tolerance)
BKSAUA:	Badan Kerja Sama Antar Umat Beragama (Committee for Interreligious Cooperation)
BMI:	Brigade Manguni Indonesia
FKUB:	Forum Kerukunan Umat Beragama (Interreligious Harmony Forum)
FPI:	Front Pembela Islam (Islamic Defenders Front)
GMIM:	Gereja Masehi Injili di Minahasa (Christian Evangelical Church in Minahasa)
HTI:	Hizbut Tahrir Indonesia
IAIN:	Institut Agama Islam Negeri (State Islamic Institute [of Higher Education])
JAJAK:	Jaringan Kerja Kasih (Labor of Love Network)
Kemendikbud:	Kementerian Pendidikan dan Kebudayaan (Ministry of Education and Culture)
KGPM:	Kerapatan Gereja Protestan Minahasa (Union of Minahasan Protestant Churches)
KKN:	*korupsi, kolusi, nepotisme* (corruption, collusion, nepotism)
Komnas HAM:	Komisi Nasional Hak Asasi Manusia (National Commission on Human Rights)
KPK:	Komisi Pemberantasan Korupsi (Corruption Eradication Commission)
KTSP:	Kurikulum Tingkat Satuan Pendidikan (School-Based Curriculum)
MAN:	Madrasah Aliyah Negeri (State madrasah [senior secondary level])
MPR:	Majelis Permusyawaratan Rakyat (People's Consultative Assembly)
MUI:	Majelis Ulama Indonesia (Indonesian Council of Ulama)

NU:	Nahdlatul Ulama
NZG:	Nederlandsch Zendeling Genootschap (Netherlands Missionary Society)
OSIS:	Organisasi Siswa Intra Sekolah (Student Council Organization)
P4:	Pedoman Penghayatan dan Pengalaman Pancasila (Training for the Application and Realization of Pancasila)
PKn:	Pendidikan Kewarganegaraan (Citizenship Education)
PMP:	Pendidikan Moral Pancasila (Pancasila Moral Education)
PPKn:	Pendidikan Pancasila dan Kewarganegaraan (Pancasila and Citizenship Education)
Rohis:	Rohani Islam (Muslim Students' Club)
Rohkris:	Rohani Kristen (Christian [Protestant] Students' Club)
SARA:	*suku, agama, ras, dan antar-golongan* (ethnicity, religion, race, and intergroup relations)
STAKN:	Sekolah Tinggi Agama Kristen Negeri (State Christian [Protestant] School [of Higher Education])

Ethics of Belonging

1

Introduction
Deliberating the Ethics of Belonging

During their afternoon civic education lesson, tenth-grade Muslim students in the public madrasah[1] of the Protestant-majority city of Manado, Indonesia, discussed the topic of diversity. The teacher, Ibu Aisyah,[2] stood in front of her class, enthusiastically leading them through the material despite it being the last period of the school day. Students sitting at wooden desks fanned themselves with their notebooks in the afternoon heat as she proclaimed: "Diversity [*keanekaragaman*] is part of Indonesia. Indonesia is extremely plural [*majemuk*] in terms of religion, tradition, culture—but these are all together in one . . . Imagine if everything were just one color. Can you imagine if everything were just white? That's boring! If there's a little red, green, and white, that's beautiful! Variation interests our eyes; it's what makes a beautiful and interesting view. Inshallah, the rest of the world will also see this as interesting." One student, Muhammad, had already voiced his conviction that Indonesia must value diversity, as the country's standing in the international community hinges on its ability to do so. Others had nodded and echoed this sentiment, repeating the imperative that Indonesians must respect difference.

However, Ibu Aisyah's follow-up question about *how* they can respect diversity and promote national unity as Indonesian citizens proved more difficult for the students to answer. Though intended to check their understanding of the material, her question has more significance than a simple textbook exercise with a predetermined answer. Indeed, the same question has become increasingly relevant in the public sphere as debates about religious and national belonging are waged in Indonesia. The problematic of maintaining national cohesion has surged to the fore with diverging visions of nation, each relying on a particular approach toward religious difference and a framework for coexistence. In the midst of these debates, one necessary measure to ensure the future integrity of the multireligious and multiethnic nation emerges as unanimous: Indonesian youth must be taught the importance of respecting and appreciating difference.

As the relationship between religion and nation and the accompanying frameworks for accommodating religious pluralism remain unsettled, schools have faced increasing pressure to shape both religiously devout and inclusive citizens, stressing a discourse of unity and coherence in a society where religious belonging is imbued with increasing social and political significance. This book aims to elucidate how schools are central sites for deliberation about the ethics and politics of coexistence and belonging in the national project.

Back in the classroom as students struggled to respond to the question, a couple of hesitant suggestions were met with critical laughter from fellow students. "We can use technology to help us?" a student named Wahyu proposed, her transformation of a statement into a question belying her uncertainty. Another's tentative remark that in order to respect difference, we must "pay attention to difference" (*memperhatikan perbedaan*) was equally sanctioned with muffled laughter. Finally, Ibu Aisyah praised Rifqi, who argued that in order to respect diversity, Indonesians must simultaneously protect the unity and integrity of the nation. As they quickly made the connection, several students spontaneously recited the national motto, "Unity in Diversity" (*Bhinneka Tunggal Ika*).

As the question of how to maintain cohesion is being raised with increasing vigor in modern plural societies, I contend that it is important to ask not only what schools teach about diversity, but how educational institutions become sites of deliberation about belonging. The question of how to approach difference and construct belonging on various levels scaling up to and including the national framework is an inherently ethical one, necessarily accompanied by ideologies and practices of inclusion and exclusion. Within the process of ethical socialization, schools are important institutions that aim to socialize citizens into particular national frameworks, encoding perspectives on difference and belonging through the negotiation and interpretation of the government-mandated curriculum. In addition, schools put forth understandings of difference through their own policies and attitudes toward dealing with diversity. However, this is not the end of the educational process—with knowledge and dispositions simply stamped onto student subjectivities—but only just the beginning.

Rather than locating schools as institutions within a faithful process of social reproduction, I emphasize the contingency of the educational process and the "deliberation" that occurs therein (Varenne 2007). Firstly, education must be considered as a multicentered process in which schools, while clearly important sites of socialization, are only one of many spheres of influence. Secondly, education does not proceed unidirectionally, as discourses about belonging—and the ethical positioning that accompanies them—do not end at the school or with the individuals who encounter them. Viewed through the lens of ethical reflection and drawing on an understanding of "reflective freedom" as central to ethical life (Laidlaw 2014, 177), the process of education is instead understood in this case as deliberation about ethical frameworks for approaching religious coexistence in a plural society.

Considering education as an ongoing process of negotiation rather than one of teleological reproduction opens up the conceptual possibility for understanding its broader connection to public ethical culture beyond simply providing context or framing. This approach, broadening the typical view of educational institutions, highlights their importance in ethical socialization in conjunction with other institutions and interactions at multiple levels. With the understanding that there is no singular foundation for ethics and ethical reasoning, I take schools as a point of departure for locating the ethical frameworks of religious difference that are channeled through them, both connecting schools to their broader political context and considering how the frameworks they circulate become grounded in subjectivities. This connection ultimately allows for a consideration of how ethical streams channeled through institutions and negotiated by the individuals and groups who constitute them can contribute to the formation of a public ethical culture regarding the question of who belongs and how to coexist.

RELIGION AND BELONGING IN MANADO, NORTH SULAWESI

The Protestant-majority province of North Sulawesi and its capital city, Manado, claim to successfully model tolerance and interreligious relations for the rest of Indonesia. The particularities of the province as a Christian stronghold that simultaneously asserts the importance of religious harmony provide an important perspective on the mediation of religious identity in the public sphere and the deliberation about the contours of plural coexistence. Part of North Sulawesi's unique position in Indonesia stems from its religious makeup when compared to the country as a whole. While 87 percent of Indonesians profess Islam and only 7 percent profess Protestant

Christianity, the majority/minority dynamics are flipped in North Sulawesi. Protestants represent over 61 percent, Muslims account for 33 percent, and Catholics are 4 percent of the province's population (Badan Pusat Statistik Sulawesi Utara 2021, 254). Hindus make up 1 percent of the provincial population, and Buddhists and Confucians together make up less than 1 percent.

North Sulawesi, with its popular motto "We Are All Brothers"[3] (Manado: *Torang Samua Basudara*), is often praised by local leaders as a model of plural coexistence for Indonesia and projects this identity at the national level. In 2017, Manado was named the most tolerant city in Indonesia, a designation celebrated among its inhabitants (Setara Institute for Democracy and Peace 2017). Discourses and performances identifying North Sulawesi in terms of its proclaimed success in religious harmony (*kerukunan beragama*) continue to circulate, framing conversations about diversity in the public sphere (Swazey 2013). Today, this important designation of North Sulawesi as a region of religious harmony fosters a local sense of purpose and identity among individuals of various religious and ethnic backgrounds.

Nonetheless, there is a lack of consensus about what guarantees peace in the region and how to secure and maintain coexistence. Furthermore,

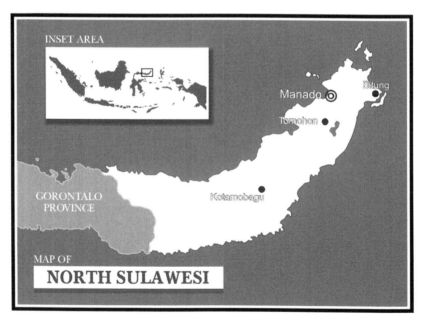

FIGURE 1.1 Map of North Sulawesi (excluding Sangihe and Talaud islands). Credit: Edhylius Sean.

ethnic identity is entangled with religious identity, as belonging to the Minahasan ethnic group (which comprises several subethnic groups) is synonymous with being Christian in the popular imagination. Yet, in reality, ethnic and religious identifications do not always overlap neatly. While many leaders and organizations praise coexistence in the province as a result of collaboration and cultural resources aimed at discouraging exclusivism, some argue that its identity as harmonious is guaranteed solely by its composition as a Christian-majority region, essentializing Christianity as a religion of love and, as a result, implicitly projecting Muslims as ethnic and religious outsiders to the region (Larson 2021).

As Indonesia ushered in a new democratic government and launched a massive decentralization campaign, ethno-religious conflicts broke out in several regions in Indonesia in the late 1990s and early 2000s, particularly in the neighboring provinces of Central Sulawesi, Maluku, and North Maluku (Sidel 2006; Wilson 2008). Significant numbers of Christian and Muslim refugees fled to Manado, and tensions ran high as many feared the region would also become embroiled in conflict (Duncan 2005). That the region was ultimately able to remain peaceful during such a turbulent time—with the help of the proactive attitude of the local government and their cooperation with community and religious leaders (Panggabean 2017)—was an important affirmation of coexistence across ethnic and religious lines. This has led to another popular local catchphrase, *"Sulut sulit disulut"* (North Sulawesi is difficult to ignite), typically indicating that Manadonese are not easily provoked into conflict, because of normative expectations of religious harmony and a tendency toward skepticism that prevents people from being drawn into divisive rumors without verification.

A network consisting of local religious leaders, intellectuals, activists, and journalists, called JAJAK (Jaringan Kerja Kasih, or Labor of Love Network), formed specifically with the goal of maintaining peaceful coexistence and resisting conflict during that time. They convinced the governor to declare both 2002 and 2003 the Year of Love, as an exhortation to maintain religious coexistence as much as to celebrate it. The monument Bukit Kasih, or the Hill of Love, was built in 2002 to enshrine religious harmony, materialized through miniature houses of worship for each of the officially recognized religions of Indonesia, set side by side against the stunning backdrop of a volcano (Thufail 2012, 365).

JAJAK produced a booklet in 2003 entitled "From North Sulawesi, We Save Indonesia," which expressed an aspiration not only to maintain peaceful coexistence but to lead the way forward as an example for the rest of the archipelago. The group praise God for maintaining peace while simultaneously admitting that the work is not done, and that the people of North Sulawesi must continue to "search for a socio-cultural mechanism with a religious foundation that is strongly rooted in the society of North Sulawesi, able to ward off violent conflicts and uphold harmony and peace" (Boroma and Alkartiri 2003).

In contemporary North Sulawesi, there remains a strong sense of pride in the province's reputation for religious harmony. While there is agreement on the importance of maintaining religious coexistence, just as for the students in the madrasah from the story above, the answer for how to do so remains more elusive. Beyond the strong efforts toward interreligious dialogue and the presence of regional organizations to facilitate dialogue and cooperation, there is little agreement about what enabled the area to avoid violent conflict and how to continue to do that in the future.

As religious belonging has come to the foreground in Indonesia more generally, there has been a strong effort to maintain a Christian-inflected public sphere in North Sulawesi through demonstrations of religiosity and political influence. Fears about the religious future of the province and about the influence of Islam, which is perceived as encroaching, shape public discussions about religious tolerance, as there is a tension between efforts to promote religious harmony and efforts to leverage the majority-Christian population to secure a strong Christian environment and influence.[4] Furthermore, many Minahasans assume causal linkages between the primarily Christian population and the history of religious harmony in the region, evoking an understanding of toleration dependent upon the goodwill of the majority, rather than the cultivation of a basis for plural belonging.

In the midst of this broad political and religious dynamic, my focus on educational institutions is intentional in its potential to demonstrate a mediation between multiple levels of analysis and societal spheres. The curriculum is developed on a national level, reflecting national concerns and normative political understandings—yet it is delivered in Manado, put into context by local teachers, and its potential resonance with students depends on their own experiences and perspectives. Furthermore, as described in chapter 2, education has the tendency to become an arena for debate about the religion-state relationship and the role of religion in public life. As various frameworks for coexistence circulate through national and local debates, they also impact the possibilities for and actual processes of ethical socialization in schools.

Observing a lack of consensus in public debates about how to respect and value difference, I began to investigate how these negotiations and deliberations extend into schools and impact the way that youth may learn about and form understandings of difference. I use this approach to demonstrate the transformative potential of these deliberations in the context of education, as schools not only disseminate and reproduce existing understandings but "scale-up" (R. W. Hefner 2021, 12) normative understandings of diversity and pluralism. This book recenters educational institutions as important and dynamic sites for understanding the relationship between interpersonal ethical deliberation and the emergence of public ethical culture.

INDONESIA'S CHALLENGES FOR UNITY IN DIVERSITY

The discussion of plural society and the possibilities for plural coexistence throughout this book focuses on the varied and divergent ethical streams in the public sphere and their ramifications for visions of nation in contemporary, democratic Indonesia. Historically, the extraordinary diversity of the Malay-Indonesian world has long attracted the attention of cultural and political observers. British civil servant and scholar J. S. Furnivall wrote of the Netherlands East Indies during the late colonial period as a prime example of a plural society, where "lack of a common will" among diverse social groups forebode instability and potential conflict (Furnivall 2010 [1939], 447). Of course, many of the social divisions noted by Furnivall materialized as a direct consequence of colonial intervention, and were subsequently leveraged to the advantage of colonial rule. Through the creation of a national project, the Indonesian archipelago has largely been able to overcome difference to maintain unity. Yet, even with a strong foundation for civic pluralism, a number of factors have posed challenges for national cohesion and religious coexistence, including more recent concerns over a climate of increasing Islamic conservatism (Van Bruinessen 2013), state repression, and democratic regression (Menchik 2019; Warburton and Aspinall 2019).

Indonesia, the world's most populous Muslim-majority country, is a multiconfessional state that recognizes six official religions.[5] Following more than three decades of authoritarian rule under President Suharto, Indonesia has since 1998 undergone a successful democratic transition and consolidation to become the third-largest democracy in the world (Künkler and Stepan 2013). Muslim intellectuals and organizations made major contributions to a public ethical culture able to support democracy, undergirded by a "civil pluralist Islam" (R. W. Hefner 2000, 12). In addition, Christian leaders have continually played important roles in supporting a nationalist project defined by a multireligious citizenship based on the national ideology of Pancasila (R. W. Hefner 2017, 99).[6] Despite the extraordinary ethnic and religious diversity across the archipelago, Indonesia managed to maintain national unity during the transition, which also entailed a massive project of decentralization to give increasing autonomy to regions outside the island of Java.

However, as mentioned above, outbreaks of sectarian and ethno-religious violence in various regions across Indonesia during the late 1990s and early 2000s have placed issues of national cohesion and management of diversity at the center of public debate, highlighting communal tensions and challenges for plural coexistence. Some analyses of these ethno-religious conflicts in Indonesia have tended to treat them as economic-resource and/or political-power grabs veiled in religious sentiments (Li 2007). Yet, others have importantly articulated that for many who experienced the violence, religion was central in how they understood and participated in or responded to the conflict (Duncan 2013, 3), and that anxieties about religious representation and threats to their religious identities impacted the evolution of violence over this period (Sidel 2006, 16). North Maluku (directly east of North Sulawesi) had previously articulated a collective identity around Christian-Muslim religious harmony, yet descended into communal violence that devastated the region (Wilson 2008). The memory of the conflict continues to organize and divide social, political, and economic life across religious lines today.

The way religion was mobilized and experienced in the communal conflicts in Indonesia indicates its important ramifications for identity, piety, and citizenship beyond the localized regions where they took place. Although the frequency and severity of large-scale conflicts have decreased, intolerance is shifting from the "radical fringe into the mainstream" (Jones 2013, 125), posing challenges for Indonesian democracy and cohesion. This book intervenes in the conversation, working to understand the ethical deliberation about religious coexistence taking place on a daily basis in a province that valorizes it as an ideal, yet simultaneously struggles to negotiate its relationship to its Christian-majority identity. In everyday practices at schools, which are viewed as important institutions in a multicentered process of socialization, how are ethical frames of religious difference circulated, deliberated, and enacted? Before turning more specifically to the theoretical concerns of the book regarding the question of education, I discuss the observed trend of increasing Islamic conservatism in Indonesia and explain how the case of North Sulawesi can contribute to understanding the national dynamics of Indonesia as well as the topics of education and minority religious groups across Southeast Asia.

Concerns about increasing intolerance are linked to developments within Indonesian Islam since the transition to democracy, notably an increasing conservatism and pluralization of religious authority. Martin van Bruinessen has characterized this as a "conservative turn" in Indonesian Islam, marked most clearly by the 2005 fatwa issued by the MUI, the Indonesian Council of Ulama (a government-sponsored assembly of Islamic scholars), proclaiming secularism, pluralism, and religious liberalism as ideologies at odds with Islamic teachings (Van Bruinessen 2013, 3). While certainly vocal and influential, this more conservative brand of Islam must be contextualized within another major trend: the pluralization of religious authority in Indonesian Islam. In addition to the influence of Salafi movements and Islamist political parties, Indonesia has seen trends of celebrity religious gurus and self-help training programs popular among middle-class Muslims (Rudnyckyj 2010; Hoesterey 2012). The recent proliferation of Muslim schools also attests to the varied organizations and movements seeking to forward their own interpretations in the context of both the fragmentation of religious authority and the increasing influence of Islamic conservatism (R. W. Hefner 2009, 97).

This conservative turn within Indonesian Islam must also be analyzed in the context of broader debates about religious plurality and citizenship, and the perspective of a Christian-majority region is strategic in this regard. Christians are not simply responding to trends in Islam; they are also working to forge a way forward and negotiate their position within the plural Indonesian nation. At its most extreme, for Christians in North Sulawesi, this trend has entailed talks of secession if there is no longer a place guaranteed for Christians in the national project, though these discussions have remained largely out of the mainstream. The national protests that erupted in 2016–2017 against Jakarta's Christian and ethnic Chinese governor Basuki Tjahaja Purnama (known as Ahok) demonstrated the continued, and even bolstered, strength of hard-line Islamic groups and their ability to mobilize followers. These protests centered on charges of blasphemy against Islam based on Ahok's comments in an edited viral online video that surfaced during his reelection campaign, a political and religious dynamic that brought concerns about belonging to the fore for many Indonesian Christians.

In contemporary Indonesia, religion is increasingly foregrounded in belonging and identity (Ricklefs 2012), and debates about the role of religion within the nation itself are taking place. While perspectives on multiculturalism tend to presuppose religious difference as a readily identifiable and necessarily salient form of difference, an ethnographic approach offers an important perspective by demonstrating under what circumstances religious difference emerges. Previous perspectives have overlooked the possibility that the salience of religious identities and boundaries may shift in various contexts. The empirical approach taken in this research, focusing on how understandings of religious difference are socialized, pushes back against an assumption that these developments in the religious and political situation have necessarily hardened religious boundaries. In investigating daily navigation of religious boundaries, these chapters demonstrate how the significance of religious boundaries shifts on various levels through embodied and discursive manifestations of religious belonging and difference, and as Muslims and Christians in North Sulawesi navigate shifting positionalities and modes of subjectivity. In this process, schools are important sites where Indonesian youth (and their teachers) deliberate about religious difference and the contours of belonging.

CONTESTED FRAMES OF BELONGING IN MANADO

Manado is a coastal city with a population of more than 450,000. In this book, I switch between discussions of the city of Manado and of the broader region, since in the local understanding Minahasa and Manado are interchangeable identifiers, loosely linked to notions of geography and ethnicity rather than referring to technically defined administrative units (Renwarin 2006, 16). Most of the ethnographic research in this book was conducted in Manado or in nearby Tomohon, a small city of just over one hundred thousand inhabitants in the Minahasan highlands with a higher proportion of Catholics in the population (nearly 25 percent) and a relatively small Muslim population (less than 3 percent) (Badan Pusat Statistik Sulawesi Utara 2021, 254).

In terms of ethnicity, the majority of Manado's inhabitants, as well as the inhabitants of nearby regencies and cities of Tomohon and Bitung, are Minahasan. The term Minahasa means "united," referring to historical alliances among groups in the region against the Bolaang to the south and political unification linked to Dutch colonization (Henley 1996, 30). Ethnic

Minahasans are primarily Protestant, resulting in an overlap of ethnic and religious identity. Widespread conversion to Protestantism took place in the mid-to-late nineteenth century among Minahasan highlanders, who had previously adhered to indigenous religious traditions. Christianization of the region was inextricably intertwined with processes of colonization and education (explored in more detail in chapter 4). In 1934, the synod in Minahasa broke from the Dutch-controlled Protestant Church to form an independent Protestant denomination: the Christian Evangelical Church in Minahasa (GMIM—Gereja Masehi Injili di Minahasa). While the GMIM remains the most prominent church in the region today, there are dozens of additional Protestant denominations active in the region. This includes another indigenous denomination, the Union of Minahasan Protestant Churches (KGPM—Kerapatan Gereja Protestan Minahasa), as well as several Indonesian and global denominations of evangelical and Pentecostal churches, and the Adventist church, among others.

Other ethnic groups represented in Manado include Sangihe, Bolaang-Mongondow, Talaud, Gorontalo, Tionghoa (ethnic Chinese), Bugis, Ternate, Maluku, Batak, and Javanese (Pomalingo 2004, 58). Muslims are from a variety of ethnic backgrounds, some indigenous to the broader region, and others present in North Sulawesi from either historical or recent migration. In Manado, there are some primarily Muslim neighborhoods, often related to historical settlements of traders or patterns of migration rather than a clear delineation of distinct religious territories, as is the case for some of the nearby post-conflict regions, such as in Ambon. In general, Christians from the island of Sangihe (who are not ethnic Minahasan) and Muslims from various ethnic groups are more concentrated in the northern part of the city, where there is also less access to public services, a distinction that may partially relate to colonial-era planning and settlements (Patandianan and Sumampouw 2016, 67). Most neighborhoods in the city, however, remain substantially diverse, providing ongoing opportunities for interreligious interaction. In the wider province, there are also many Muslim communities within predominantly Christian Minahasan villages that have had little difficulty in establishing mosques and participating in the local democratic processes (Rusli 2020, 24). The rising middle class in this relatively prosperous province includes both Christians and Muslims, making it difficult to give blanket statements about the intersection of class with ethnic and religious identity. Yet, political representation and land ownership remain disproportionately concentrated in the hands of Minahasan Christians.

FIGURE 1.2 Jesus Bless Monument (Monumen Yesus Memberkati) in Manado.

Despite the pride of Manadonese in their region's ability to avoid widespread conflict during democratization and decentralization at the turn of the century, plural coexistence remains an unfinished project, requiring ongoing work and negotiation. Social actors employ a variety of normative frames and draw on varying ethical streams as they consider how to deal with religious diversity. Although invoking a commitment to religious harmony is generally required for legitimacy in the public sphere, these invocations do not refer to a shared understanding of how to enact religious coexistence in practice. Rather, the different ways the discourse is interpreted and the political and religious stances that accompany it actually reflect ongoing contestation about living in a religiously plural society.

Throughout this book, I demonstrate how deliberation about belonging takes place in and beyond educational settings in Manado. Two major frameworks for approaching religious difference emerge. On the one hand, there is collective striving toward aspirational coexistence, where belonging is guaranteed by mutual recognition, dialogue, and the assurance of religious freedom. This vision is often justified in relation to national principles, understood as in alignment with religious teachings from all traditions, and also linked to Minahasan culture and tradition. In many ways, aspirational coexistence has become normative in local discourse, but this does not mean it is an empty signifier; for many teachers, students, and other citizens, it is a real goal. This aspirational coexistence underpins the province's identity as uniquely poised to exemplify religious harmony, a desirable status that brings national recognition.

However, on the other hand, a vision of majoritarian coexistence often emerges, particularly when the principles of this aspirational coexistence are perceived as threatened or tarnished by local or national events. The belonging of Others under these terms becomes guaranteed exclusively by the goodwill of the majority: Minahasan Christians. In this sense, Christians project themselves as the source of and guarantors of peace, which is threatened only by outsiders. In the chapters that follow, I trace the circulation of and tension between these two frameworks.

THE SIGNIFICANCE OF BELONGING AND COEXISTENCE

The case of Manado and Indonesia provide important insights for the question of how to maintain cohesion and shape belonging, which is an ongoing concern for many contemporary plural societies. In this book, I have chosen the term "belonging" to indicate a relation to identity and an articulation with an affective dimension rather than drawing attention to the more formal tone of citizenship and the ideas of rights and statuses it may invoke. Belonging also encompasses an ethical dimension in relation not only to individual identity and positioning but also to projecting understandings on others—who should be included, who should not, and on what grounds.

Writing on the notion of belonging in island Southeast Asia, Renato Rosaldo considers the relationship between the center and the margins in terms of the identity of "hinterland minorities" and the political and moral questions raised about who can belong in the nation (2003, 4–5). Rather than focusing on an ethnic minority whose inclusion in the national project is under question because of their identity as indigenous or tribal (see Li 2000), or one that has resisted national participation, I consider a national ethnic and religious minority—Minahasan Christians—who believe their cultural traditions to be inherently democratic and conducive to a maintenance of religious harmony (Pinontoan 2018, 125), allowing them to fashion the identity of the region as uniquely positioned to realize nationalist goals. Tom Boellstorff (2005) has given insight into the pursuit of belonging in Indonesia among those considered on the margins through his ethnographic investigation of gay men in Indonesia. He importantly demonstrates how the cultivation of minoritized identities can precisely depend on the national level of belonging as the scale where local and global not only intersect but become constituted.

Instead of assimilating to a form of nationalism dictated by the Javanese center, in this post-Suharto era of increasing possibilities of identity expression in the public sphere, Minahasans have reinscribed their own claims to national belonging. As these claims negotiate new relationships between *adat* (tradition), religion, and ethnicity (Swazey 2013; Thufail 2012), they are not only about belonging in the Indonesian nation. They are also about who belongs in the region, as Minahasan Christians position themselves as having the ability to act on behalf of Christians as a national minority, leveraging their local majority status to carve out a desired national position for Christians. In this province that carefully manages its image relative to religious harmony and projects its example outward, limits to aspirational coexistence typically appear when the future of the province as majority Christian is perceived as threatened.

These deliberations about belonging relate to conversations taking place in the public sphere in Western liberal democracies as well, as societies contend with developing a public ethical culture that is capable of drawing together various streams and elements within society. Some multicultural theorists, drawing on Western examples, typically call for an individual rights-based approach to multicultural citizenship (Kymlicka 1995; Taylor and Guttman 1994). Jeremy Menchik has pointed out that in Indonesia, Islamic organizations' embrace of communal tolerance (rather than liberal notions of tolerance) has provided a way for some organizations to espouse democracy, belief in God, and support for minority rights (2015, 158). Furthermore, it is important to realize that recognition not only takes place through formal political rights, but also has moral and affective dimensions. My ethnographic approach, therefore, seeks to understand which ethical frameworks regarding coexistence are in operation, and how they define national belonging in relation to religious difference.

Throughout the book, I prefer to speak about religious coexistence rather than tolerance, recognizing both the linkage of the concept of "toleration" to liberalism and contemporary deployment of the term to indicate a Western superiority vis-à-vis nonliberal others (Brown 2006). In addition, I use the term "religious coexistence" as going beyond toleration in requiring work to understand and respond to differences. However, my interlocutors do often speak about *toleransi* (tolerance), and for this reason it is important to empirically approach these concepts to better understand what they imply, how they are deployed, and what frameworks of inclusion and exclusion they entail.

Education is undoubtedly central to disseminating notions of citizenship and circulating discourses and practices related to belonging. Benedict Anderson's highly influential perspective on nations as "imagined communities" explicitly links the role of mass education in the formation of a nationalist consciousness and an indigenous intelligentsia in colonies that would go on to spearhead independence movements (2006 [1983]). Schooling is directly linked to nation building, socializing individuals into new hierarchies, national languages, and values to cement a basis for social cohesion (Weber 1976). At the same time, youth are socialized not only as citizens of a particular national identity, but also as members of local communities and ethnic or religious groups, into gendered social roles, class milieus, and other subjectivities that transect or go beyond national identity. Based on my ethnographic research in a madrasah, a public high school, and a private Catholic school, I provide a broad perspective on schools as important spaces that are intimately intertwined with the ethics and politics of belonging. I will outline in more detail below the methodologies applied in the course of the research.

EDUCATION: DISCIPLINARY AND DELIBERATIVE

This book argues for a multicentered approach to education, requiring ethnographic attentiveness to the plural ethical streams in society, the institutions promoting them, and the deliberation about ethical values that takes place both in and beyond them. This attention to deliberation is not meant to override or ignore the disciplinary aspects of schooling, which are certainly present in the Indonesian schools discussed here, and to some extent in all educational endeavors. Indeed, striving toward the goals of the national curriculum by implementing it in schools represents a strong disciplinary trend, as educators often seek out pedagogical strategies to help youth internalize state ideologies and principles such that they become normative. The disciplinary nature is also evident in each of the schools studied in the emphasis put on religious practice and diligent piety as a mechanism of self-transformation and collective improvement.

To understand the modes of deliberation occurring in schools, I consider the relationship between deliberation and discipline, which Charles Hirschkind (2001) has elaborated as one of interdependence and coconstruction. David Burchell's (1995) description of the development of early modern European ideas about citizenly attributes and their acquisition provides an account of how ethical discipline can create "the nondiscursive background of sentiments and habits on which public deliberation depends" (Hirschkind 2001, 5). Even in examining the "technologies of the self" (Foucault 1997, 225) that emerge in educational projects, there still remains space for the exercise of deliberative agency in the process. This becomes even clearer when adding ethics as a frame of analysis, in paying attention to the "reflective thought" (Foucault 1997, 117) inherent in the practice of ethics. Analyzing the relationship between discipline and deliberation is particularly important in a multicentered understanding of education, with the recognition that there are many spaces of socialization that are not necessarily tied to the same telos.

Why is it important to focus on the level of institutions at all, particularly since it is clear that "the socializing function of schools . . . is not hegemonic" (Adely 2012, 20)? A call to focus on institutions does necessarily represent movement toward a deterministic "effacement of the individual in the institution" (Fortna 2003, 21–22). Technologies of the self also relate to institutions, the particular modes of power they deploy, and the potential emergence of relevant publics (Hirschkind 2001, 6). Therefore, recognizing the socially embedded nature of ethical learning, grounded in social institutions, can elucidate the relationship between individual and interpersonal ethical learning and the formation of a public ethical culture. Ethical frameworks for approaching religious difference are not simply the result of discipline executed as a top-down internalization, and do not neatly emerge as a product of a political doctrine or national ideology. Rather, they are related to broad ethical streams in society and the pedagogical process of "deliberation" (Varenne 2007) that takes place in and beyond educational institutions. The ethical values undergirding the forms of coexistence—aspirational and majoritarian—that emerge in this case study of Manado are formative of public virtues and therefore relevant to deliberation taking place on interpersonal levels as well as in the public sphere.

EDUCATION, RELIGION, AND THE DELIBERATING PUBLIC

Educational institutions are important sites where the religious and secular are mutually constitutive (Stambach 2006), underscoring their significance as arenas of debate where the place of religion within the nation is contested and negotiated. However, analyses of modern educational systems have tended to characterize them as secular extensions of the state. The conceptualization of education as an agent of modernization has likely played a role in entrenching these assumptions. In the early twentieth century, both Émile Durkheim and John Dewey argued in their respective social contexts for mobilizing education to disseminate a secular morality based in rational, modern science, as religion was deemed fundamentally irrational and unable to serve as a unifying force in plural societies (Dill 2007, 224). The role of modern education has also been emphasized in disseminating ideas of national belonging, "shaping individuals to fit into societies and cultures broader than their own, and persuading them that these broader realms are their own" (Weber 1976, 330–331). Yet, these shifts in modern approaches to mass education did not simply produce novel educational institutions and processes, but rather demonstrated how education becomes a site where the secular and religious are intertwined (Fortna 2003, 39).

An orientation toward education that has obscured its relation to the religious sphere requires an interrogation of education as both a contested domain and a process. Toward this end, insights from existing ethnographic studies of religious education can inform this reconceptualization of education as fundamentally multicentered. As modern educational institutions have often been viewed as arms of the secular state, they have been portrayed as relatively separate and isolated institutions with regards to the surrounding community. Yet, studies of Islamic education in particular (Eickelman 1985; Berkey 1992) can provide renewed attention to the social relationships sustaining the transmission of knowledge and the social and political context of educational institutions, recognizing that education is always socially embedded.

Ethnographies of contemporary Islamic education also address the question of how religious and political institutions work to sustain a transmission of knowledge without assuming that their goals necessarily coincide with or serve a singular interest. Islamic education has been impacted by both the spread of mass education and religious reform movements throughout the Islamic world, and has continued to negotiate its position in relation to modern mass education throughout the process (R. W. Hefner 2007, 12). Because Islamic schools are now often in competition with secular state schools and under the purview of the state, their contextualized position is often addressed in relation to the educational field. Although modern mass education tends to "functionalize" religion to serve nationalist goals (Starrett 1998, 18–19), religious education still defies being contained to a formal subject throughout the school day. Fida Adely's account of education at an all-girls secondary school in contemporary Jordan (2012) demonstrates how religious education takes place while students chat between classes, teachers couch curricular subjects in Islamic discourse, and students encounter religious lessons at home and in their communities. Recognizing that education, even including schools in their modern and standardized forms, is fundamentally multicentered is an important reminder for the study of schooling and education more broadly.

Furthermore, all forms of education, whether classified as religious or secular, seek to shape subjects according to a set of moral values. Amy Stambach, writing on Christianity and education in East Africa, argues that education cannot be studied merely as a tool of the nation-state or as the activities that make up schooling, because it also necessarily encodes "moral disposition" (2010, 12). Adely and Seale-Collazo stress the insights that can be gleaned from studies of religious education: "Ethnographic analyses of religious education and its pedagogical methods . . . also sheds light on the moral projects that undergird *all* educational efforts" (2013, 342, emphasis in original). This particular lens outlines the importance of schools as sites of ethical deliberation and subject formation, the result of which can never be predetermined or assumed but must be examined as a process.

The study of education within anthropology and sociology has been highly influenced by Bourdieu's account of social reproduction, focusing primarily on the ways in which social relationships of domination become reproduced through various means, including through educational structures. Although his theoretical perspective is often dismissed as overly deterministic, Bourdieu's practice theory (1977) outlines a circuit model of social reproduction based in the habitus as a catalogue of generative schemes. This circuit offers an explanation for cultural reproduction, but also recognizes various social fields and leaves room for at least incremental change at various points. Furthermore, additional ethnographies of education espousing this theory have paid attention to how the norms promoted by educational institutions are appropriated, resisted, and negotiated, with varying effects (Eckert 1989; Willis 1977), at times unwittingly contributing to the further entrenchment of their status. In this book, rather than focusing on cultural maintenance and the transmission of values that undergird the existing social structure, I instead attempt to integrate the insights discussed above regarding the multicentered and processual nature of education.

Furthermore, I examine the process of education as one of contingent deliberation. Hervé Varenne has argued that education should be a central concern for anthropologists as they work to explain and study cultural evolution (rather than conservation), asserting the "radical impossibility of reproduction" (2008, 363). Drawing on liberal theories of education that have focused on its potential as a vehicle for social change (Cremin 1976; Dewey 1916), Varenne proposes an understanding of education as deliberation: "the activity of people talking about something that happened outside their immediate setting; making practical decisions about what is to happen next; and then publicly reflecting on what just happened" (2007, 1569). This definition opens up a conceptual locus for separating education from its supposed aim of cultural reproduction, yet also avoids equating its aim of social change with its actual result. In doing so, it eschews top-down or resistance-based approaches to education, underscoring a process that is also fundamentally social—not exclusively personal.

An account of education as deliberation emphasizes the processual nature of education, and also avoids reducing it to a simple matter of reproduction and/or discipline. Yet, its genealogical link to liberal theories of education also brings theoretical baggage in its assumptions about rational debate as the primary mechanism of deliberation in the public sphere. Rejecting these assumptions, I approach deliberation through the lens of ethics, with the perspective that education is an arena for ethical deliberation about the normative visions of society, the nation, belonging, and difference. Instead of assuming that the outcome is singular and necessarily clear, however, looking at education as ethical cultivation requires a recognition of subjectivity as "premised upon multifaceted and contradictory intentions" (Boutieri 2013, 377). As all educational projects are linked to moral ones, deliberation is understood here as a process of situated ethical learning and practice in a context where there are multiple normative visions of religious coexistence being deliberated.

In applying the term "public" in the context of the public sphere or public ethical culture, I do not refer to a fixed site or location, but recognize that its usage is always contextual and in relation to that which is deemed "private." For Habermas (1989), the public sphere is significant because of its potential to facilitate social integration, accomplished through discourse. Many critiques have been leveled at Habermas for his historical account of the rise of the public sphere in Western bourgeois society, including his failure to take into account the gendered distinctions of public and private that were necessarily inscribed within the rise of the public sphere (Fraser 1992; Warner 1992). Particularly relevant here, however, is the concern about disregard for religion (Calhoun 1992, 31) and the way in which religion was reformulated as a component of "private" life so as not to impinge on the public sphere as a space for rational discourse normatively designated as secular (Asad 1993, 205).

In his critique of liberal assumptions regarding the public sphere based on an ethnographic investigation of Islamic cassette sermons in Cairo and their listeners, Hirschkind also challenges an assumed clear distinction between public and private. He points out how the ethical dispositions grounded in Islamic discipline sought out by the sermon listeners "create the moral space within which public argumentation takes place, orienting the interlocutors towards the goals and goods that define that space" (Hirschkind 2006, 136). Furthermore, the "fractal distinction" between public and private is reproduced across different institutions and scales, allowing the personal to become public in particular contexts (Gal 2002, 78–79). These critical insights regarding the way in which the public relates intimately to the personal have shaped my own thinking in this investigation of how the religiously inflected ethical self-making that takes place in Indonesian educational institutions can have broader consequences beyond individual and interpersonal interactions. Considering religious diversity and belonging as fundamentally ethical questions helps to bridge various interconnected social scales by understanding the kinds of "ethical affordances" (Keane

2016, 27) individuals draw on as they engage in deliberation, and how they voice their justifications as through "public reasoning" (Bowen 2010, 6).

Employing the lens of deliberation underscores the complicated, messy, and dynamic coconstruction of education as opposed to a unidirectional internalization. Focusing on individuals as "deliberating subjects" in this sense emphasizes the fact that deliberation is in part a rational endeavor but is also highly intertwined with moral and affective registers. It also encourages us to consider the consequences particular moral frameworks can have on a broader scale as they are engaged by a deliberating public. Finally, this perspective draws in the entanglements at the level of the school, family, region, and nation, and the discourses that are driven by a complex set of institutional, political, and economic circumstances before entering into an individual's lifeworld.

ETHICAL REFLECTION AND DELIBERATION

Reframing the socialization of belonging and recognition of difference as processes of ethical deliberation underscores the processual nature of education as described above. As opposed to being outcome oriented with regards to what is learned at school about approaching religious difference and belonging in the nation, I use the concept of deliberation to draw attention to the contingent and unsettled nature of the considerations of these topics. This strategy is intentional in order to examine learning as more than internalization, and as a process involving reflection. Furthermore, ideologies and practices relating to the inscription of difference are fundamentally ethical questions, connecting not only to a political context and discourse but also to individual subjectivities. In this vein, this book considers how processes of ethical self-making and interpersonal ethical reflection might link up with a public ethical culture. How do educational institutions circulate ethical frameworks, and how do individuals and groups employ these varying approaches toward religious difference and belonging?

Studies regarding the influence of cultural context on moral development and socialization (Shweder, Mahapatra, and Miller 1987; Shweder and Much 1991) and models of subjectivity in which individuals are constantly monitoring and revisiting their positioning vis-à-vis normative social frameworks (Kleinman 1988) provide a basis for understanding the process of ethical deliberation as a continuous negotiation between multiple ethical frameworks. I examine the role that institutions play in this process, particularly in circulating various ethical frameworks that may resonate with individuals and become grounded in subjectivities. As schools implement a national curriculum aiming toward educating tolerant and pious citizens, the teachers who are charged with this task disseminate ethical frameworks about ways to approach religious difference. I seek to further outline how deliberation about these frameworks takes place for individuals and among groups, and to clarify the stakes both within and beyond the schoolyard.

An emerging literature on the ethical dimensions of social life has enriched understandings of how individuals navigate and negotiate ethical frameworks, particularly in the context of aspiration and self-work toward a deepened religious engagement (Mahmood 2005; Hirschkind 2006). Within these debates, the approach of "ordinary ethics" (Das 2010; Lambek 2010) has indicated how ethical reasoning emerges from everyday interactions, recognizing that normative ethical work happens at "diffuse and tacit levels and not only in the terms set by the audit culture or with respect to what have been discursively produced as largely, specific, and public ethical 'problems'" (Robbins 2016, 782). Yet, this perspective also risks a flattened view of the institutions that play a role in disseminating various frames, omitting an important direction of inquiry in how the framing of public ethical issues shapes reflection on a diffuse and interpersonal level, and how these interpersonal interactions might feed back into and interact with the institutional or public levels.

In developing and operationalizing the concept of ethical deliberation, I draw on James Laidlaw's outlining of "reflective freedom" as intrinsic to ethics (Laidlaw 2014, 177), elaborated through a reading of Foucault's "reflective thought" (Foucault 1997, 117). Laidlaw argues that reflective freedom is a precondition for ethical life, tied "to the reality of consciousness and the constitution of the subject through socially instituted practices and relations of power and mutual recognition," and linked to the management of value pluralism (2014, 177). Ethical reflection takes place "through socially instituted practices and power relations," which leads to varied forms of ethical constitution (Laidlaw 2014, 149). I contend that this provides an opportunity to understand how educational institutions channel ethical normativities and act as arenas for individual deliberation, and how they are also relevant for public ethical deliberation. This perspective foregrounds pedagogical processes, positioning education—broadly conceived—as a critical site of ethical reflection. The quality of reflection as a temporal process parallels that of deliberation, as various possibilities are considered and decisions or actions are taken with ramifications beyond the interpersonal interactions in which they take place. Using this concept of "reflective freedom" and connecting it with an understanding of education as deliberation provides theoretical leverage in understanding how schools, as institutions of socialization, act as an important link between interpersonal ethical deliberation and a public ethical culture in channeling ethical frameworks.

This approach, therefore, seeks to ascribe a nuanced role to institutions provided by engagement with the anthropology of education, to bear on a consideration of ethics that has been preoccupied primarily with the level of subjectivity. Despite ethics having been described as a "pedagogical primal scene" (Faubion, quoted in Laidlaw 2014, 150), referring to ethical striving between an individual in relation to a moral exemplar, the pedagogical aspects of ethical self-making have been largely sidelined in the anthropological literature (Laidlaw and Mair 2019, 352). This reality is perhaps indicative of a larger devaluation of the study of education and a continued oversight of schools "as sources of new knowledge and value, new configurations of difference, which interrelate in complex ways with the other educational relations and practices of everyday life" (Levinson 1999, 599). Bringing together the affective and rational aspects of deliberation through an analysis of ethical life allows for a reconsideration of pedagogical processes, relating to the ethical dispositions individuals acquire in the process and their consequences for the broader political context.

This perspective has not been without its critiques, for example, claims that a focus on the pedagogical dimension of ethical subject-making will unnecessarily privilege an examination of the technologies and exemplars themselves rather than the perspectives of the individuals who engage in deliberation about the best course of action (Mattingly 2014a, 479). Yet, the particular understanding of education employed here avoids this pitfall in a careful analysis of education as deliberation, rather than considering only the aims of the project or assuming that the frameworks for approaching religious difference will simply be the result of a top-down internalization of a national ideology. In addition, the examination of several different schools as research foci aims to provide insight into the way that the national curriculum is concretely enacted in these different school environments.

The approach to ethics here also recognizes the subjective experience of ethical pluralism, not always experienced as a clash of cultural systems (Robbins 2004), as a moral breakdown (Zigon 2008), or as a unique consequence of modernity (Berger 2014), but as central to the human experience (Ewing 1990). Living in light of ethical values or an ethical tradition is not about being inculcated in and internalizing values such that action according to the principles is automatic, but rather about "the ability to manage the conflicts between these and other demands through reflective and thoughtful self-direction" (Laidlaw 2014, 168). Critiquing portrayals of religious individuals as singularly motivated by pious aspirations, several anthropologists have examined the tension, ambiguities, and contradictions that mark the judgments and decision-making undertaken by religious individuals in their everyday lives (Marsden 2005; Deeb and Harb 2013; Simon 2014; Schielke 2015; Slama and Hoesterey 2021).

The existence of seemingly contradictory moral registers at play should not be surprising, and is possibly even necessary for approaching complex, real-world situations. Self-representations may give an "illusion of wholeness," but are ultimately inconsistent, contextual, and fleeting (Ewing 1990). For example, Gregory Simon's (2014) investigation of moral subjectivity in Minangkabau society demonstrates the tensions between perceptions of selfhood based on social expectation and from pious aspiration, which appear to conflict on the surface but emerge as coexisting cultural ideals. Samuli Schielke has argued that one should not expect to find people operating according to coherent moral systems, but rather an "incoherent and unsystematic dialogue of moral voices that exist parallel to and at times contradict one another" (2015, 53). His focus, however, is primarily on what takes place at the level of individual subjectivity and how ambiguity and contradiction manifest there. I argue that these individual-level ethical concerns must be linked to institutions and the socialization into various ethical dispositions that may drive or channel some of the ethical frames that resonate with individual concerns. Ambiguities and contradictions exist on multiple levels—not just on the level of individual subjectivity—and analyses should focus on how these emerge, disseminated through institutions in particular sociopolitical contexts as well as experienced through grounding in individual subjectivities (Larson 2022).

Finally, in this project of bringing localized, interpersonal deliberations in connection with institutions and public ethical culture, I also ask what it means to live in a plural society where individuals are not only deliberating about ethical frameworks within their own religious identity or ethnic traditions, but are constantly engaging with others who may apply or consider different ethical values. In bringing institutions centrally into this analysis, I aim to move out of an overly narrow conception of ethical lifeworlds and consider what ethical pluralism might mean both on the individual level of subjectivity and on a public level.

METHODOLOGY

To investigate these questions about education, religion, and politics on the ground, I conducted seventeen months of ethnographic fieldwork in North Sulawesi, including one-month visits in 2014 and 2018, and an extended period of research in 2015–2016. Research took place mostly in the provincial capital, Manado, and in the nearby smaller city of Tomohon, though school activities, interviews, and other events often took me beyond these city limits. Following a methodological approach that views schools as arenas of deliberation and moves outward to follow connections to broader societal debates, I began my research by identifying schools with varying religious affiliation and public/private status to serve as the main foci of my research. I selected three senior high schools: a public high school (Sekolah Menengah Atas Negeri, SMA from here onward), the public Madrasah Aliyah Negeri (MAN from here onward), and a private high school with informal Catholic affiliation referred to as Lokon School.

At each of these three schools, I attended civic education and religious education courses regularly. I took field notes related to both the delivery of the course material and student responses and interaction. During the school day, when I was not observing classes, I typically spent time in the teachers' lounge or in the cafeteria to casually chat with teachers and students. I attended numerous school events at each of the schools, including flag ceremonies, worship sessions, parent-teacher meetings, and morning announcements. While conducting research, I lived on the campus of Lokon School, the only school of the three studied that requires students to board. I stayed in housing allocated for teachers, but also spent time with students and staff at the girls' dormitories in the evening, and ate dinner with students in the cafeteria. From time to time, I also assisted in English-language courses in the high school and middle school (on the same campus), and for several months ran an after-school English game activity with middle school students at the dormitory.

Because my strategy involved getting to know teachers first by spending time with them throughout the school day, students quickly began to perceive me as an authority figure, most assuming I had come to their school to teach English. Through participation in extracurricular activities, such as school retreats, I was able to get to know students better and soften their initial perception of me as an authority figure. In my interactions with students, I relied more heavily on informal conversation and observation as opposed to formal interviews. In-between classes and after school, I conducted semistructured interviews in Indonesian with several religious and civic education teachers at each of the schools to better understand their philosophical approach to teaching their respective subjects and addressing religious difference within the scope of the course material and beyond. I also interviewed school administrators in order to understand the practical and theoretical frameworks in regards to the place of religion within the school, approaches toward religious and moral education, and ways of dealing with religious difference.

I collected and took notes on religious education and civic education textbooks in circulation at the schools, as curriculum analysis remains an important tool for understanding the visions of nation and coexistence proposed as normative by the state and other organizations and institutions that are influential in curriculum development. Various privately produced textbooks were in circulation at the schools in addition to official government-supplied textbooks. In chapter 2, I draw my analyses specifically from the state-produced textbooks. In cases where I discuss particular delivery of the curriculum in a classroom setting, I focus on the material presented in the classroom context, whether from privately or state-produced textbooks.

Aiming to connect what is taking place in educational institutions to broader debates about the religious difference, I also examined public debates engaging questions of plurality and interviewed religious and community leaders in Manado.[7] For this research on broad public-level debates, I expanded my network and engaged with additional religious organizations, community leaders, politicians, women's organizations, and local traditional organizations, among others. In addition to interviews conducted with leaders and participants, I attended public events (both religious and nonreligious) of these organizations. I also participated in an interreligious exchange program facilitated by several religious universities (the subject of chapter 6), which provided an important case study of interreligious interaction and dialogue among university students.

Throughout my research, I focused heavily on processes of religious and civic education in schools, but continually made an effort to follow these processes both upstream and downstream, recognizing that schools are but one of many potential sources contributing to education and socialization. This particular methodological approach was developed with an eye toward moving beyond an ethnography of the classroom alone, and rather examining schools as arenas for deliberation, where a plurality of discourses is present, impinging on social life inside and outside the school walls. I connect these processes to the debates taking place in the public sphere to examine attempts toward a public ethic, asking how formal education links up with and contributes to these processes.

OUTLINE OF CHAPTERS

The structure of the book reflects the methodological approach taken in focusing on schools as arenas of deliberation about religious coexistence and belonging within the national framework. I treat each of the three schools individually in its own chapter before broadening outward to focus on university-level interreligious initiatives, and finally, public-level debates related to plurality and citizenship. It struck me that starting with the societal-level context of public debate and then addressing individual schools may unwittingly work against the injunction to investigate education as more than a top-down endeavor. The structure is intended to further underscore the message that schools are more than simple microcosms of the broader public sphere where messages are filtered down and disseminated. Public-level debates about religious coexistence are not analyzed to simply provide context for what is taking place in schools, but rather examined as an additional ethnographically investigated site to offer insight into their articulation with the level of individual schools and illuminate the circulation of ethical frameworks on various scales.

In chapter 2, I establish how schools become arenas for debate about the national imaginary and politics of difference, highlighting the central role that religion and secularism play. I do so by weaving together a theoretical consideration of secularism, religion, and education with an analysis of the historical shifts in moral education from the authoritarian New Order regime (1966–1998) to today's character education efforts in democratic Indonesia. I argue that visions of nation and political doctrines of secularism do not simply produce a public ethical culture, but that this ethical culture and the values underpinning it are continuously under deliberation, particularly in the sphere of education.

Chapters 3, 4, and 5 are in-depth ethnographic analyses of three different high schools in North Sulawesi, where teachers and students engage in deliberation about moral personhood, national belonging, and religious difference, framed by the regional political context, the national curriculum, and its interpretation by teachers in the moment. SMA, a religiously and ethnically diverse public high school, and the discursive and embodied frameworks for religious belonging circulated in the school are the subject of chapter 3.

An examination of school policies and responses to them related to the allocation of space for religious worship, the use of greetings and prayers, regulations on food in the cafeteria, and school uniforms demonstrates how embodied forms of religious belonging are promoted in the school. These forms shape the encounter of religious difference, at times in opposition to a circulation of discourses about respect for religious diversity.

Chapter 4 examines Lokon School, a private boarding school with informal Catholic affiliation which "missionizes" for the development of the nation in its approach to build up individual faith and character as the first step toward producing Christian elites from eastern Indonesia. A historical perspective recasts the influential status of Minahasa in the colonial past to imagine a more central role for North Sulawesi in developing Indonesia's future. The chapter considers the way in which the future of the nation is "rendered ethical," not as a matter of neoliberal individualization, but as deliberation about the role Christians can play in the nation's collective future.

Next, chapter 5 turns to the public madrasah, where the approach toward teaching tolerance relies on a model of moral action referring back to the perfection and truth of Islamic teachings, resulting in a particular understanding of personhood. Although students deliberate about the application of Islamic ethical principles in a plural society, teachers refer back to moral codes presented as clear-cut, focusing on the principles themselves rather than their imperfect application. The community beyond the school is simultaneously projected as a potential place for students to enact the religious values they have learned (including tolerance) and as a potential source of negative influence and temptation that could dangerously influence Muslim youth, especially in a context where they are part of the religious minority.

Chapter 6 discusses ethnographic data from an interreligious exchange program that brings together Protestant, Catholic, and Muslim university students for interreligious dialogue, as well as data collected from various interreligious events across Manado. Through the frame of "commensuration" and "incommensuration" (Mair and Evans 2015), I demonstrate the strategies that students use to render religious traditions similar yet incomparable. In doing so, they encounter religious boundaries as sites of not only ethical but political entanglement, and their approach simultaneously fortifies and chips these boundaries away. I consider the linkage of these frames to narratives of belonging encountered in all three of the high schools, demonstrating how they emerge in multiple environments.

Chapter 7 zooms out to debates taking place in the public sphere related to questions about plurality and citizenship, revealing the tensions that can emerge between a vision for North Sulawesi as a bastion of religious harmony and as a Christian stronghold. Focusing the role that both interreligious organizations and self-described *adat* (traditional) organizations play in framing the terms of debate in the public sphere, I analyze controversies that brewed as a result of plans to build a local religious theme park, drawing into question the very principle of religious harmony the park was meant to enshrine. The public acceptance of a discourse of religious harmony in Manado is as an aspirational norm that must be invoked for legitimacy in the public sphere, yet remains in tension with ongoing efforts to maintain a Protestant majority and Christian influence. These contending frames for belonging are based on a redefining of the relationship between religion and *adat* and a strategic leveraging of minority/majority positioning by religious and political actors.

Throughout these chapters, the tensions between aspirational and majoritarian coexistence manifest on multiple levels and are engaged through various forms of deliberation. In the public sphere in Manado, an aspirational coexistence is promoted as normative through plans to build the religious theme park, celebrating the principle of religious harmony. Yet, contention that arises about the logistics of building the theme park effectively emboldens groups that advance a clear position of majoritarian coexistence, seeking to establish the Christian majority as the gatekeepers who enable and ensure religious tolerance. In integrating ethnographic perspectives provided by the three schools, I demonstrate that these contestations are taking place through the application of school policies as well as in everyday interpersonal interactions on school grounds. Schools become important sites that can link the dynamics of interpersonal deliberation and the normative work of institutions to the level of public ethical culture. This underscores the importance of what takes place in schools, not only in linking the events that take place there and the visions of coexistence promoted to societal concerns, but in representing the stakes and potential consequences of these interactions. As the scope of the book shifts to also consider deliberation on different levels, these two frames of coexistence remain salient, and the high stakes of both public debates and interpersonal interactions come into focus.

2
Religion, Nation, and Politics of Difference through the Lens of Education

The parameters of belonging within the national imaginary are never fully secured, but are continually contested and questioned. Religion is undoubtedly a major axis of group belonging that has impacted the trajectory of national imaginaries and public culture, in both avowedly secular countries and those in which religion is the very foundation of and claim to legitimacy by the state. In Indonesia, which represents neither of these extremes, religion has been influential in both social organization and in politics since colonial times, but especially since the country experienced a religious resurgence several decades ago. Though the world's most populous Muslim-majority country is often referred to as secular because Islam does not serve as the basis of state, Indonesia's constitution is multiconfessional in affirming the existence of a supreme God. Although approximately 87 percent of Indonesians are Muslim, religious relations are far from straightforwardly majoritarian, partially due to the fact that several regions and provinces have a majority religion other than Islam. While North Sulawesi is majority Protestant, Bali is majority Hindu, and East Nusa Tenggara (including the island of Flores) is majority Catholic, to give a few examples. With this dynamic, the question of religious coexistence is equally important at formal political levels in maintaining national unity, as well as at local and interpersonal levels in addressing various arrangements of religious diversity across the archipelago.

In this chapter, I focus on the place of religion within the national imaginary and approaches to religious difference as they manifest within the educational realm. The religion-state relationship or the establishment of a democracy does not necessarily create a normative hegemony as the ideal for citizens of a particular nation. Constitutional arrangements, therefore, are neither purely the source nor the product of an emergent public culture. So, how can we understand the way in which a public ethical culture—not as fixed but continually deliberated—precipitates, in this case, particularly when it comes to the treatment of religious difference and the contours of national belonging? Taking the literature on secularism and the religion-state relationship as a starting point, I demonstrate how public deliberation about education and its goals has ethical consequences for how national imaginaries and approaches toward religious difference manifest. Although education has often been studied as an arm of the secular state, introducing modernization and inculcating national values, this view flattens the interplay of religion and secularism that takes place in the realm of education and oversimplifies the complex and contingent process of education. In continuous negotiation, the realm of education and educational institutions themselves become critical loci of deliberation as the actions of students, teachers, and administrators intersect with state curricular directives and ideologies charged with shaping the young generation.

Anthropologist Amy Stambach, through her fieldwork on education and modernity in East Africa, has shown how "debates about education provide a lens into social life beyond classrooms. They help us understand the connections people make between textbooks and the wider society" (2000, 2). In this chapter, I aim to examine these connections to uncover how schools become arenas for debate about the national imaginary and the central role that religion and secularism play, weaving together a theoretical and historical narrative. I locate education as the site of this contestation and underscore the relation of educational institutions to public ethical culture and approaches to diversity and coexistence. The place of religion within the nation has a historical trajectory as well as a variety of contemporary normative understandings that shape the direction of and possibilities for the relationship of religion to state, as well as the role of religion in the public sphere. Indonesia serves as a telling case study for unpacking this theoretical assertion and moving across time from the educational approaches to religion and diversity during the country's authoritarian rule to new directives on the topics in contemporary democratic Indonesia. Discourses about ethnic and religious difference disseminated through an educational program during the authoritarian New Order regime (1966–1998) were highly controlled, a measure that had often been assumed to signal the project's success. In contrast, contemporary efforts to redefine Pancasila for a democratic era and the proliferation of discourses about diversity in textbooks indicate not one clear direction or framework for plural coexistence within the nation but several deployed at the same time as schools are called upon to emphasize religious principles as the foundation of good character and address the growing religious intolerance facing Indonesian society.

SECULARISM AND THE POLITICS OF RELIGIOUS DIFFERENCE

Secularization, or the assumption that religious belief and practice will necessarily decline and be reduced to the private sphere as societies modernize, has retreated as a normative theory in the social sciences, the situation of Western Europe having been recognized as an anomaly rather than an inevitable occurrence for all societies. It is clear that religion is not likely to wane or become reduced to the private sphere in the majority of societies across the world, yet this has not diminished the impact that secularism (as a political doctrine) has by virtue of its entanglement with modernity. Secularization, defined in this context as the differentiation of religion and religious practice into a separate sphere, has the potential to reorganize social domains and challenge or create friction with other spheres (Casanova 1994, 2006). Charles Taylor (2007) has critiqued the mistaken assumption that as religion becomes confined to a discrete sphere, other social spheres remain unaffected (Calhoun, Juergensmeyer, and VanAntwerpen 2011, 11). For Taylor, Western modernity and the slew of processes that it entails—including secularization—have contributed to the emergence of a space conceived of as the public sphere and a range of possible social imaginaries (2002).

Secularism as a worldview or a political ideology that involves a reorganization of the religion-state relationship does not necessarily result in the privatization of religion as transformation into atomized individual practice. Indeed, in some forms, it leaves room for the deep involvement of religion in public life through civil associations, and through the ethical resources religion affords regarding not only individual piety but also public order (Casanova 1994). In other words, religion can and does still figure in debates about politics, education, and economics to "challenge the very claims of secular spheres to differentiated autonomy exempt from extrinsic normative constraints" (Casanova 2006, 14). The particularities of any given variety of secularism do impact the understanding and treatment of religious diversity and the guarantee of religious freedom. In contemporary liberal democracies, secularism is often applied as a buffer to better attain equality and to adopt a measure of "principled distance" (Bhargava 1998, 520) and nonpartisanship that can act to mediate and incorporate religious difference.

However, the capacity of the political doctrine of secularism to mediate particular identities (including religious ones) and guarantee neutrality as the basis of tolerance has been called into question, particularly as modern capitalist nation-states continue to legitimize violence precisely through their role in guaranteeing liberal principles (Asad 2003, 5–8). Because secularism is tied to the modern nation-state and national identity, its practice is also still shaped by minority-majority distinctions and relationships (Asad 2003, 7–8; Mahmood 2016). Both Talal Asad and Saba Mahmood analyze secularism not exclusively as a political doctrine, but as part of the hegemonic project of modernity that also impacts individual experience of the categories of the secular and the religious.

While national ideologies and political doctrines can serve as anchoring principles and frame the terms of public debate, they cannot be assumed to produce a public ethical culture in a straightforward manner. To make an initial connection to the realm of education, I bring the work of anthropologist Reva Jaffe-Walter into the conversation. She details how public policies and anxiety about Muslim immigrants are channeled through secular liberal Danish schools and experienced by Muslim students. Ultimately, she argues that the "technologies of concern" enacted on behalf of Muslim students are used to justify an exclusivist and xenophobic vision of nation within schools typically lauded for their inclusivity (2016, 6). Drawing on Asad's perspective on secularism and liberalism, she argues that these technologies originate from the false promises of Western liberal democracy as able to achieve neutrality and secure religious freedom. However, ascribing the source of these policies as political doctrines and ideologies risks reducing schools to places where policies are implemented—rather than focusing on their potential to occupy a central position in coconstructing existing orientations toward Islam in particular and religious difference more broadly. In the assumption that secularism and liberalism have necessarily given rise to a distinct public ethical culture, the role of educational institutions again becomes reduced to one of mere dissemination of national ideologies, rather than sites of potential deliberation or contestation.

Adopting an ethnographically driven approach, I argue that the existing religion-state relationship and political ideology cannot be assumed to simply produce an emergent public ethical culture. It is important to empirically determine the various ways in which the religion-state relationship is being reimagined in contemporary Indonesia, and uncover the roles that schools play in the process. To this end, perspectives of secularism from political science are useful in their emphasis on how the political doctrine has been advanced in practical terms: often in a piecemeal fashion and through on-the-ground (often elite) coalitions. Furthermore, it has become increasingly clear that secularism is not a simple, one-size-fits-all doctrine, but takes on varied formations in different political regimes (Stepan 2011), and that very few states actually have what is typically assumed to be secularism's basic tenet: strict separation of religion and state (Fox 2008). These particular approaches demonstrate how secularism operates in a practical sense as a constitutional arrangement regarding religion, rather than as a pervasive normative hegemony that necessarily reflects or produces a public ethical culture. Furthermore, it is often education that becomes the arena of deliberation about the very nature of this relationship.

INDONESIAN NATIONALISM: RELIGIOUS OR SECULAR?

Although Indonesia is often described as a secular nation because the constitution does not establish an Islamic state or privilege Islam, it is more accurately a multiconfessional or multireligious nation. The state ideology of Pancasila privileges religion generally by affirming belief in a supreme God, but does not allocate special privilege to Islam. This agreement was reached in part because the main nationalist faction against an Islamic state was not advocating for a strict privatization of religion, but tended to envision the possibility for religion to play a public role (R. W. Hefner 2000, 237n3). The state is highly involved in the support and regulation of religious affairs, including defining and outlining state-approved religions. The Indonesian government recognizes six official religions (*agama*): Islam, Catholicism, Protestantism, Hinduism, Buddhism, and Confucianism. Some traditional belief systems (*aliran kepercayaan*) are recognized, though they are accorded a different legal status.

Accounts of the rise of nationalism generally, and also specifically in the case of Indonesia, have tended to emphasize secular factors in developing a sense of connectedness through the spread of language, administration, and print media (Anderson 2006 [1983]). Anderson's influential account of nations as "imagined communities" in former colonies such as the Netherlands East Indies is centered on the importance of the colonial administration, the provision of education, and modern forms of organizations and associations in laying the foundation for a nationalist consciousness.

However, as Michael Laffan highlights, a secular-focused narrative of the rise of the nation and nationalism ignores its religious foundations, such as the role of Muslim institutions and networks in the Netherlands East Indies that paralleled those of the colonial elite. Muslim religious networks were indeed an integral part of the Indonesian independence movement, shaping a vision of Indonesian nationalism with "deeper roots in an Islamic ecumenism within archipelagic Southeast Asia" (Laffan 2003, 3). For both Protestants and Catholics belonging to the emerging class of colonial educated Christian elites, religion also impacted their effort for the nationalist cause. A unique combination of religious background, class status, and educational opportunity produced Christian elites who also contributed to the nationalist movement, pushing for the creation of an independent Indonesia (Van Klinken 2003).

Supporters of the multiconfessional and Islamic visions of nation both took part in the independence struggle, but the split between the contending multiconfessional and religious nationalism still persisted in 1945, when Indonesia declared its independence. The committee tasked with providing a blueprint for independent Indonesia "deadlocked on the thorny issue of Islam's role in the state" (R. W. Hefner 2000, 41). Sukarno, the multiconfessional nationalist who would become Indonesia's first president, introduced the doctrine of Pancasila in a draft preamble to the constitution as a compromise between secular and Islamic nationalism. The doctrine is composed of five major principles: commitment to belief in one supreme God, just and civilized humanitarianism, national unity, consensual democracy, and social justice. Muslim nationalists offered one draft version that included the Jakarta Charter, a clause added to the first pillar stating an obligation for Muslims to carry out shari'a. The clause ultimately disappeared under somewhat murky conditions, though certainly in part due to concerns that its inclusion would have lead the Christian-majority regions of eastern Indonesia to withdraw their participation from the national project (Lindsey 2012, 38). The drafting of the constitution in Indonesia played an important role in establishing a multiconfessional rather than Islamic state, though its future as such was far from guaranteed.

The question of the role of Islam in the Indonesian state was not simply "fixed" at the time of independence, and has continued to reemerge throughout its history. Following Indonesia's democratic transition, which began in 1998, ushered in by the *reformasi* movement, the question was posed once again in a major way. As part of the process of constitutional review and revision, the legislative body of the People's Consultative Assembly (MPR—Majelis Permusyawaratan Rakyat) formally considered a proposed amendment that would have reintroduced the Jakarta Charter, obligating Muslims to adhere to shari'a. Ultimately the vote by the democratically elected MPR representatives in 2002 rejected the proposal, reaffirming the multiconfessional basis of the state established at the time of independence (Lindsey

2012, 48). The decision to found Indonesia as a multiconfessional nation at the time of independence and the reaffirmation of this status during the period of democratization represent "critical junctures" (Pierson 2000, 263), setting the relationship between religion and state down a particular path and bringing consequences for negotiation of national and ethnic identity (Bertrand 2004, 24) in addition to religious identity. Furthermore, the compromise that lies at Indonesia's founding as multiconfessional has not prevented religion, particularly Islam, from being a strong and even at times democratizing force within civil society (see R. W. Hefner 2000).

While Indonesia's political ideology does provide a basic foundation for support of religious coexistence, it has not guaranteed a clear template for accomplishing it. Indeed, in his description of what he dubs Indonesia's "godly nationalism," which binds together the state and religious organizations in their orthodox theism, Jeremy Menchik argues that bolstering nationalism actually depends on the exclusion of faiths considered heterodox (and the restriction of individual religious freedom) (2015, 90). Although Christianity would be considered part of the acceptable religious expressions delineated by this godly nationalism, the particular situation of Minahasa helps to show the way in which religious minorities have at times used their status to question belonging in the Indonesian national project.

INDONESIAN NATIONALISM: THE VIEW FROM MINAHASA

Looking at this national history from a regional perspective, it becomes clear that the role of Islam in relation to the state remains a particularly charged subject for places like Minahasa, or contemporary North Sulawesi. As mentioned above, at the time of independence, there was concern that majority-Christian areas of eastern Indonesia like Minahasa would abandon the national project if an Islamic state were established. While there were many Christians active in the nationalist movement, including the Minahasan Sam Ratulangi, their status as minorities and as elite Christians made their relationship to the nationalist movement more "problematic" (Van Klinken 2003, 2). Among other reasons, this was because their religious status positioned them more closely with the colonial order, and more ambiguously in relationship to the mainstream nationalist movement.

In the particular case of Minahasa, while the nationalist movement ultimately crystallized around the intent to join the Indonesian nation, there was an assumption that the national model would be more federal than unitary (Henley 1996, 142). In chapter 4, I discuss in more detail the shifting position of Minahasa and North Sulawesi within the national imaginary over time from its popular conception as the "twelfth province of the Netherlands" to being viewed as part of eastern Indonesia, or the underdeveloped "outer islands." In considering the relationship of Minahasa to the nation, it is also important to mention the historical significance of Permesta (Perjuangan Semesta—Universal Struggle) for the region. While many Minahasans still prefer to call it a movement (*gerakan*) rather than a rebellion (*pemberontakan*), Permesta was an armed struggle against the government from 1957 to 1961 with ambiguous goals on a number of fronts that evolved over time, yet primarily focused on demands for increased autonomy for the regions of eastern Indonesia (Liwe 2010, 244). Though the movement led to a civil war based in Manado and involving covert military intervention from the United States on its behalf, its leaders never openly argued for separatism and largely continued to operate within the assumption of a nationalist Indonesian framework (Liwe 2010, 18). The memory of Permesta within the national context remains largely unresolved, highlighting the fact that the relationship of Minahasa and North Sulawesi to the nation has in some ways been historically fraught. Although the decentralization that has taken place since the fall of the New Order has offered new possibilities for regional autonomy, it has also led to new uncertainties.

Anxieties regarding the place of Islam in the nation and the consequences for North Sulawesi were particularly heightened in the early 2000s, before the vote on the proposed amendment regarding the Jakarta Charter in newly democratic Indonesia. Considering that Indonesia could conceivably become an Islamic state, political figures and Protestant religious leaders in Minahasa organized a meeting they named the Kongres Minahasa Raya, or the Great Minahasan Congress. The unofficial congress lacked legal authority, yet effectively drew the participation of prominent leaders in the region who publicly discussed the possibility of secession if Indonesia were to become an Islamic state. On August 5, 2000, the lieutenant governor of North Sulawesi, the regent (*bupati*) of Minahasa, along with several youth representatives closely linked to the mainline indigenous Christian Evangelical Church in Minahasa (GMIM) and representatives of each of the Minahasan subethnic groups, issued a declaration from the congress (Kosel 2010, 302).

At the congress, the participants proclaimed the commitment of Minahasa to the nation of Indonesia based on the 1945 Constitution, demonstrating that their actions originated from a place of pro- rather than anti-nationalist sentiment. They rejected sectarian politics based on religion and any "attempts to divide the unity and togetherness of the Indonesian nation by incorporating the Jakarta Charter or any similar formulation into the constitution."[1] Furthermore, they asserted that if the commitment of the constitution were to be revised in any way on this matter, the "Minahasan people" (*rakyat Minahasa*) would separate from Indonesia and withdraw their commitment to the Indonesian nation. The document does not indicate whether it is referring to Minahasa as an ethnic marker or a geographical one, but it notably uses this identifier rather than referring to the political and administrative unit of North Sulawesi. Overall, the statement remains clear in its rejection of an Islamic state and conditional threat of secession, even if political mechanisms for doing so were not specifically outlined.

Relating squarely to the politics of religious difference, the declaration made by the congress also condemned the communal violence that had broken out in several neighboring regions in the early 2000s, calling on the national government to take swift action. In their recommendations, however, it becomes clear that they were speaking on behalf of Christians in their call for the government to pull the Muslim paramilitary group Laskar Jihad and any police or military personnel implicated in the conflicts in Maluku, Poso, and other regions of Indonesia, and to prosecute "perpetrators of Christian massacres" (*para pelaku pembantai umat Kristen*) (Talumewo n.d.).

Movements suggesting the possible secession of Minahasa or North Sulawesi have continued to emerge from time to time in different permutations, ranging from being relatively mainstream (like the first Kongres Minahasa Raya) to remaining on the fringe. Before the proposed vote on the Jakarta Charter, a second Kongres Minahasa Raya was held in 2001. President Abdurrahman Wahid (referred to colloquially as Gus Dur), just prior to his impeachment and removal from office, attended the congress as a guest of honor, and was praised by Minahasans for his commitment to a multireligious Indonesia (Kosel 2010, 303–304). In 2006, the Movement for Minahasan Independence (Gerakan Minahasa Merdeka) was founded by Dolfie Maringka, who organized a rally in support of President George W. Bush later the same year to show solidarity with the United States (Kosel 2010, 292).

More recent discussions of secession were precipitated by the trial of Jakarta's Christian and ethnic Chinese governor, Basuki Tjahaja Purnama (known as Ahok), who was charged with blasphemy against Islam and sentenced to two years in prison for controversial comments that surfaced in a video circulated on social media during his campaign for reelection as governor of Jakarta. As hard-line Muslim groups appeared to hold growing sway in the national public sphere and exploited ethnic and religious divisions, many in North Sulawesi viewed Ahok as something of a national political martyr. His high position had represented for them a real demonstration of the possibility for Christians to play a prominent role in shaping the nation's future, ultimately cut off by hard-line Muslim groups. In response, conversations about the possibility of secession reemerged, though they have continued to remain largely outside of the mainstream. Protests organized at the governor's office in December 2016 and May 2017 called for the implementation of a "Referendum Minahasa Raya," or a referendum about the possibility of secession. Those calling for the referendum insist that it is not a separatist movement but aims to assess the possibility of breaking from Indonesia through legal avenues because the country has failed to uphold the Pancasila principles upon which it is based.

The declaration from the first Kongres Minahasa Raya establishes a commitment to an Indonesia based in the principles of Pancasila, yet also clearly speaks from a particular religious (Christian) perspective. The positioning evident in the declaration demonstrates one way that Protestant Christianity "mediates Minahasan ethnics' participation in national culture, playing a role in their expression of their version of the local" (Swazey 2013, 16). Looking at the enactment of nationalism mediated through religious identities is a way to understand how the contours of the state-religion relationship are being reimagined, but it also brings up important questions about how religious freedom and pluralism are conceptualized and enacted within these frameworks.

EDUCATION: ARENA OF DEBATE ABOUT THE RELIGION-STATE RELATIONSHIP

Even in secular liberal democracies like France that view communitarianism—particularly around religion—as a threat to the nation, debates continue about the extent to which religion can be involved in the public sphere (Bowen 2010). This is also the case for the United States, where there is a long history of religious groups as a core contingent of civil society, yet negotiations persist about the extent to which the state can regulate religion. Understanding how political ideologies provide a foundation for a role for religion in the public sphere, analyzing groups that are active in the public sphere and their own interpretations of these ideologies, and understanding historical change can all illuminate various aspects of this ongoing contestation.

The important position of education in negotiations about religion in the public sphere has been recognized in several different contexts. In his analysis of the manifestations of secularism in the United States, France, and Turkey, political scientist Ahmet Kuru discerns education as the main arena for public debates about state policies on religion (2009, 8). Speaking about the relationship between Islam and the state in the late Ottoman Empire, historian Benjamin Fortna claims that education, "situated at the juncture of social, institutional, intellectual, political, and economic history, affords a unique vantage point from which to observe this interplay" (2003, 25). Fortna uses this perspective to question the assumed secular nature of education as well as its association with a unique, hegemonically Western modernity. Though schooling is often theoretically associated with the project of modernization and secular nation-state building, recognition of the recursive relationship between religion and education "opens up a conceptual locus and mode for analyzing how the public realm is being newly transformed" (Stambach 2006, 3). Debates taking place *about* and *within* the realm of education participate in collective deliberations about the place of religion in the nation, with the politics of religious difference and possibilities for coexistence at stake.

Educational institutions are central to this analysis because of their position and their potential to engage in a project of "normative work" that orients toward possible frameworks of coexistence in a plural society (R. W. Hefner 2014, 131). In this kind of normative work, educational institutions are equally important as sites of deliberation and as sites of scaling, or advancing ethico-political positions that may have social resonance. Schools are also important in their transformation of "experiences of 'the everyday' . . . into categories of social differentiation and identification" (Stambach 2006, 10). The permutations of the religion-state relationship do have an impact, though not necessarily a straightforward one, on possible frameworks for national belonging and the ethical frameworks for approaching difference that inform them.

The formal curriculum presented in schools is one major mechanism of normative work and scaling, though it would be a mistake to equate its messages with those that students internalize, or even those that teachers deliver. Nonetheless, the curriculum remains a useful resource for understanding the approach to the project of nation building and the visions of nationhood and belonging conveyed (Doumato and Starrett 2007), particularly when analyzed in conjunction with ethnographic evidence to understand the educational process as a multicentered phenomenon. A highly controlled curriculum may present a unified state vision of nationhood and a unitary moral code for enacting it, such as during the authoritarian New Order regime under President Suharto (Shiraishi 1997). Yet even in this case, religious organizations and political groups with religious affiliations sought to influence how material about religion and the national ideology would be presented. Thus, the finalized curriculum must be seen as the state-approved product of curriculum development involving input from various interest groups. An analysis of curricula is instructive for grasping the shift in the imagined contours of religion and religious coexistence in relationship to the national framework in Indonesia.

RELIGION AND DIVERSITY UNDER THE NEW ORDER REGIME

The New Order regime under President Suharto was established following an attempted leftist coup that was attributed to the Indonesian Communist Party, and the subsequent violent anti-communist campaign that resulted in the killing of an estimated half million or more Indonesians. The New Order government sought to combat left-wing ideologies partially through a mobilization of religion in service of state development goals. At the same time, the regime was wary of political Islamism and sought to bring religious organizations under clear state control. In walking this line, the New Order initially strongly controlled Muslim political parties but allowed and indeed provided strong support for social initiatives from Muslim organizations later on (R. W. Hefner 2000, 92). The initiatives positioned religion and religious organizations as apolitical and clearly subordinate to the state and its development-oriented agenda.

Ideological control was enacted largely through the elevation of the existing Pancasila, which was the "New Order's answer to the problem of opposition and political conflict," presented as a necessary ideological alternative to communism, Western liberalism, political Islam, and any other ideologies considered anti-state by the Suharto regime (Weatherbee 1985b, 134). Through the *asas tunggal* (sole principle) legislation enacted in 1985, all organizations—including social and religious ones—were required to recognize Pancasila as the sole foundation of their organization. This measure was not universally accepted by Muslim organizations, though most of the mainstream ones eventually accommodated the requirement (Ricklefs 2012, 42). The ideology, wielded for purposes of control, was also intended to serve as the foundation for a national Indonesian culture able to encompass disciplined and limited expressions of a regional, ethnic, and religious difference.

Under Suharto, an authoritarian effort toward repression and domestication of difference was enforced to promote nation building through a variety of discourses emphasizing national unity across cultural groups. The national motto, *Bhinneka Tunggal Ika* ("Unity in Diversity"), transformed diversity into a state-managed project that involved foregrounding aspects of static and nonthreatening cultural representations, creating something of a "national standard upon difference" to provide a measure of unity (Spyer 1996, 26). New Order–era development projects aimed at integrating indigenous groups often involved forced resettlement programs or transmigration to physically impose a tangible measure of integration (Li 2000). Manifestations of difference were largely suppressed in public discourse, and the taboo categories were widely known through the acronym SARA, referring to ethnicity, religion, race, and the catch-all category of intergroup relations. Forms of difference available for public expression served the purpose of integration through their abstraction and projection into a national identity.

The Beautiful Indonesia in Miniature Park (Taman Mini Indonesia Indah), a theme park that was conceptualized by Ibu Tien Suharto, President Suharto's wife, is an apt representation of the state project delimiting the acceptable forms of difference and their relation to national unity as they were conceived under the New Order (Pemberton 1994, 12). The theme park, opened in 1975 and still in operation today, includes a Pancasila Monument as the main attraction that visitors are led directly toward upon entering the park. In addition, the large pond in the center of the park contains man-made islands as a re-creation and representation of the Indonesian archipelago. Miniature houses of worship for official religions and miniature representations of regional houses and displays of regional dress—one from each province—are on display. The various regional houses surround the pond so that it "captures on its shimmering surface the varied reflections of the mini houses, which thereby are cast as manifestations of the same underlying unity" (Spyer 1996, 26). In this version of nation building, where the state clearly plays a significant role in mandating the framework for unity, cultural, religious, and ethnic differences are displayed in a nonthreatening material form that ultimately casts the differences as aesthetically beautiful, and also superficial, in the face of national unity. However, in these representations of the project to control regional identities, their effectiveness is often exaggerated, with a lack of attention to how these state directives were interpreted and implemented on a local level and by individual citizens.

Suharto's broad strategies for managing the relationship between religion and state and delineating the parameters of diversity through the frame of Pancasila were also translated into educational programs. An examination of the regime's intensive focus on expanding education and the deployment of particular frameworks for understanding religion and diversity gives insight into how the principles were presented in the curriculum, and how they were meant to be internalized by Indonesian youth. In this case, it also becomes clear that previous studies of the moral education program implemented by the New Order regime failed to take into account the reception of these ideals and overestimated the power of the state. These previous oversights help to point out that an examination of the ideologies being presented in the curriculum without paying attention to their reception—even when taking place in an authoritarian context—often results in unwarranted assumptions and oversimplifications about the process of education itself.

RELIGION-STATE NEGOTIATIONS THROUGH EDUCATION UNDER THE NEW ORDER

The significant expansion of education under the New Order regime was enacted in tandem with development, as funds from economic growth were invested in education to develop an increasingly skilled workforce to continue acting as the motor for development. State revenues from the oil industry were funneled into the construction of primary schools to work toward the fulfillment of universal primary education. By 1987, levels of primary school enrollment were ten times the 1945–1946 levels (Leigh 1999, 42). Accordingly, rates of literacy among the population increased significantly, from 40 percent of the population in 1965 to 90 percent by the year 1990 (R. W. Hefner 2000, 119). The language of instruction in schools was (and remains) Indonesian, an important symbol of the unity of the country, carrying with it a valence of progress and development (Leigh 1999, 44). Furthermore, New Order classrooms were designed to function as a space of socialization into a nation modeled on the structure of the family, with

Suharto cast as the paternalistic "Father of Development" (*Bapak Pembangunan*) (Shiraishi 1997).

The institution of required religious education allowed for the state to encourage piety among its citizens while imposing some control on the versions of religious orthodoxy promoted in schools. Because of its importance as a safeguard against communism, religious education implemented as instruction in one's professed religion became a required subject in the national curriculum in 1966, from elementary school through higher education (Suhadi et al. 2014, 10–11). As part of the New Order's efforts to depoliticize religion and religious organizations, in the late 1980s, existing student religious organizations were banned from operating inside schools and replaced with the alternative religious extracurricular clubs based on religious belonging (Suhadi et al. 2014, 40–41). The basic structure of these religious clubs, referred to as spiritual organizations (*organisasi kerohanian*, such as the Muslim students' club Rohis and the Protestant student club Rohkris), still exists as part of the extracurricular offerings of schools, though today there is typically little control on their affiliation to outside religious associations.[2]

Although the analysis in this chapter focuses most heavily on the intended state goals and directions of education, it is important to remember that the educational arena at this time was still a sphere in which various interest groups sought to impart their visions for the future of the nation. In his analysis of Muslim-Christian relations during the New Order, Mujiburrahman has shown that debates over education were waged as a mechanism to gain the power to shape cultural identity, and that these debates typically involved Christians aligning with secular nationalists to stave off those who advocated for stronger Islamic influence in the educational system (2006, 207). The tension between these two major factions influenced the creation of a dual administration whereby public schools and universities were placed under the purview of the Ministry of Education and Culture, and state-run Islamic schools were placed under the Ministry of Religion (Mujiburrahman 2006, 223). Although there were attempts to unify this system during the New Order era, mutual suspicions between these two main factions impeded this agenda. In 1989, new legislation required madrasahs to implement a curriculum based on the national educational standards defined by the Ministry of Education and Culture, even as they were (and are) still allowed to implement their own curricular materials to provide an Islamic perspective and add religious coursework from the Ministry of Religious Affairs (Azra, Afrianty, and Hefner 2007, 187).

The mandatory teaching of religious education at all levels—in both public and private schools—gave a public importance to religion while also giving the state a significant measure of control over how religious teachings were presented. Political debates over the provision of religious education in private schools became a thorny subject during this time as well. Many private Christian schools offered only Christian religious education courses for religiously diverse student bodies, a practice denounced by Muslim groups as proselytization (Mujiburrahman 2006, 244). The practice continues today in many private Christian schools, still opposed by some and remaining a sensitive point for groups on both sides (Crouch 2014, 20–21). Indeed, most of these issues, from the dual structure of educational administration to the provision of religious education in private schools, remain controversial in contemporary Indonesia as various interest groups attempt to shape the system according to their respective goals. These concerns show how during the New Order era, even though education was highly state controlled, public debates about the role of religion in the state did emerge in this context.

NEW ORDER EDUCATION FOR A PANCASILA NATION

One of the major attempts to educate youth to be loyalist and nationalist was enacted through the Suharto regime's development and implementation of a moral and civic educational program, Pancasila Moral Education (PMP—Pendidikan Moral Pancasila). In 1975, PMP was instituted as a required component of the curriculum at all educational levels for at least two hours each week to educate students in the national ideology (Nishimura 1995, 311). The curriculum was imposed as a technology to shape citizens who were loyal not only to Indonesia but to the Suharto government in particular. The government initially planned for PMP to replace religious education within the national curriculum, but the proposal was met with opposition from Islamic groups; the compromise was that *both* PMP and religious education would be part of the national curriculum (Mujiburrahman 2006, 230). PMP was engaged in fashioning and disseminating a particular vision of nation, intent on using the educational system to reproduce the beliefs and norms of that particular vision of nation in the next generation.

The foundational component of the PMP moral and civic education program was the five principles of the Pancasila, as laid out in the preamble of the 1945 Constitution. Because of its symbolic weight as the multiconfessional (rather than Islamic) basis of the nation, Pancasila served as a broad foundation for national unity amid religious and ethnic difference (Rudnyckyj 2010, 191). The principles were reinterpreted and turned into the basis of an educational program training citizens to enact them in their daily lives, with the assumption that knowledge about the principles could be neatly transferred to the moral character of students (Nishimura 1995, 310). This emphasis on enacting rather than simply believing is linked to the regime's strong focus on development that required action and sacrifice from all citizens. Complicity or shared belief was considered insufficient to unite the country and drive the economy forward. An example of this focus on enacting Pancasila principles can be seen in PMP's teaching of mutual assistance (*gotong royong*). Under the New Order, national values were cast as reincarnations of traditional indigenous values of social harmony that provide guidance for self-conduct in all social relationships in a plural society (Weatherbee 1985a, 188).

Prior to 1980, PMP course textbooks were not standardized, and several versions were produced and approved by the state for implementation within schools. One version of the textbook in use prior to official approval by the state led to significant controversy in its highly Islamic interpretation of the first pillar of Pancasila, belief in *Ketuhanan Yang Maha Esa* (the One Almighty God). The textbook included the statement that "God does not have a father and mother. God does not have a son and is not labeled as a son," openly repudiating the Christian doctrines of the trinity and the incarnation (quoted in Mujiburrahman 2006, 231). Enacting a further measure of control over the curriculum and its presentation in textbooks, the state later entrusted the development of the PMP curriculum to the Pancasila Laboratory at the Teacher Training Institute in Malang, East Java. The laboratory had been established in 1967 to further elaborate on the doctrine of, collect public opinion about, and produce educational materials based on Pancasila (Song 2008, 176).

Education in the Pancasila principle of belief in the One Almighty God, covered at all grade levels, also encoded normative stances toward religion and religious difference within the national framework. Religious difference was clearly mentioned and pointed out through differences in houses of worship and religious holidays in the PMP curriculum. Ultimately, difference was framed in the curriculum as easily overcome, with a focus on how all religious believers (and followers of the state-approved traditional belief systems) are united through their belief in the One Almighty God. Such portrayals of difference, however, were met with backlash and critique from modernist Muslim circles. One junior high school textbook that alarmed modernist Muslim groups had instructed that religions take different paths, but are all leading toward God, using the metaphor of different modes of transportation (train, bus, ship) to arrive at the same destination (Mujiburrahman 2006, 232). Focusing on the lens of national unity, textbooks projected religious difference as existent but ultimately superficial, easily overcome in the service of national unity.

The PMP curriculum was designed to provide instruction in Pancasila values suited for each grade level, which in practice meant that the same themes were continually stressed and reintroduced at each grade level. As is also true for the elementary school PMP textbooks, the first chapter of a tenth-grade PMP textbook is about building up one's life based on belief in the One Almighty God (Kemendikbud 1983a). It includes sections about the obligation of Indonesians to believe in God, the requirement to value followers of other religions, and the meaning of religious holidays. At this grade level, students are required to read about the legal basis for the principle of belief in a supreme God from the constitution and other important sources. Exhortations to enact religious tolerance are prominent within the textbook and defined by examples of allowing others to celebrate their respective religious holidays, with the clarification that tolerance does not involve the mixing of religious teachings. Furthermore, religious harmony is positioned as a necessary attitude and behavior in service of national development, rather than an end in itself: "With the behavior of mutual respect and honor, a life that is harmonious, orderly, and peaceful will be created so that national development can be accomplished" (Kemendikbud 1983a, 7).

Discussions of regional and cultural differences in the context of integration were also part of the PMP curriculum geared toward teaching students how to implement the third pillar of Pancasila: national unity. In the twelfth-grade PMP textbook, the relationship between regional and national identity is directly addressed, with the assertion that regional cultures are the foundation for national culture. Students are told that they must recognize and honor religious, ethnic, cultural, and regional differences, as they are continually reminded of the national motto, "Unity in Diversity," which they would have certainly memorized by this point in their education. Students read that the Indonesian nation is made up of many different ethnic groups, but that, consequently, "we should not foreground our ethnic groups because that will lead to our disintegration" (Kemendikbud 1983b, 49). The wealth and beauty of difference within the country are continually emphasized in the chapter, with regional dances discussed as a model form of cultural difference to which students should contribute by learning and performing.

Rather than creating educational programs exclusively geared toward the young generation, the regime also sought to indoctrinate government employees and public figures through the implementation of the "Training for the Application and Realization of Pancasila," referred to in Indonesian with the name P4.[3] The program was first instituted in 1978 and was required for all civil servants, including teachers, and employees of state-owned corporations. Government employees were required to undertake the two-week P4 training every five years, and their performance was recorded and taken into consideration for promotions (Rudnyckyj 2010, 196–197). At the program's inception, the goal was to ensure that all Indonesian citizens would be exposed to the Pancasila training at some point, and the expansion of the program was carried out over time. By 1984, the target trainees also included religious leaders, and by 1985, P4 was launched in junior and senior high schools, where PMP was already a part of the standard curriculum (Weatherbee 1985b, 188). Many social organizations and associations also undertook P4 training voluntarily as a way to signal their alignment with the politics of the Suharto regime (Morfit 1981, 838).

Analyses of PMP and P4 programs often focus on their operation as a "corporatist system of state control" (McGregor 2002, 47), again echoing assumptions about educational institutions as a secular arm of the state. This view not only obscures how religion and religious groups continued to shape the scope and content of the project, but also tends to focus on the ideological content itself rather than the ethical imperatives it promoted. The educational programs, beyond teaching national values, implicitly introduced an acceptable range of action or belief, anything outside of which could be deemed anti-state or anti-Pancasila. The state education programs position the individual in relationship to "a curriculum that demands overt, unquestioning acceptance" (Leigh 1999, 52). However, accounts of the state-run moral education programs have narrowly focused on their intended purpose, rather than a careful ethnographic account of educational process. As a result, many assumed that the programs were highly effective, without examining the potential interpretations that could be drawn from them.

There was clearly a strong interest on the part of the regime in maintaining as much authority as possible over the curriculum and its transmission. Apart from the state control over the development of textbooks and educational materials, educators themselves were required to undergo P4 educational programs. In addition, the PMP curriculum promoted an environment where the textbook, and not the teacher, was meant to be the authoritative source of knowledge (Leigh 1999, 46–47). Ethnographic observations by Lyn Parker (2002) and Pam Nilan (2003) indicate that teachers often enthusiastically relied on textbooks, teaching by reading directly from the textbook, and students were directed to learn by memorizing or copying down sections of the text. The existence of a national examination system encourages students and teachers to rely heavily on the material as presented in the state-produced textbooks. The official goals of the PMP and P4 educational programs were to inculcate a framework for enacting Pancasila in daily life, and to combine moral and civic education to cultivate moral attitudes and instill a sense of nationalism. The implicit goal of the educational program, however, was to promote one specific vision of nation, of which the Suharto regime was understood as both the exemplar and protector.

The methodological control that was exerted over the PMP educational program indicates an attempt to prevent alternative interpretations of the material from arising at several levels. This authoritarian level of surveillance led many to assume that education under the New Order functioned as a hegemonic instrument, unquestioningly effective in the transmission of national values from the level of state ideology directly onto students' characters (Shiraishi 1997; Leigh 1999). However, the same youth who had been exposed to the national civic and moral education programs throughout their educational careers became a major driving force in the pro-democracy movement of the late 1990s, spearheading critiques of the regime.

Thus, an analysis of educational programs remains an important tool for understanding the visions of nation and coexistence presented as normative by the state and other organizations that influence curriculum development (Doumato and Starrett 2007; Kaplan 2006). As emphasized above, state efforts to control the curriculum, even under an authoritarian regime, cannot fully control its reception or the interpretations that are drawn from it (Starrett 1998; Coe 2005). Within the pro-democracy *reformasi* movement that swept Indonesia and forced authoritarian president Suharto to step down from power, Indonesian youth—particularly university students—played an important role in galvanizing public support for their increasingly critical and confrontational political stance. Although the New Order regime had attempted to depoliticize college campuses through the Campus Normalization Law, youth were able to position themselves as a moral rather than political force with the aim to correct, not challenge, the regime (Aspinall 2005, 118).[4] This suggests that not only were many youths capable of escaping the narrow ideological control enacted upon them, they were also able to consider another framework of ethical action that still oriented itself toward nationalist ideals.

REDEFINING PANCASILA FOR A DEMOCRATIC ERA

In contemporary Indonesia, the terms of the nation itself and the resulting consequences for religious pluralism are still under negotiation. The shift from an authoritarian regime to a democratic government where freedom of expression is possible has led to new manifestations of identity politics. Religious resurgence over the past several decades has led to an increasing social and cultural emphasis on piety and morality, at the same time as restrictions have been lifted on the manifestations of religious identity in the public sphere. Limits on the founding of political parties have been removed, and religion has increasingly become a mobilizing factor. Furthermore, this emergence of new forms of identity politics has taken place during a massive decentralization campaign aimed at giving greater autonomy to provinces outside of Java, such as North Sulawesi.

One of the most devastating manifestations of identity politics that emerged was the ethnic and religious violence that broke out in various regions of the archipelago in the late 1990s and early 2000s. Indonesia as a national project is challenged by the incorporation of profound ethnic and religious diversity, but this sudden escalation and boiling over of tensions elicited questions about the future of a nation with a historical legacy of pluralism that had previously seemed more or less settled, or at least highly controlled by the state. Many Indonesian observers have suggested that rising levels of intolerance are strongly related to a new social climate where religion is foregrounded in belonging and identity. Michel Picard has described the communal tensions of the post-Suharto era, largely organized around oppositional religious identities, as due to the fact that the "Pancasila state ideology gave way to confrontational identity politics" (2011, 17). Such a characterization brings up an important question about the contemporary role of Pancasila in a state where an interpretation and indoctrination of the ideology have established a normative framework for understanding religious difference and approaching interreligious relations.

The question of how Pancasila is being redefined in contemporary, democratic Indonesia is important for understanding whether it retains any legitimacy in shaping the relationship between religion and state and the relationships among religious communities. Political scientist Alfred Stepan argues that, in principle, Pancasila provides a model for a "multivalued" secularism because it historically enabled the rejection of an Islamic state and gives a positive value to diversity of religion, a condition for the ability of the state to provide respect and support for all recognized religions (2011, 130). Stepan maintains that democracy does not require a strict separatist variety of secularism, but does require "twin tolerations," defined as "the minimal degree of toleration that democracy needs to receive or induce from religion and the minimal degree of toleration that religion needs to receive or induce from the state for the polity to be democratic" (2011, 116).

As the state ideology had been turned into a vehicle for propaganda and control under the New Order regime, it was largely discredited as a meaningless ideology in the public sphere at the turn of the twenty-first century (Lindsey 2012, 45), which complicated its ability to serve as a rallying cry for religious pluralism and freedom in contemporary democratic Indonesia. The MPR even issued a statement recognizing that the Suharto regime had misused Pancasila, and that Pancasila "should become a national ideology that is 'open to discussion for the future of Indonesia'" (quoted in Lindsey 2012, 45). Serious consequences have resulted from the shift, even in terms of legal interpretations of the doctrine and the relationship between religion and state that it encodes. But there has also been a strong effort in recent years to revive and revitalize Pancasila, visible not only in political circles but also in public discussions and in the civic education curriculum.

The reaffirmation of a multiconfessional nation and the adoption of a constitutional amendment to uphold principles of freedom of religion and worship are positive indicators of the strength and extent of democratic commitment to citizens' rights on issues of religion. However, the state also used Pancasila to legitimate its deep involvement in religious affairs by citing the upholding of piety as within its purview, thereby "facilitating a state role in Islam and vice versa" (Ricklefs 2012, 448) that is not compatible with strong twin tolerations in practice. The strength of movements calling for the implementation of shari'a-based legislation (especially at the provincial level in the context of decentralization), the increase in legal action against religious groups labeled as heterodox, and the increase in high-profile blasphemy cases illustrate this trend. While those opposed to the adoption of shari'a-based legislation have rallied around and in some ways revived Pancasila, it is also important to note that pro-shari'a actors are often working within the democratic system to enact legislation (Lindsey 2012, 3). Further complicating matters is the diversity of actors backing shariʻa-inspired legislation; many regulations have been proposed not by Islamic but by secular political parties in attempts to establish their moral legitimacy (Bush 2008, 182). Furthermore, many of the groups in favor of shariʻa legislation argue that the principles of Pancasila do not conflict with legal Islamization (Bowen 2013, 157).

The legal debates and questions related to Pancasila demonstrate the importance of the various meanings given to the national ideology and its social and political consequences. It is clear that religion and religious institutions play a prominent role in contemporary Indonesia, though public deliberation continues about what the religion-state relationship should look like and what it means for a deeply plural society. The parameters of this relationship are particularly important because of indicators that Indonesia, following a global trend, has begun to experience a democratic regression among indications of illiberal repression (Menchik 2019; Warburton and Aspinall 2019).

EDUCATION FOR PANCASILA-MINDED DEMOCRATIC CITIZENS

As Indonesia began the process of democratic transition, the national curriculum required an overhaul to educate a new generation of Indonesian citizens in democratic attitudes and values. The 2003 National Education Act was intended to reform the educational system, declaring the objective to educate democratic citizens who are pious (*beriman dan bertakwa kepada Tuhan Yang Maha Esa*) and of noble character (*berakhlak mulia*), indicating a commitment to both democracy and state-endorsed religiosity (Syafruddin 2011, 27). Since the passing of the 2003 National Education Act, however, there have been several rounds of curriculum changes that have presented their own visions and generated new deliberations about how to educate democratic citizens and the role that religion can play toward this goal.[5]

Introduction of the 2006 School-Based Curriculum, KTSP (Kurikulum Tingkat Satuan Pendidikan), involved a comprehensive overhaul of the national curriculum. Against a backdrop of massive government decentralization and ongoing democratization, KTSP intended to allow schools to play a greater role in developing curricular materials (Suhadi et al. 2014, 21). In other words, individual schools could have more autonomy in choosing how to implement broad directives in accordance with local needs, availability of resources, and the training level of teachers, among other factors. However, before the new curriculum had even been fully implemented across the country, a new round of curriculum development began, once again promising major changes, development of new textbooks, and new rounds of teacher training regarding implementation.

A revised version of the national curriculum, referred to as the 2013 Curriculum (Kurikulum 2013) was developed for implementation in schools across Indonesia. The curriculum sought to address two major concerns: the poor performance of Indonesian students on math and science assessments, and the perceived increase in moral failings among Indonesian youth. In backing the 2013 Curriculum, the government argued that the earlier KTSP and its methods of evaluation were overly focused on cognitive performance, and that the increasing prevalence of violence and corruption across the nation needed to be addressed through an education program that focuses on character development (Suhadi et al. 2014, 24).

The new emphasis on character education in the 2013 Curriculum entailed shifts in both civic and religious educational directives. In terms of civic education, the curriculum requires two hours per week of instruction for senior high school students in Pancasila and Citizenship Education (PPKn—Pendidikan Pancasila dan Kewarganegaraan), showing a renewed vigor for Pancasila as an integral component of democratic civic education. However, a major challenge has been the reinvention and reinterpretation of Pancasila to make it a suitable basis for democratic citizenship education after its initial de-emphasis during the democratic transition (Gaylord 2007, 48). The MPR had passed legislation to stop the P4 program after Suharto's resignation in 1998 (Lindsey 2012, 45), and a new civic education curriculum was in development, called Citizenship Education (PKn—Pendidikan Kewarganegaraan), which replaced Pancasila-based civic education (Fearnley-Sander and Yulaelawati 2008, 115). The initial de-emphasis of the national ideology in the democratic civic education curriculum related to its general loss of currency in the public sphere (Lindsey 2012, 45). Among civic educators in Indonesia today, however, there is significant support for implementing a more strongly Pancasila-centric democratic civic education curriculum. Debates about the meaning of Pancasila for the democratic era in Indonesia and how it should be taught in schools are centrally about the role of religion in contemporary Indonesia and the question of how to live together in difference.

Renewed support for a Pancasila-centric civic education is based on two major discourses among educators. The first of these discourses posits that the lack of Pancasila education during the early period of democratic transition is directly related to the perceived moral degradation among youth, and argues that a renewed Pancasila civic education program will facilitate the teaching of uniquely Indonesian moral values. This particular perspective often assumes that teaching only democratic values in civic education courses has led to an excessively liberal and individualistic interpretation of democracy that is not compatible with Indonesian tradition and values. Therefore, some civic education researchers have encouraged a Pancasila foundation in order to give democratic civic education the moral basis needed for the success of democracy in Indonesia (see Triyanto 2013). Notably, the focus is on the transformation that an understanding of Pancasila can provide to change individual students' characters.

Today, Pancasila is taught as a moral foundation, meant to protect against liberal ideas deemed incompatible with indigenous values, as well as against political Islamism. In early 2016, when there was widespread panic about the spread of what was referred to as an LGBT "lifestyle" among Indonesian youth, Minister of Education and Culture Anies Baswedan announced that the educational system would counter the trend through increased focus on religious values and Pancasila (Republika 2016a). In early 2016, as there was also increased concern about the spread of Islamic radicalism in the country, several government figures and educators spoke out against radicalism and for the need to implement the Pancasila ideology to protect against radicalism on college campuses (Republika 2016b). This line of reasoning resonates with concerns about simply importing Western educational materials and methods without infusing them with Indonesian cultural values, and also recognizes that students may be influenced by ideological media outside of school with which discourses encountered in the school must compete.

The second common discourse calling for a Pancasila revival in education, more concerned with how Pancasila can collectively transform society, links the lack of Pancasila in civic education during the early reform era to the outbreak of ethnic and religious conflicts across the archipelago. The two perspectives on the need for Pancasila education are certainly not mutually exclusive, but this particular one addresses the need for a framework to manage a diverse society and the important role that Pancasila can play toward this end. A senior lecturer in civic education at a private Muhammadiyah university in Central Java who has seen several rounds of curriculum changes over the course of his career explains: "Upon entering the reform era, it was like people were allergic to Pancasila, and so the name and the material related to Pancasila decreased. . . . After the experience of *reformasi,* ten years in, the effects of that emerged. For example, the impacts on tolerance, and then, people did not understand the importance of diversity. There were horizontal conflicts everywhere, and like now, when the 2013 Curriculum was developed, Pancasila material was included again with the name 'Citizenship and Pancasila Education.'" A prominent civic education professor in North Sulawesi similarly connects the near disappearance of Pancasila in the early reform-era curriculum to the serious communal conflicts that plagued Indonesia at the time. He argues that Pancasila is necessary to provide national unity, and this is why it has been rightly reinstated as an important component in the 2013 Curriculum.

Among civic educators, there remains a tension between the desire to respond to the new needs and opportunities in a burgeoning democracy and the nostalgia for the subject's highly accorded status and the clear moral directives of the PMP and P4 programs implemented by the New Order regime. At a meeting in Central Java for the regional Indonesian Professional Association of Pancasila and Citizenship Education in 2015, attendees expressed dismay about the lack of prestige given to civic education and brainstormed ways to increase the standing of the subject in universities. While agreeing on the need for a more scientific and academic approach in order to be taken seriously by other disciplines, at the same time, they waxed nostalgic about the greatness of PMP and P4 during the New Order era—especially the moral foundation they had provided students. One teacher at the meeting complained that Pancasila and Citizenship Education had become a "leftover subject" (*mata pelajaran titipan*) expected to address all topics that do not fit in other academic subjects, ranging from anti-corruption education to the importance of obeying traffic laws. The invited speaker, himself a professor of civic education, countered that this approach was not wrong, as these do all fall under the broad scope and purpose of civic education: "to form citizens who are good, smart, and able to live together in society" (*membentuk warga negara yang baik, cerdas, dan bisa hidup bersama masyarakat*).

EDUCATION FOR MORAL AND PIOUS DEMOCRATIC CITIZENS

As part of the state's approach to character education, the 2013 Curriculum requires three hours of instruction per week for senior high school students in the subject of Pendidikan Agama dan Budi Pekerti (Religious and Character Education)—according to one's professed religion—intended to emphasize the moral aspect of religious education. Although the subject's name uses the Indonesian (by way of the Javanese language) term *budi pekerti,* which has the connotation of moral values related to custom and politeness, the foundation for morality in this case is unequivocally assumed to be religion (Suhadi et al. 2014, 33). However, in bringing concerns of character education beyond specified courses, the 2013 Curriculum for high school students also requires students to meet spiritual competencies in each grade level and each academic subject. In this sense, students are evaluated by all their teachers on their application and realization of religious teachings based on professed religious beliefs. For example, one of several spiritual core competencies for the subject of Indonesian history for tenth grade requires that students "live up to the example of leaders in interreligious tolerance and practice it in everyday life" (Kemendikbud 2013, 62). Students are also evaluated on social competencies in each subject, including honesty, cooperation, politeness, and tolerance. While subjects like religious education and civic education often do explicitly address these topics in the curriculum, many other subjects do not. Thus, the extent to which these competencies are emphasized in class, and particularly how they are evaluated, depends significantly on individual teachers.

High school teachers often pose questions about grading students on their spiritual and social competencies at teacher-training events, focused mostly on the practical difficulty of keeping track of the academic and character grades for each student they teach. At an in-house curriculum training put on by the regional education office at the state madrasah MAN in Manado, the speaker explained that teachers must observe and evaluate students on their behavior. He detailed the kinds of actions teachers should look for: Do students pray to begin class? Do they regularly perform the five daily prayers required in Islam? Do they always greet teachers? Do they leave without permission during class? He proceeded to present a series of PowerPoint slides with a dizzying array of tables as a model to organize the grading and evaluation of students, claiming that grading in accordance with the new curriculum is simple. During the training, a science teacher turned around and leaned over the table to talk to me about her exasperation with the seemingly never-ending evaluation that the 2013 Curriculum requires, summarizing her feelings with her declaration that "it gives me a headache!" *(bikin pusing).* She takes the process seriously, but finds it exhausting. When a student greets her appropriately outside of school—at the market or the mall, for example—she tries to remember the name and class of the student so that she can later record the encounter and add points to their grade.

Indeed, the speaker at the training had explained that the spiritual and social competencies are not limited to students' performance within that particular course subject, or even on school grounds, but also include students' behavior outside of school in terms of their confidence, curiosity, discipline, cooperation, and concern for the environment.

At the private Catholic Lokon School, students receive a behavioral grade to evaluate their social competencies as well as an academic grade to evaluate their performance for each academic subject. Students are required to achieve a grade of C or higher in behavior in order to pass, assuming that their academic grade also meets the D minimum. When students are chattering amongst themselves in civic education class, the teacher, Ibu Sandra, reminds them that they are graded on their behavior as well as their academic performance. Because it is a boarding school, students also receive marks from the dormitory staff in three areas, delineated by the school's motto: *Veritas, Virtus, Fides* (Latin for "Truth, Virtue, Faith"). Of the many criteria upon which students are evaluated, two examples are their ability to "socialize with anyone" (*bergaul dengan siapa saja*) and to "value difference of religion, tribe, ethnicity, opinion, behavior, and the actions of others who are different" (*menghargai perbedaan agama, suku, etnis, pendapat, sikap dan tindakan orang lain yang berbeda*).

The emphasis on morality in the most recent version of the curriculum is not new, since the New Order PMP and P4 curricula were also extremely focused on implementing a particular moral order through education. Indeed, it is not an overstatement to say that all educational projects relate to some moral agenda. But the way in which the specific moral values to be imparted are made explicit and designed to infuse the entire educational endeavor do signal the centrality of religiosity within the state project to shape a new generation of Indonesians. The curriculum is also based on the assumption that these moral imperatives must be learned as individual traits, as it requires that each student be graded individually on their ability to demonstrate a level of character deemed acceptable in order to justify continued academic progress.

RELIGION AND DIVERSITY IN THE 2013 CIVIC EDUCATION CURRICULUM

Discourses present within the government-produced and distributed high school religious and civic education textbooks represent another way in which education acts as a site of deliberation about the relationship between religion and state, the place accorded to religion in public life, and how to approach religious diversity. In line with the view of education as an arena of debate about religion and difference, the textbooks reflect the influence of varying actors and their particular visions of Indonesian nationhood, negotiated and packaged within a textbook format. When they are examined together, it is clear that current religious and civic education textbooks provide varied ethical frames for understanding religious difference rather than one unitary view. Consistent with the focus on individual moral development monitored through competency requirements, tolerance of diversity is often approached as an individual trait to be extolled and encouraged in students, supported by religious and nationalist discourses in the curriculum. At the same time, as religious education curricula convey the importance of respect for diversity (including religious diversity) in the name of national harmony, several also recast it as a potential strategy of proselytization.

The civic education textbooks produced by the state for the 2013 Curriculum and the PMP textbooks of the New Order era both assert a relatively strong role for the state in regulating religious affairs. However, a major difference between the textbooks is an increased emphasis in the 2013 Curriculum on individual religiosity and religious practice as an enactment of citizenship. Furthermore, there is a stronger emphasis in the new curriculum on the rights and obligations of citizens and on human rights in relation to religious freedom. The textbooks for the 2013 Curriculum position religiosity as a necessary component of enacting Indonesian citizenship, in line with the government's educational program to promote character education and moral development. At the same time, the textbooks also implicitly demonstrate the strong role that the state plays in religious life, particularly through its role in defining and legally enforcing what counts as religious orthodoxy or as blasphemy.

In civic education textbooks that follow the 2013 Curriculum, religion is discussed in its importance for the Indonesian nation as a whole and for individual belief and character. Emphasis on individual religious practice is evident mostly through discussion of implementing Pancasila values in daily life. For example, in the eleventh-grade PPKn textbook, students are asked to complete a self-evaluation on actions clearly intended to index morality (ranging from showing up to school on time to helping victims of natural disaster) by checking one of the boxes to indicate how often (always, often, sometimes, or never) they engage in such behaviors. The statements related to individual religiosity are as follows: "1) I don't bother others who are worshipping 2) I join religious activities 3) I don't choose friends on the basis of religious difference" (Kemendikbud 2014e, 56–57). Within the instructions, students are advised to change their behavior regarding any of the items for which they checked "sometimes" or "never." The main body of the textbook presents information about citizen rights, obligations, and principles, and discussion of their practice comes mainly through the assignments or activities students are asked to complete to check understanding at the end of each chapter.

Respect for diversity—religious, ethnic, and cultural—is framed in terms of a need for national integration in the face of both internal and external threats. In the tenth-grade PPKn textbook, this topic is addressed in the chapter titled "Knitting Togetherness in Diversity" (*Merajut Kebersamaan Dalam Kebhinekaan*) (Kemendikbud 2014d). The treatment of the topic of diversity remains similar to that under the New Order in its formalistic discussion of difference, although there is a recognition of the conflicts that have plagued Indonesia in recent times and the need to address intolerance through education. The framing of respect for diversity in terms of rights is what most distinguishes the discourse from the more coercive and integralist application present in the New Order textbooks. In addition, in the exercise portion, students are asked to reflect on a conflict in Indonesia that they have heard about or found out about through the media and discuss the causes and consequences of the conflict. Ultimately, the extensive diversity of the country is recognized and presented as both a potential challenge (as it increases the nation's vulnerability to conflict) and an enrichment through potential opportunities to enhance development prospects. While intercultural tolerance does figure in the discussion, the only concrete example provided to students on how to accomplish it is to perform various regional ethnic dances, which will "give rise to interethnic sympathy" (Kemendikbud 2014d, 64).

Religious harmony is also an important topic in the civic education textbooks, and is presented in three parts: internal harmony, interreligious harmony, and harmony between religious groups and the government (Kemendikbud 2014e, 48). Internal harmony is defined as respect and tolerance for those within one's own broader religious community, with the qualification that it is required as long as their beliefs/practices do not deviate from religious teachings. The explanation of interreligious harmony clarifies that it does not entail any kind of "mixing" of religious teachings, and gives an example of implementation through an interreligious dialogue centered around peace and harmony rather than a discussion of difference. The last principle about the relationship between religious communities and the state gives a reminder that people should obey religious rules and obligations, but are also required to obey Indonesian national law. The principle specifically rejects Islamism by clarifying that religious law does not negate or override national law, but that citizens have an obligation to both.

DIVERSITY IN THE 2013 RELIGIOUS EDUCATION CURRICULA

A consideration of religious education curricula requires an analysis of the textbooks for multiple religious traditions, as students are separated by professed religion. In this section, the focus is on Muslim, Protestant, and Catholic religious education textbooks. In Indonesia, Protestantism (*agama Kristen*) and Catholicism (*agama Katolik*) are considered separate religions according to the Ministry of Religious Affairs, and therefore have separate religious education courses and curricula. Textbooks for each religion include material on both religious dogma and ethics, in line with the approach of pushing religious values as the foundation of students' moral characters.

All religious education textbooks examined consider the position of religion within the Indonesian state, and explicitly focus on religious teachings that relate to tolerance. The Center for Religious and Cross-Cultural Studies has published a report on the politics of religious education in the 2013 Curriculum (Suhadi et al. 2014), with an in-depth analysis of the new curriculum and textbooks, focusing particularly on the teaching values related to multiculturalism. The authors argue that religious education is an extremely important forum for presenting the values of tolerance and multiculturalism to students, but that the curriculum ultimately prioritizes teaching religious dogma rather than ethics. In addition, the researchers determined that the Protestant and Catholic religious education books include material about respecting religious diversity in the context of Indonesia as a plural society, but that the material for Islamic religious education was more limited in providing students with an orientation toward respecting religious diversity (Suhadi et al. 2014, 39).

In the state-produced eleventh-grade Islamic education textbook, there is one chapter devoted exclusively to the subject of "Tolerance as the Unifying Mechanism of the Nation," including the importance of interreligious harmony for national unity (Kemendikbud 2014a). The three levels of religious harmony (internal, interreligious, and between religious groups and the state) mirror those presented in the civic education textbooks. Furthermore, there is an admission that these principles have not always been upheld in Indonesia, and that it has led to conflicts that endanger the unity of the nation, such as in Poso and Ambon during the early reform era. The text provides Qur'anic verses and hadith to showcase religious teachings related to enacting tolerance and avoiding violence.[6] However, within the same context, it also positions Islam as a missionizing or proselytizing religion, a characteristic that has been noted in regards to the revised Islamic education curriculum in general (Suhadi et al. 2014, 35). One section that presents the "tolerant behavior that must be fostered in accordance with Islamic teachings" explains the importance of enacting mutual respect between people of different religions as follows: "We cannot force our will on others so they join our faith. People of other faiths also cannot force their will on us. Upon seeing noble behavior, God willing, others will be interested. The Messenger of God [Muhammad] always demonstrated noble character to all, including his enemies, and many unbelievers were drawn to the character of the Messenger of God and converted to Islam because of its glory" (Kemendikbud 2014a, 196).

Up until this point in the textbook, living with mutual respect for other religions is presented as a necessary part of living in a plural nation and upholding this unity, one that is supported by Islamic teachings. The connection to proselytizing occurs late in the chapter and certainly presents the possibility that the reader will reorient their understanding of tolerance as required insofar as it serves the purpose of spreading the faith.

In the Protestant religious education textbooks, values related to living in a plural society are discussed in relation to several different topics, such as maturity and honesty, becoming a responsible person in society, resisting exclusivism within the Christian community, and loving one's enemies. The focus on broad Christian ethics as opposed to dogma is somewhat due to the existence of many Protestant Christian denominations in Indonesia, which might have slightly different dogmatic interpretations. As a result, the textbooks focus more on broad Christian values, the assumption being that the students will learn dogma from their respective churches (Suhadi et al. 2014, 33–34).

In the state-produced tenth-grade Protestant religious education textbook, the chapter titled "God's Work through Diversity" (*Karya Allah dalam Kepelbagaian*) introduces diversity as a blessing from God that must be respected and requires each person to work for the unity of the Indonesian nation through the frame of "Unity in Diversity" (Kemendikbud 2014c). The chapter also includes Bible verses related to the respect of diversity and calls on students to follow the example of Jesus Christ in interacting with those who are different.[7] At the same time, the requirement to maintain a strong Christian identity in these interactions is reinforced by scripture, asking students to demonstrate their faith and Christian identity so that "people can witness a full Christian life" (Kemendikbud 2014c, 83). A more in-depth or concrete explanation for how students should express this identity while enacting the values of respect and tolerance in interactions with others is not provided.

The Catholic religious education curriculum addresses the importance of respect for religious difference through the frames of both the Second Vatican Council (Vatican II) and human rights. The eleventh-grade textbook has a chapter on human rights that includes articles from the Universal Declaration of Human Rights as well as a consideration of human rights in accordance with Jesus's teachings. The role of the Church in the broader society is asserted: "*The Church must try to build cohesion among citizens* in the spirit of love and peace. Upholding cohesion in a society is a unique contribution of religious groups. Together with those of another religion, and those who are good-willed, Christians must fight for justice in brotherhood with all people" (Kemendikbud 2014b, 130–131, emphasis in original). The chapter also discusses building up a culture of nonviolence and love. One notable difference in the Catholic religious education textbook, compared to the Islamic and Protestant textbooks, is the extensive use of current events and news articles within the lessons, and exercises about these events that require critical analysis. Within the Catholic textbook, several sensitive issues are addressed, including protests against building churches in Java (presented as a clear human rights violation), the increasing gap between the rich and the poor, the conflict in Syria, and the death penalty.

Overall, all the religious education textbooks reflect an increased focus on ethics and character building, in line with the goals of the 2013 Curriculum. The textbooks project the assumption that in order to be good citizens, students need a strong religious foundation of morality. There are clearly attempts to address current social issues of intolerance and religious conflicts through the inclusion of material related to diversity and respect for difference for the sake of national unity. The material is supported by religious teachings and is presented from a religious perspective that preaches interreligious tolerance, though at times tolerance is discussed as ultimately for the sake of proselytizing or for demonstrating one's religious identity to others.

CURRICULUM ON PAPER AND IN PRACTICE

Analyses of educational projects and their textbooks serve as a starting point for linking the realm of education to broader public debates about the place of religion in the nation and the accommodation of religious diversity. By examining secularism, we can see the importance of education as a site of deliberation about the relationship between religion and nation, and the potential consequences for the accommodation of religious diversity. A historical look at the treatment of diversity under the New Order regime and its control through the PMP educational program demonstrates how the national ideology of Pancasila, providing a foundation for the multireligious character of state, became a major tool to delimit acceptable forms of difference.

While Pancasila as the state ideology may provide an orientation for a public ethical culture regarding the religion-state relationship and the question of how to live together in difference, it certainly does not determine it, or even give a clear template for accomplishing it. The ideology may be able to serve as a basis for coexistence in theory, but in post-Suharto Indonesia it has also been used by the state to justify increased support and regulation of the religious domain, as non-state actors vie to impart their own interpretation. As new manifestations of identity and difference have become possible in the public sphere, some groups and organizations have called for a Pancasila revival, urging its reinterpretation for a democratic era to counteract the new forms of exclusion and identity politics that have emerged. Civic educators maintain that the ideology needs to be brought back to impart values as a moral corrective at the individual level, in addition to its ability to serve as a unifying framework for the country.

An examination of the current civic and religious education programs and textbooks aptly illustrates the negotiation occurring between religion and state, and the uncertain consequences for the future of religious pluralism. The curricula clearly focus on individual character building, delineating spiritual and social competencies that students must meet to advance to the next grade level, in addition to the academic requirements. However, rather than providing a singular frame for approaching diversity and expressing tolerance, the civic and religious education curricula shine a light on the varying ethical frames presented in this ongoing deliberation. In the chapters that follow, the interpretation of these textbooks in the classroom setting, the physical organization of schools, extracurricular clubs, and more, will further stitch together the connection between schools as educational institutions and the deliberation that takes place in and through them in relation to broad public debates and public culture.

These analyses interrogate the typical association of educational institutions with a strictly secular state, and show how the inscribing of religion in the realm of education illuminates the intersection of many social processes. But what exactly does the curriculum tell us? It is important to be clear about the insights it can provide, as well as its limitations. On the one hand, it is easy to overemphasize the importance of the curriculum, as was done in analyses of the New Order's highly controlled educational project, informing assumptions that the highly controlled educational system was unequivocally effective. Of course, we now know that students played a central role in giving legitimacy to the pro-democracy movement, going against the regime. On the other hand, it is also too easy to downplay the significance of a textbook passage, noting that it may ultimately be overlooked or ignored in the classroom. This reality underscores the necessity to observe and examine education as a contingent and multicentered process, rather than a straightforward, top-down, and instantaneous transmission. Educational institutions are central to maintaining democratic institutions, and this is precisely because of their potential to scale up ethical frames that may resonate with individuals. Still, deliberation about the curriculum is not the end of this process, but the beginning.

Finally, it is important to underscore what is at stake. A rise in identity politics coupled with indications of democratic regression means that deliberations about the role that religion plays in public life and about its relationship to the state and the national imaginary are consequential. To understand the role that state ideologies like Pancasila or expressions of religious belonging might play in shaping public ethical culture, we need to investigate deliberations taking place *about* schools and curricula in addition to those taking place *within* them.

3

Public High School
Influence of the Protestant Majority

More than three hundred Protestant students from the public high school gathered at a private villa in Manado for an overnight religious retreat prior to the National Exam (*Ujian Nasional*), required for high school graduation in Indonesia. A giant printed poster with an image of Jesus teaching a group of children announced in bold capital letters, "I GOT ALL I NEED WHEN I GOT JESUS." A few Muslim students were also at the retreat, helping to prepare and organize meal service for their Christian classmates. In the evening, after several worship sessions with religious songs and sermons given by teachers and students, Pak Daniel took over the microphone to deliver an impassioned sermon. Pak Daniel is a Protestant religious education teacher who has been teaching at the school for nearly thirty years and tends to grab students' attention with his booming voice and fire-and-brimstone style of preaching. As students sat under a large tent in red and blue plastic chairs, Pak Daniel looked over the rim of his glasses and encouraged students to give up sinful behavior:

> Do you want to crucify Jesus a second time? Are there any boys who brought cigarettes to the retreat? Please, bring them up to the altar now to show your faith. Did you bring alcohol? We're not here for fun, we are here to praise God! We're going to start the process of self-evaluation [*periksa diri*] to think about our sins. Humans are sinful, but God gives us a chance to confess our sins, and we are forgiven. In a moment, we will confess our sins by writing them down on a piece of paper and throwing them into a bonfire. This will transform us.

Though no one gave up contraband in response to his sermon, the students did express enjoyment when throwing pieces of paper in the crackling bonfire at one o'clock in the morning to burn their sins. As teachers

66 : CHAPTER 3

FIGURE 3.1 Protestant students from SMA sing praise songs under a tent at a weekend retreat.

supervised, they continually reminded students the purpose of the bonfire was for worship and not for fun. The retreat was intended as spiritual preparation for national exams, for the students to undergo purification through the confession of sins before undertaking this trial. Catholic students, Muslim students, and Hindu students in the twelfth grade organized their own religious retreats for spiritual preparation in advance of the exams.

In this chapter, I focus on the public high school in Manado, called SMA, as a locus of deliberation about both religious belonging and coexistence. Although a public school, SMA is focused on deepening the religious character of its ethnically and religiously diverse student body to provide all students with a strong moral foundation. As is required of public schools by law, SMA provides religious education for all students in their respective religions. Moving beyond these basic legal requirements, teachers and administrators work to weave religion and religious practice into the daily routine of the school, encouraging participation in a number of religious activities.

In the context of this heightened attention to religion at the school, the analysis focuses on the ways that teachers and students produce an embodied religious belonging. The scene above provides a powerful sense of redemption and renewal through fire, asking students to participate in a religious ritual that promises to transform those involved, by first engaging in self-reflection and then watching their sins literally disappear, turning to ash. Embodied religious belonging is produced through explicitly religious practices and rituals, but is also produced through daily experiences at the school involving space, sound, food, and dress. Each of these elements shows how religious embodiment arises not only through individual religious experience, but also in the physical encounter with religious difference that manifests in various forms.

Everyday practices at the school and the production of embodied religious belonging are related to the conversations and reflections they incite about religiosity and the accommodation of religious difference beyond the school walls. These deliberations link to the contested frames of belonging in the province, drawing on the status of the province as both a Christian-majority region and one known for its respect of religious difference, deploying forms of both aspirational and majoritarian coexistence within the specific context of the public school.

The landscape of embodied religious belonging at SMA reveals a strong Protestant majoritarianism, even in an environment where the administration and students tend to support the principle of religious diversity and a deepening of religious practice in general. Protestant students and teachers further entrench this position by discursively focusing on their minority positioning on a national level while leveraging a majority position in practice. The importance of majority/minority positioning and the contextual shifting between the two relates to the ongoing deliberation about coexistence, demonstrating that the question continually applies both at the local and at the national scale.

The linkages between the local and national contexts are also forged as teachers deliver the national curriculum, negotiating its meaning and offering their own interpretations that make sense in Manado. Similarly, students apply their own understandings in participating and deliberating. This chapter underscores the many forms that deliberation may take. The ability of certain ethical frames about religious difference to take hold is not based exclusively on rational debate. The concept of "deliberation" (Varenne 2007) and its inspiration from liberal theories of education (Cremin 1976; Dewey 1916) risks conveying the assumption that rational debate in the public sphere is the primary mechanism of education and the formation of a public ethic. In this case, deliberation takes place as students make choices about what style of uniform to wear, and as they encounter and react to policies about halal food at the cafeteria, creating a sense of belonging through embodiment that is continually negotiated in response to religious others.

PUBLIC HIGH SCHOOL (SMA) PROFILE

I arrived at the public high school SMA for my first day of observation, relieved to see that the entrance gate on a bustling street of Manado was still unlocked, even though it was several minutes past the seven o'clock morning bell. Two school administrators remained stationed at the entrance, smiling and shaking the hands of students and teachers as they continued to arrive. Students were easily recognizable in their brown scouting uniforms, some pouring out of blue vans (*mikrolet*) that blared pop music, and others emerging from the sea of motorbikes parked on the sidewalk.

The gate opens up to the large central court of the school, surrounded by the rectangular three-story building that accommodates more than two thousand students every day. The court is open, but sheltered from both the piercing sunlight and the heavy downpours during the rainy season by a sloped corrugated metal roof. The edges of the court are peppered with trees and greenery. I soon discovered that the court is multifunctional, easily transformed to accommodate a range of activities: basketball games, worship sessions, student competitions, and informational meetings for parents. As I walked toward the teachers' lounge, I studied the one-story-high poster featuring a formal photo of all teachers and administrators at the school dressed up in matching bright-blue batik print uniforms and a slogan printed in English: "The Right Choice, The Bright Future."

SMA has a notable academic reputation in North Sulawesi, and is often referred to as a "favorite school" (*sekolah favorit*) among Manadonese because of its prestige and record of high academic achievement. The student body is ethnically and religiously diverse, loosely approximating the social diversity of the city of Manado. The majority of students are Protestant, with a sizable minority of Muslim students, a smaller group of Catholic students, and several Hindu, Buddhist, and Confucian students. Most Protestant students are affiliated with the mainstream GMIM denomination, but several other Christian traditions are represented as well, including Seventh-day Adventists and Pentecostals. Ethnically, the majority of students are Minahasan, but there is significant diversity on this front as well. In particular, Muslim students are mostly from Bolaang-Mongondow or Gorontalo ethnic groups.

Principal Jeiny always shows up to school events polished and well coiffed. Her face is seen throughout the school on printed posters and banners wishing students well on their national exams or marking the school's celebration of national holidays. Though she speaks in formal Indonesian when dictated by protocol, she prefers to talk to students and teachers in the local Melayu Manado in a lively and familiar manner. The first time I came to the school to seek her permission to conduct research there, I waited outside her office while she gave students a heartfelt pep talk before they set off to represent the school in a national academic competition. Jeiny is a devout Protestant, and is personally close to several of the Protestant religious education teachers at the school. The twelfth-grade Protestant student retreat took place at a villa she owns in Manado, and she was present for the entirety of the event, coordinating logistics and even delivering a sermon during one of the worship sessions.

Since her appointment as principal, Ibu Jeiny has made several important changes on the academic front. The most consequential was the decision to switch back to the 2006 KTSP Curriculum instead of moving forward with the 2013 Curriculum her predecessor had already started implementing at the school—a decision that has since been reversed to bring the school in line with national requirements. While teachers admitted having mixed feelings about sticking to the earlier curriculum and textbooks, few complained that the schedule allowed for a Monday–Friday school week, as opposed to the typical Monday–Saturday school week implemented at almost all other high schools in the area.

At SMA, I most often joined the Protestant and Islamic religious education classes. There are several Protestant religious education teachers, all of whom are affiliated with the GMIM Church. They teach the religious education courses, facilitate the small weekly student worship sessions, and coordinate larger school-wide events for Protestant students. In addition, several of them also take on roles as counselors at the school. The Islamic religious education teacher is also a lecturer at another Islamic institute in Manado and has many other commitments that often cause him to miss his scheduled classes. Muslim students had grown accustomed to his regular absence, and passed the time in the classroom chatting, eating, praying, taking selfies, or quietly reading. Due to the situation, I was able to more quickly get to know the Muslim students at the school and spent a significant amount of time conversing with them during their scheduled class time. I also joined civic education classes, spent time in the counseling room, participated in extracurricular activities (especially religious clubs), accompanied students on field trips, and attended school-wide assemblies.

DEEPENING RELIGIOSITY AT SMA

For the teachers and administrators at SMA, the clear path forward for ensuring effective character education is to increase the religious focus of the school. As a public school with students from varied religious backgrounds, this means that each student should deepen religious knowledge and practice within their own religious tradition. In addition to the required three hours weekly of religious instruction in students' professed religions, worship during school hours or religiously based extracurricular activities or events regularly take place.

As I arrived at the school one morning before the bell, I witnessed several students and teachers scattered on the sidewalk around the school entrance stop mid-step to bow their heads and fold their hands. The voice of Pak Daniel came crackling over the loudspeaker. On this day, he began to pray for the school, the students, and the teachers and administration, in a formal and rhythmic Indonesian, audible not only within the school, but on the surrounding street, competing with the concert of honking horns from morning commuters. Pak Daniel asked for God's wisdom and guidance as everyone carried out their daily activities. After several minutes of solemn prayer, with teachers and students frozen in place, the final phrase "in Jesus's name we pray, Amen" cued the recommencement of the hustle and bustle as students and teachers went in and prepared for the school day. Typically, one of the Protestant religious education teachers leads the morning prayer, although one teacher joked that Pak Daniel shouldn't be given the microphone again, lest he be tempted to perform an entire sermon.

Prayer is used to ritualize not only the opening of the school day but all major school activities and events as well. At an after-school ceremony to induct new members into the school's Red Cross (Palang Merah) club, the principal asked the Protestant religious education teacher Ibu Sonia to open the event with a prayer. When parents of seniors at SMA were called to the school for an information session about the national examinations, the principal again asked Ibu Sonia to lead a prayer in front of the parents before the meeting began.

The school's schedule is designed to accommodate one-hour worship sessions on Fridays in addition to the mandated time spent on religious education each week. The Protestant students stay in their homeroom class to carry out a student-led worship session with prayers, hymns, and a short sermon, with responsibilities rotating among the students throughout the academic year. At the same time, Muslim students meet with the Islamic religious education teacher to walk to a nearby neighborhood mosque and pray. Catholic and Hindu students also hold their own religious activities at the same time in different unoccupied classrooms. The principal regularly decides to shorten or even cancel academic classes on certain days to accommodate a worship session. These gatherings are often in celebration of particular holidays, such as Easter or Valentine's Day,[1] or to prepare students for academic competitions or events, such as the national examinations. These events are major productions that bring all of the Protestant students and teachers together in the main central court of the school to worship as one congregation.

There are also several religious clubs at SMA that allow students to spend additional time after school on religious activities—such as planning the execution of these extensive worship sessions—and encourage student-led worship. Although there are several religious extracurricular activities available at the school, I focused primarily on the activities of the Islamic students' club, Rohis, and one province-wide Protestant club, Pelsis, which had recruited several students from SMA. Muslim students gathered in a classroom after school to participate in the club Rohis, which is found at schools across Indonesia but can vary enormously in programming. The local club Pelsis (Pelayanan Siswa Kristen—Christian Student Ministry) gathered Protestant students to organize school worship activities and prepare for province-wide events and competitions. Previous studies have shown the importance that extracurricular religious clubs can have in Indonesian schools, acting as an arena where students debate ideas about coexistence, and also as a place where various social actors can gain influence among youth and spread ideas that impact plural coexistence in the broader society (Salim, Kailani, and Azekiyah 2011). Their place outside of the official curriculum makes them particularly important because they are potentially more susceptible to pressure and influence from local groups.

Pelsis is a province-wide organization active in identifying and recruiting Protestant students with leadership potential. The club is most active at public schools in North Sulawesi, and is founded on the principle that Christian students must be aware of their mission to preach the gospel everywhere, including in their respective schools. The organization's leader, Pastor Steven Liow, plans to expand the organization to the national level. He appeals to both Pancasila and Christian teachings of love in order to affirm the dedication of Protestant Christians in North Sulawesi to nationalist principles. The number of students active in Pelsis from any one school may be small, because those participating are typically identified specifically as leaders among their peers. Part of their training in Pelsis encourages them to take initiative within their schools to become leaders in other Christian groups and activities in the school and their community.

In short, the administration has instituted several policies that promote a strong emphasis on religion, integrating religious practices into the daily and weekly rituals of the school. As SMA is a public school, the administration is required to accommodate students of all religions by providing them with religious education according to their professed religion, and it does so enthusiastically and readily. Principal Jeiny also provides support for all of the extracurricular religious clubs and activities, promoting religious education and activities as a strong moral foundation that is intended to provide students with the skills they need to excel academically, spiritually, and socially.

EMBODIED RELIGIOUS BELONGING: RELATION TO SELF AND OTHER

In the school, however, religious practice is not the only instance where embodied religious belonging is produced and where students encounter its implications for a religiously diverse student body. In other words, religious belonging does not emerge in a vacuum exclusively focused on religious practice. Religious belonging takes on meaning in the quotidian reality of the school, particularly as youth encounter those from different religious backgrounds. These interactions are also mediated by school policies about the organization of space, the use of greetings and prayers, the provision of food in the cafeteria, and school uniforms. These physical realities do not determine understandings of religious difference, but they do propose ethical frames for approaching religious difference.

The tension between Manado's desire to model interreligious harmony and simultaneous efforts to secure the Protestant majority and influence in the region play out in this environment of the school. Schools act as arenas for debate about the position of religion within the national framework and scale different ethical normativities oriented toward religious difference. Administrators and teachers are strongly supportive of all religious activities, yet the way that religious activities are implemented at the school evinces a de facto Protestant majoritarian influence. These frameworks, related to both aspirational coexistence and majoritarian coexistence, become tangible for youth at the school, which in turn impacts how students encounter and interpret religious belonging.

Embodiment relates to subjectivity, and is an important mode beyond discourse whereby youth develop a sense of belonging and ideas about diversity, partially through encountering the self in relation to others. Students contend with the religious belonging of others primarily through the practical and embodied realities of what their friends can eat and what they wear, and in this physical and tangible way, the abstraction of the Other becomes real. In learning an embodied modesty, Hasidic Jewish girls in New York City are socialized to recognize an embodied difference between Hasidic women and women outside of the community: Gentiles, secular North American women, and Orthodox Jewish women (Fader 2009, 32, 147). It is not only the religious education and teachings they receive, but the consistent everyday exchanges and interactions with the largely secular outside environment that gives these embodied signs of religious belonging particular significance.

Understanding religious difference through embodiment underscores the ways that youth actually perceive and act upon religious difference in their everyday physical environments. In addition, it is also useful in demonstrating a particular way that deliberation happens. The process of ethical reflection is not an exclusively individualized and cognitivized process of weighing different options in the abstract. Deliberation, as a model for education as proposed by Varenne, is a social rather than a personal or individual activity, and herein lies its power for social change (2007). In this chapter, deliberation emerges mostly as a response to the Other and their embodied religious belonging, acted upon in an environment that itself not only proposes but naturalizes a Protestant hegemony. These interactions work in tandem with discourse, as youth become socialized to contextualize their religious belonging in terms of a shifting majority/minority identity, based on context.

The religious makeup of Manado's SMA students is broadly reflective of that of the population of Manado, and the school prides itself on being a diverse public institution dedicated to educating youth while also providing them instruction in religious education and opportunities to worship. The overall dynamic of the school also reflects the tensions present in the broader public sphere: an ideal of religious diversity and coexistence that is important and even a source of pride, but also a feeling among Christians that the public sphere should remain visibly and audibly Christian. The way in which the majority of teachers and administrators take steps to accommodate other religions while effectively maintaining a Christian atmosphere at the school is itself an example of a certain kind of normative work related to broader collective deliberations. In the classroom, some teachers preach the importance of religious harmony and tolerance in the abstract, but when faced with concrete questions, propagate ideas and opinions that go against the ostensibly public ethical norms of aspirational coexistence.

The increasing majoritarian religious influence in public schools is not isolated to this particular case, but has also been noted in Muslim-majority Java, and has been located within the larger trend of the foregrounding religious identity in the post-Suharto era. Many public schools in Java have instituted Qur'anic recitation to open the school day, and require all Muslim students to wear the Muslim version of the school uniform (which includes a veil for female students) (Kwok 2014). Furthermore, religious associations outside schools have proved influential in promoting, through extracurricular religious activities, an effective Islamization of the environment within some public schools. For example, some schools have enforced policies about the separation of boys and girls in school activities, and rules requiring or pressuring female Muslim students to wear the *jilbab* (veil)—in particular, styles that are considered more modest (Salim, Kailani, and Azekiyah 2011).

At SMA, the integration of religiosity and religious activities into the school inscribes the environment of the school as Protestant, despite the official appeal to and concern about accommodating other religions. This majoritarian influence can be seen in the allocation of worship space, food policies in the cafeteria, greetings and prayer in various contexts, and through school uniforms. The de facto majoritarian influence and understandings of majoritarian coexistence that accompany it arise in the school as a coherent scheme, not necessarily explicitly planned, but emergent from policies and practices. As teachers and the administration channel ethical normativities about plurality and coexistence encountered in the public sphere that impact the functioning of the school, they deploy particular understandings of what it means to coexist and to accommodate other religions.

A PROTESTANT SPATIAL ORGANIZATION OF INCLUSION AND EXCLUSION

Spatial organization in educational institutions, both as intended and imposed by policy and as materialized through daily social interactions, influences the emerging dynamics of inclusion and exclusion. In this sense, "knowing one's place" (Gulson and Symes 2007, 2) becomes a learning process as spatial divisions come to be naturalized as social ones. Ethnographies of education that have attended to the organization of space have demonstrated its influence on socialization processes where embodiment as racialized (Bucholtz 2011) and gendered (Kjaran 2017) individuals and groups is learned. This is often the case in spite of embraced discourses of multiculturalism and progressivism that are intended to discursively mark spaces as inclusive.

Politics regarding the religious environment of public schools in Indonesia have at times brought them into the spotlight as objects of debate about the accommodation of religious difference in public space. In the city of Manado, spatial organization indicates strong efforts to maintain a public religiosity that is Christian, when the frame of majoritarian coexistence projected into public debates about belonging often implies the toleration of Muslims on a recognizably Christian land. When discussing his calling to help form the Protestant club Pelsis in the 1990s, one founder of the organization recounted to me that he was living in Jakarta at the time and had heard about proposed plans to build prayer rooms for Muslim students in public schools in Manado. This proposal convinced him to return to the city and petition that if prayer rooms for Muslim students were to be built in public schools, schools would also need to provide chapels for Protestant students. He claimed that his strategy effectively put a halt to the construction of most of the prayer rooms. This instance shows how schools and their policies are often deliberated about as spaces that convey messages about and institute practices of belonging. However, even when the allocation and the actual interaction with space in schools appears banal and does not become a focus of public attention, it still contributes to producing an embodied sense of belonging for the students who encounter it on a daily basis.

The administration at SMA encourages a deepening of religiosity for all students, and abstract discourses about religious harmony are often promoted in Protestant and Muslim religious education classes. However, one of the ways in which SMA effectively imposes a majoritarian influence is through the allocation of worship space in the school. During worship events (invariably held near Christian holidays), the central court is transformed into a Protestant worship space large enough to accommodate all Protestant students and teachers. Students work together to build a makeshift stage in the central courtyard, and collaborate to hang a printed poster for the occasion. Students designated as worship leaders play instruments, say prayers, and perform dance routines to Christian worship songs, anointing the court as a sacred space through the ritual before transforming it back into its multipurpose state.

At the designated worship times, Muslim students organize their own worship activities in collaboration with their religious education teacher.

However, there is no place within the school that is large enough to accommodate the hundreds of Muslim students at the same time. The school has one designated classroom for Islamic education, where students gather for their religious education courses and meet after school for the Rohis club. This particular room has a green-carpeted floor and green walls, which visually mark it as a Muslim space. The room is on the third floor of the school building, and is slightly smaller than most regular classrooms. Some students stop by during the day to carry out daily prayers, and there is a stack of prayer rugs on top of the bookshelves for their convenience. The classroom has no student desks, which allows it to function as a prayer space and as a classroom where students sit on the floor in a circle around their teacher, Pak Ustad, in a nod to traditional Islamic education. Students can conduct individual or small-group prayers in the room, but there is no space where all Muslim students can gather to worship as a group on school grounds. When meeting as a large group, Muslim students typically leave the school grounds for a nearby mosque, accompanied by their teacher.

During a normal school day, students remain in the same classroom all day, as teachers move from classroom to classroom to teach classes, and spend time in the teachers' lounge or the cafeteria when not teaching. For the students, this means that they remain with the same group of twenty to thirty students throughout the school day, and stay in the same space with their homeroom classmates. Students are sorted into homerooms by grade

FIGURE 3.2 Islamic education classroom at SMA.

and by track (either natural science or social science), and are religiously mixed. During their religious education class time, Protestant students remain in the classroom. Upon arrival, the Protestant religious education teacher dismisses all of the non-Protestant students, who then go to their respective meeting locations.

On Friday afternoons, the school holds regular worship sessions, the timing of which does accommodate Muslim students' participation in Friday prayer. At this time, as well as during the special worship sessions (when Protestants use the central court), Muslim students typically gather and walk to a nearby mosque with Pak Ustad, who often delivers a short sermon after leading prayers with his students. While the central court of the school can and is regularly transformed into a Protestant space of worship, Muslim prayers and sermons either take place as limited gatherings in a sequestered room, or are taken off school grounds.

One morning, during the scheduled religious education class, I asked eleventh-grade Muslim students about religious activities and celebrations at the school. The charismatic Pak Ustad was absent that day, and students decided to cover some material by sitting in a circle and reading aloud from a section in the textbook called "Islam in the Modern Era." After about fifteen minutes, attention spans began to reach their limits. As Taufik, the student who was reading at that moment, encountered a large chunk of text in the book, he abruptly came to a stop. The lesson started to evolve into a group conversation. Ani, who had taken charge to get everyone organized in a circle and pass out books, seemed to accept this turn of events, though she also clearly wanted to take part in facilitating them as well. She looked over at me, seated on the floor as part of the circle, and asked if I had any questions for them. She caught me off guard. I was used to students asking me to tell them about life in America, and I usually had to work hard to turn the conversation around to find out more about their lives and experiences. Here, suddenly, the floor was opened to me. I started blabbering on, trying to demonstrate my interest and knowledge about Islam in Indonesia, and realized I was squandering an important opportunity to learn about their experiences. I quickly shifted gears, asking if they would be willing to talk about religious activities at the school. As the students responded, they reflected on the treatment of religious differences at the school, considering Islamic teachings, school policies, and their own beliefs and everyday experiences.

One of the students started to explain that, logistically, they were separate from the Protestant students for any kind of religious celebration at the school, but that these celebrations usually involved the Muslim students "accommodating the others" (*menyesuaikan dengan yang lain*), implicitly referring to the Protestant majority. The student leader of Rohis then jumped in to explain that in Islam, there is a teaching that "I have my own religion, and you have yours," referring to a verse in Surah Al-Kafirun in the Qur'an (109:6). I often heard Muslims in Manado refer to this verse as a guiding ethical principle toward acceptance of religious difference, though its practical consequences were not always interpreted in the same way. In this case, the student used it to argue that there was no issue with the school's method of organizing worship sessions, saying "It's not a problem."

His fellow students began to push back slightly on his claim, several citing concerns about always needing to coordinate and adapt to "them" (the Protestant majority). One student in the circle piped up, saying "Well, honestly, we're the minority, right? So, it's always us who have to adjust to 'them' [Manado: *dorang*]." Before we moved on to another topic, his friend offered another interpretation particularly related to being a religious minority, stating that it is not always easy, but they must continue to "struggle for the sake of *dakwah* [*berjuang untuk dakwah*].".[2] This discussion is an instance of deliberation about the significance of school policies and how to interpret them in light of students' own positions, experiences, and understandings of religious coexistence.

In our conversation, Muslim students continually referred to themselves as in a minority position, despite living in a country that is overwhelmingly Muslim. Their daily experience of space, as well as other aspects of the school discussed below, crystallizes this sense of religious belonging—not only as Muslims but as minoritized Muslims.

PROTESTANT SOUNDSCAPES: *SYALOM!*

Sounds travel through, fill, resonate, and dissipate within spaces, marking them through the production of soundscapes. The religious elements of these soundscapes can inflect neighborhoods or spaces with a particular atmosphere or character, as cassette sermons in urban Cairo leave the mark of Islamic piety on the "acoustic architecture" of the city (Hirschkind 2006, 8). In Muslim-majority areas of Indonesia, soundscapes are shaped as recognizably Islamic through the amplification of the five daily *adzan* (calls to prayer) and through sermons and recitations being pumped out of loudspeakers for the sake of passersby beyond the walls of the mosques. At SMA, Protestant greetings and prayers with all students throughout the school day contributed to marking the space of the school as Protestant, reflecting efforts to inflect the religious atmosphere of the region through the creation of a recognizably Christian soundscape.

Each morning as I awoke in the Christian-majority city of Tomohon at sunrise, a nearby Protestant church played the prerecorded hymn "Good Morning, Father" ("Selamat Pagi, Bapa"), thanking God for having watched over us during the night. This particular rendition features the pure and angelic voice of a child, accompanied by a soft piano to evoke a heavenly soundscape. After playing several other hymns, often more dynamic and percussive ones, a church member announces all the upcoming church events and meetings. Lasting around ten minutes, this use of sound marks the start of the day in a religious manner. The sonic ritual permeates the area surrounding the church—not only the public space, but penetrating into the private spaces of homes as well. This emission of religious sound waves is a clear assertion that the space is Christian. In addition to expressing religiosity, its deployment is also related to the fear of Islam encroaching, and to the desire that the area remain majority Christian.

In other words, the use of sound in this way represents in part the response of a national minority working to maintain an atmosphere that is recognizably and audibly Christian. In a majority-Christian Kenya, Muslim neighborhoods work to assert their own autonomy, though not in a legal sense, through creating Islamic soundscapes that penetrate beyond the public space, and in doing so, challenge existing models of citizenship (Eisenberg 2020). In Manado, Protestants use the loudspeaker as a response to dominant forms of Islamization visible in the region to some extent, but more so nationally, through building mosques—which occupy not only space but the sound waves as well. The use of sound by Christians in Manado reflects their position both as a national minority, responding to the creation of a national Islamic atmosphere, and also as a local majority, easily able to cultivate this Christian soundscape.

The ways that Protestant-style greetings and prayers at SMA are used at communal school gatherings and amplified through daily school-wide announcements also have an impact on creating a Protestant soundscape. At formal events, particularly those involving parents, other schools, or the broader community, a range of religious greetings are used to signify attention to religious plurality and demonstrate a respect for diversity. However, in the less formal everyday announcements and events at the school, these greetings are often shortened and consist exclusively of recognizably Protestant forms. The use of greetings and prayers at the school therefore further underscores an environment that appeals to respect for religious diversity while simultaneously asserting a Protestant dominance.

For context, at formal public events in the region, it is customary to hear religiously inflected greetings from all speakers. Each person typically offers at least both the Muslim greeting *"assalamu'alaikum warahmatullahi wabarakatuh"* and the generic Christian greeting *"salam sejahtera"* (considered appropriate for both Protestants and Catholics) in tandem. On occasion, the Hindu greeting *"om swastyastu"* is added. In Indonesia, using a range of greetings is considered an important gesture of accommodation toward different religious groups. In Manado, a more specific call-and-response Protestant greeting based on GMIM Church practices is often added at local events. In this greeting, the speaker begins with *"syalom"* (after the Hebrew *shalom*), to which the audience responds *"damai di hati"* (peace in my heart). The speaker then comes back with *"damai di hati,"* and the greeting closes with a final *"syalom"* from the audience. My local informants indicated that this call-and-response format was a relatively recent convention, within the past decade or so, and that the Protestant greeting of choice had previously been a simple *"syalom."*

Greetings are often considered a measure of inclusiveness in religiously mixed settings in Indonesia, with conventions used to recognize various religious groups for gatherings ranging from small local events to presidential addresses. At any formal event that takes place at the SMA, the principal and other administrators hew to the typical formula, giving multiple religious greetings to those present. One morning, when parents came to pick up their children's report cards and attended an informational session, they were greeted with *"syalom"* and a short *"assalamu'alaikum"* from Principal Jeiny. At the same meeting, Principal Jeiny had invited Protestant religious education teacher Ibu Sonia to open the meeting with a prayer. Before bowing her head, Ibu Sonia notified the parents that she would pray according to her own religion, Protestantism, inviting them to join her in prayer according to their own religion. The invitation for others to pray according to their own religion is considered another measure of accommodation to allow and even encourage religious rituals at public events without excluding diverse religious backgrounds.

As classes in nonreligious subjects begin at SMA, teachers greet students with the standard and nonreligious "good morning" (*selamat pagi*) or "good afternoon" (*selamat siang*), and students stand up to return the greeting in unison. In religion classes, students are grouped separately, and therefore use specific religious greetings with their teachers. However, for most everyday school events at SMA, teachers do not typically make an effort to use multiple religious greetings as they do for more formal events. For example, when the extracurricular Red Cross (Palang Merah) club held their event to induct new members, Principal Jeiny began the event with a simple *"syalom!"* and then proceeded to call Ibu Sonia to lead them in prayer. Although teachers at SMA are religiously diverse, Protestant teachers are by far the majority, and are almost always leading school events.

During the morning announcements over the intercom, different teachers take turns saying the morning prayer, but it is always a Protestant teacher who takes on the task. When Ibu Sonia prays, she makes reference to "the Lord Jesus" (Tuhan Yesus), and Pak Daniel typically closes by saying, "in Jesus's name we pray, Amen" (*dalam nama Yesus kami berdoa, Amin*). Although the morning prayer is not always said by a religion teacher, according to my observations, it is always said by a teacher who is Protestant.

Furthermore, the allocation of worship space discussed in the previous section contributes to a Christian soundscape. On Friday afternoons, as Muslim students leave the school for Friday prayer, their Protestant classmates stay inside, filling their classrooms with Protestant songs and sermons that overflow into the central space of the school. For major school events, where Protestant worship is carried out in the central courtyard, microphones and speakers are set up for singing and preaching, amplifying Protestant songs and prayers to echo through the school.

Through the religious soundscape of the school, shaped by both greetings and prayers, administrators are able to adhere to the principle of inclusivity. For formal events, teachers and administrators at SMA use multiple religious greetings and take care to invite others to pray according to their respective religions when addressing the diverse student body, parents, or others from the community. At the same time, the daily use of prayer and greetings during announcements and activities creates a recognizably Christian soundscape in the school as formalities are dropped, and the use of Protestant greetings and prayers dominates. The SMA soundscape is not simply created at the school but echoes a broader public sphere in which the soundscape of Manado and North Sulawesi is continually established as Protestant, in response to and in anticipation of Islamic soundscapes that mark certain neighborhoods in the province, and Muslim-majority provinces elsewhere in Indonesia, as Muslim.

HALAL FOOD DESERT

At SMA, one can follow the smell of fried food to get to the cafeteria by ducking under a stairwell to enter a room with a cement floor and walls, where a handful of local food vendors come daily to cook rice, the local specialty *tinutuan* (a vegetable porridge typically eaten for breakfast), noodles, fried fish and chicken, sweets, and to sell prepackaged snacks and drinks. There is not one official food provider for the school, but each has to gain approval from the administration in order to become a vendor at the school. As in most Indonesian public schools, there is no official lunch or snack time, and the small room is able to accommodate only about fifty people at a time at the wooden tables and benches. The school day at SMA runs from seven o'clock in the morning to one-thirty in the afternoon, and students may choose to stop by to eat a meal or buy snacks in-between classes or after school. Parents often give their children a small daily or weekly allowance to cover the food expenses. None of the vendors are allowed to serve pork in the school cafeteria, as per the administration.

I learned about the cafeteria policy during a casual conversation one afternoon with Muslim students when I asked them which vendors serve halal food. Iqbal, a popular boy active in the Muslim students' club, hesitated before responding. He explained that although no pork is cooked or served in the cafeteria, none of the vendors sell freshly cooked halal food. Surprised, I asked how the students navigate the daily reality of buying and eating food at the school. He explained that some students who are concerned bring their own food from home to avoid the cafeteria altogether, while others opt for buying exclusively processed and prepackaged snacks that bear the seal of halal food certified by the Indonesian Council of Ulama (MUI). Iqbal then shrugged, admitting that, for the most part, Muslim students still tend to buy food from the school's vendors. The cafeteria policy at SMA requires Muslim students (and their parents) to make daily decisions about how best to follow religious requirements in an environment where freshly prepared certified halal food is not readily available.

Policies about food in schools emerge from a broader socialization agenda related to cultural beliefs, tradition, and morality, and orientations toward difference (Allison 1991; Karrebæk 2012). At SMA, the administration's policy on halal food is related to particular visions of multiculturalism in Manado that openly welcome the idea of religious and ethnic diversity while simultaneously imposing a strong framework for how others—specifically Muslims—are accommodated. Although SMA's student body includes several hundred Muslim students, the school does not have any food vendors that prepare fresh halal food for sale. Instead, the administration instituted a policy that none of the food vendors are allowed to cook or serve pork products at the school. The measure, intended to accommodate Muslim students, adheres to the common assumptions among Christians in Manado that equate halal requirements to not eating pork and/or that cast Muslims who follow dietary restrictions too closely as fanatic or radical. Furthermore, the public school's policy is an example of one of the ways in which it is assumed that Christians are securing the religious harmony of the region: through the voluntary accommodation of a Muslim minority.

Among youth in Manado, food is an extremely salient example of embodied religious difference. When asked about their experience with friends of another religion, both Muslim and Christian students often bring up food as a potential source of tension but also as an opportunity to demonstrate tolerance. Several Muslim students from the madrasah and from SMA said that they were aware of the need to "be careful" (*berhati-hati*) about the source of their food, especially when among non-Muslims. They also readily recounted instances of being moved by their non-Muslim friends going out of their way to provide halal food for them, or avoiding eating in front of them during Ramadan, the fasting month. These concerns about halal food in Manado's schools may be a relatively recent issue, as several middle-aged Christian informants claimed that it had not been a concern among their Muslim peers when they were younger. However, this claim is also sometimes used to justify a positioning of contemporary Muslims concerned with eating halal as unnecessarily fanatic, projecting them as responsible for drawing stronger social boundaries between religious groups.

SMA's restriction on pork products is one strategy for accommodating a Muslim minority, while other public schools in Manado have taken different approaches. However, there is no consensus about the best way to accommodate the dietary restrictions of Muslim students, including among Muslim students and educators. One morning, I was having a coffee at the exclusively halal cafeteria of the State Islamic Institute of Manado (IAIN— Institut Agama Islam Negeri) in Manado while speaking with a group of lecturers about the history of Islamic education in North Sulawesi. As I explained briefly that my research related to education and tolerance, one of the lecturers immediately offered up a culinary example of what he referred to as an effort to "create an atmosphere of tolerance" (*menciptakan suasana toleransi*). At one of the local public middle schools, he recounted, the administration recently decided to designate a specific area as the Muslim cafeteria (*kantin Islam*), with a vendor serving only halal food. Farizky, a younger lecturer active in a subbranch of the Islamic organization Nahdlatul Ulama, confided later that he disagreed with the professor's statement about the cafeteria, although he did not dare to openly contradict his senior.

Farizky worried that the act of creating a separate cafeteria, regardless of the intention behind it, could potentially harden the divisions among students based on religious identity due to the physical separation of students it would induce.

SMA's policy about food in the cafeteria also links to common assumptions in Manado about the centrality of Christians in securing a working arrangement of religious coexistence through their tolerance on a number of different fronts. Just as the prohibition of pork is meant as an accommodating gesture toward Muslim students, so is the provision of food for Muslim guests at Minahasan events and celebrations (birthday parties, weddings, funerals, etc.). Although a roast pig (*babi putar*) is central in these celebrations, there is typically a separate table featuring dishes made without pork, dog, bat, or any of the other typical meats used for festive Minahasan fare. This table is consistently referred to as the "national food" (*makanan nasional*) table rather than explicitly as halal food, but it is always understood to be for Muslim guests. The provisioning of food for Muslims is framed as an enactment of Christian and Minahasan hospitality toward guests and neighbors.

The presence of Muslims following strict dietary restrictions in Manado plays into existing fears of a Muslim encroachment, or the idea that there has been an influx of Muslim "outsiders" in the region, and that it endangers the status quo. For many Christians in Manado, the presence of halal foods is indicative of an ongoing Muslim intrusion into the public sphere. At a few local restaurants and food stalls (*warung*), the designation "100% NON-HALAL" (*100% TIDAK HALAL*) is splashed across signage and menus. At one such restaurant, the fact that the house specialty was pork noodles rendered it immediately obvious that the food was not halal. Rather than being simply informative, these symbols work to reinforce the public space as Christian.

In this framework of majoritarian coexistence, Muslims are praised for their tolerance in not requiring the Christian majority to accommodate them. In some areas of Indonesia, including across Java, restaurants often remain open during fasting hours in the month of Ramadan, but install curtains to shield the food and dining customers from the sight of those passing by. Minahasan Christians often remark upon and praise the tolerance of Muslims in Manado for not requesting that restaurants install curtains during the fasting month, suggesting it is an exemplary model of coexistence. Consequently, Muslims who advocate for restaurants to be covered up, or those who choose not to eat pork, are projected as radical. At the same time,

FIGURE 3.3 Restaurant sign claiming "1000% Non-halal."

this manifestation of majoritarian coexistence positions Muslims as tolerant when they accept the conditions of the hegemonically Christian public sphere.

Food is a highly significant mode of embodied religious belonging for youth, particularly in Muslim–non-Muslim student interactions, as it impacts how they socialize with each other and emerges as a salient marker of religious difference. In addition to shaping through its cafeteria policies how this interaction happens, SMA also channels frameworks for coexistence from the public sphere that argue for accommodation in principle, but ultimately reinforce a majoritarian Christian environment where Muslims are congratulated as tolerant when they adapt themselves to this environment.

*JILBAB*S IN A CHRISTIAN SPACE

Parallel to statements about Manadonese Muslims and their relationship to halal food, Minahasan Christians often claim that Muslims in Manado do not wear the *jilbab* because they are moderate, as opposed to being fanatical (*fanatik*).³ The practice of veiling in the Muslim-majority Java has increased in tandem with a general Islamic resurgence over the past several decades. Just a few short decades ago, veiling was considered a departure from local traditions in Java, and those who started donning the veil were often considered religious fanatics (Brenner 1996, 675). However, since then, veiling among Muslim women in Java has become largely mainstream and even normative in some circles and educational institutions. Smith-Hefner (2007) analyzes the donning of the veil by young middle-class women in Java who want to signal their pious commitment while simultaneously taking advantage of new opportunities of education and employment in a rapidly changing society. A relative increase in the number of veiling women is often remarked upon by Christians in Manado, particularly for those advocating for a strong Christian atmosphere and who view the expansion of Islam in the region as a threat. From their perspective, an increase in veiling offers tangible evidence of the growth of the Muslim community and the spread of less-moderate forms of Islam in the region.

There is not sufficient space here to fully delve into the history of veiling and its myriad meanings across Indonesia and the Muslim world, but veiling as part of Islamic piety movements is linked to embodiment through ethical self-work and aspiration toward becoming an ideal (and gendered) subject (Mahmood 2005). Such an analysis of veiling is important as it challenges secular liberal assumptions about the practice, and acts as a much-needed corrective to politically reductive analyses of agency. In this section, the focus is shifted from the ethical projects and aspirations undertaken by those who wear the veil to the production of embodied religious difference through the presence of the veil, and how it is mediated by Muslims and non-Muslims at SMA and beyond. Taking care not to reduce veiling to a political question, I point to ways in which mediations of the practice shape ethical frameworks in operation regarding approaches to religious difference and possibilities for coexistence.

At a public school like SMA, all boys wear the same standard school uniform of collared shirts and slacks, whereas Muslim girls are faced with a choice of which version of the school uniform to wear. They can select between the standard school uniform with short-sleeved collared shirts and knee-length skirts, or the Islamic version with long-sleeved shirts, floor-length skirts, and a *jilbab*. Most Muslim girls at SMA choose to wear the standard uniform (without the veil), in the same style as Christian girls in their class. At SMA, wearing the veil is discussed as a requirement of Islam in the religious education course in the standard religious education curriculum, but it is not implemented as policy and does not emerge as a major topic of discussion in the classroom.

Many girls who wear the Islamic version of the school uniform on a daily basis have a shifting and contextual practice of veiling. Irma, who wears the complete Islamic school uniform on a daily basis, showed me her pictures on Facebook one day while waiting for class to start. I noticed that in nearly all of her pictures, she was not wearing the veil. Before I could ask about it, she laughed and brought up the topic herself, openly declaring, "There's a lot of pictures of me without a *jilbab*." I then asked her why she wears the veil to school, hinting that perhaps her parents had encouraged her to do so. Irma quickly shook her head and replied, "No, it's my choice." Students who veil on school grounds do not necessarily do so outside of the school. However, like Irma, many asserted narratives of personal choice rather than influences or pressure from their families, religious community, or peers.

Two Muslim girls from the southern part of the province of North Sulawesi attend SMA through a scholarship program, and do veil on a regular basis, at school as well as in their daily activities outside the school. Far away from their families, they stay together at Ibu Sonia's house. During the retreat for Protestant students that Ibu Sonia helped coordinate, the two Muslim students came along with her. As students and teachers met at the school that Saturday morning before taking buses to the retreat location, the students showed up with Ibu Sonia in jeans and T-shirts, and had each chosen not to wear a *jilbab*. As I sat down with them in the school's lounge, one of their friends passed by. Surprised, she commented that they weren't wearing their *jilbab*s. One of the students shrugged off the question, and neither responded directly.

Many Muslim students who choose to wear the regular school uniform are still pious and concerned about maintaining modesty. Indeed, a large proportion of participants in the club Rohis are Muslim girls who do not wear the Islamic school uniform on a daily basis. At Rohis events outside the school, all students do wear matching uniforms: black long-sleeved collared shirts with the Rohis logo, the Indonesian flag, and the student's name embroidered on the fabric. Girls also wear a veil when representing the Islamic students' club outside the school campus, signaling their membership and piety. On a daily basis in the classroom, however, wearing the standard school uniform has practical implications for maintaining modesty in the classroom. In the Islamic education classroom at SMA, as there are no desks or chairs, students sit on the carpeted floor in a circle for their weekly two-hour lesson. Girls who wear the knee-length skirt of the general school uniform deal with concerns about maintaining modesty while sitting on the floor by placing prayer mats over their laps for the duration of the class.

Muslim girls at SMA do participate in other extracurricular activities, like the dance team, which also requires them to navigate ideas about modesty in dancing and in selecting costumes for their performances. In these negotiations, they consider religious rules as well as social norms, engaging in deliberation as they "navigate complex moral terrain in order to have fun while feeling good about themselves," just like Shi'i Muslim youth in Beirut who want to socialize in cafés but must choose those they consider appropriate (Deeb and Harb 2013, 136). There are several Muslim girls at SMA who participate in the school's dance team, but none of them regularly wear a *jilbab*. When the team competes in dance competitions or performs at basketball games, the Muslim students wear the same dance costumes as the other members of the dance team. In the video of their dance routine one of the students played for me on her smartphone, they wore leggings with basketball shorts over them and jean jackets over loose T-shirts. When I asked how they felt about wearing these costumes, they quickly distinguished their own costumes from what they described as the shockingly immodest costumes of other schools' dance teams. Their stories of girls wearing scandalous crop tops or short cheerleading-style skirts caught the attention of a student wearing a *jilbab* who was quietly sitting nearby. She offered her opinion that it is not right for anyone, but especially for students, to go around wearing such revealing and immodest clothes. The girls on the dance team nodded in agreement, affirming their participation in the dance team as appropriate by distancing themselves from teams that wear immodest clothing.

Muslim students who are making choices about which school uniform to choose and how to fulfill religious requirements related to modesty must also consider how their uniform might be perceived by others. At public religiously mixed schools in Manado, veiling students are at times perceived as evidence of the expansion of Islam (or a more radical form of Islam) in a Christian space. At one religiously mixed public school in Manado, it was rumored that the principal had privately instructed the admissions committee at the school to not accept too many Muslim girls who wore the veil, implying that it might negatively impact the image of the school. Note that the goal was particularly to avoid accepting students who would visually transform the space and potentially call into question its assumed religious character as Christian.

Normative frames related to majoritarian coexistence in Manado project *jilbab*-clad Muslims as radical outsiders, as opposed to tolerant Manadonese Muslims. Christian interlocutors often issued blanket claims that Manadonese Muslims do not wear *jilbab*s, even though this was clearly not objectively the case. Eka, an eleventh grader at the public high school who wears a relatively long and modest *jilbab,* is well aware of how she is perceived when out in public. As we sat on the floor of the Islamic education classroom, students fanning themselves with paper in the midday heat, I had started another informal discussion with them about what it was like to live as Muslims in Manado. While her classmates praised the city as harmonious (*rukun*) and peaceful (*damai*), Eka drew from her personal experience, stating bluntly that people in Manado often eye her suspiciously because of her choice to wear a long *jilbab*. The practice of veiling, an embodied sign of religious belonging, is fraught in Manado, tied into questions about plurality and coexistence as well as individual piety and morality.

Just as in the Muslim students' discussions about worship space at the school, there is a tendency for them to position themselves as a minority based on their everyday experience of adjusting to accommodate the majority. All students, not only Muslim students, consider which kind of clothing to wear outside of school and must weigh the pressure to follow popular fashion trends, religious ideas about maintaining modesty, and familial expectations. Yet, for the Muslim students, there is also a clear question of relating to a local mainstream culture for which they do not set the terms.

PROTESTANTS: LEARNING TO SHIFT MAJORITY/MINORITY POSITIONING

Policies regarding the allocation of space and the allowance of food in the cafeteria assert the majority position of Protestants in setting the norms for how other religions are to be accommodated at the school, producing an embodied religious belonging for Protestants not only as Christians, but as a local majority. On the other hand, in classes and extracurricular clubs at SMA, Protestant students and teachers emphasize their own position as a national minority when discussing interreligious relations. Teachers, and sometimes students, tend to invoke the position of Protestants as a local majority only when encouraging a deepening of religiosity, drawing attention to the dangers of complacency that a majority status can bring. The situation at the school relates to the way that Protestants in Manado use their status as a local majority to advocate for Christians across Indonesia, aiming to publicize their plight as a national minority in the public sphere as they respond to a variety of incidents and concerns. At SMA, embodied forms of religious belonging produced through space, food, sound, and dress are deliberated by Muslim students as they come to understand and discursively express their position primarily in terms of being a minority, requiring them to adapt to school policies and requirements.

In the Protestant religious education classroom, discourses support the principle of tolerance in the abstract, promoting aspirational coexistence, but they also focus concretely on the difficulty for Christians as a religious minority. Teachers thus use a national frame to reflect on the situation of Indonesian Christians as a whole. During a Protestant religious education class at SMA, a discussion about living in a religiously diverse society involved students drawing on discourses about the importance of respecting and valuing difference. Their teacher, Ibu Sonia, launched into a lecture about both the good intentions of all religions and the importance of love in Christian teachings. When speaking in the abstract, she proclaimed the good nature of all religions: "If we were all able to follow our religion well—whether Muslim, Catholic, Hindu, or Confucian—if we were all able to follow our respective teachings, there would be no conflict on earth!"

The topic of the lecture prompted an eager student in the front row to ask about a Facebook post she had recently seen about demonstrators in Java opposing the construction of a church. She wondered what had motivated the protesters, and how she could respond to them in a Christian way. In addressing this concrete example, the same teacher explained that Christians are continually taught about love, but "they"—Muslims—are taught that Christians are *kafir,* infidels or unbelievers. She lamented how difficult it is for Christians to worship in Indonesia, where they are a minority and their neighbors might report them just for clapping their hands in worship, while Christians tolerate Muslims shouting *Allahu akbar* early in the morning. In this example, Ibu Sonia draws attention to a national soundscape in which Christian sounds are suppressed, rather than the soundscape of the school or the region, where Protestant sounds of worship and greeting saturate the environment.

When Ibu Sonia started addressing the question, she said, "We are a minority," sticking to the national context the student was addressing, also occupying the particular subject position through use of "we" (*kita;* Manado: *torang*). In addition, throughout her answer, she used "they" (*mereka;* Manado: *dorang*) to implicitly refer to Muslims, the majority. At the end of her monologue, however, Ibu Sonia implied that none of this matters when they consider the bigger picture. "Everyone is searching for salvation," she explained to the students, "but salvation is already in our hands, through the flesh and blood of Christ!" Through her statement, she moved away from her earlier positive characterization of all religions, fixating on Christianity as the ultimate truth.

Ibu Sonia spreads the official discourse of religious harmony and respect for difference, aligned with a framework of aspirational coexistence, yet she also expresses assumptions about Christian love and tolerance that attribute the religious harmony in Manado to its majority Christian population. The teacher's understanding that Christians guarantee coexistence, based on the essentializing equation of Christianity to love, is quite common in Manado and relates to the frame of majoritarian coexistence. It resonates with the broader discourse of Manado as an example of religious harmony, but attributes this achievement to the fact that the majority of people in Manado follow Christianity. For example, one Protestant pastor affiliated with Manado's Interreligious Harmony Forum (FKUB—Forum Kerukunan Umat Beragama) claimed that religious harmony in the city is declining. He argued that increasing the level of tolerance would be difficult so long as Muslims remain opposed to building churches in other regions of Indonesia. Suspicion of Muslims is thus framed as a reasonable response and is justified using essentialized portraits of both religions.

In the tenth-grade civic education course, students learn about respecting others as citizens and valuing difference rather than discriminating based on ethnicity, religion, race, or intergroup relations (represented by the acronym SARA), or gender. When teaching the topic to tenth-grade students, the teacher, Ibu Pricilia, gave them time in groups to brainstorm ways to enact national unity and avoid differentiating based on each of the categories. Each group was asked to give examples of behavior that does not discriminate based on religion, and present these answers in front of the class. From the first group, one boy stated that it's important not to denigrate other religions (*jangan menjelekkan agama lain*). One student, Evan, shouted out without being called on: "Don't compare religious teachings!" (*jangan membandingkan ajaran*). Grace spoke up for her group: "We have to safeguard harmonious interreligious relations" (*harus menjaga kerukunan antar umat beragama*).

Considering the responses from the students, Ibu Pricilia summarized that "religion is sensitive," qualifying that this is especially so when we talk about majority versus minority. She went on to say that she is Protestant because she considers it the best religion for her, but if someone is Muslim, it is because they consider it the best religion for them. Bringing up the question of how to value religious difference, she offered her own response with the concrete example of the Protestant governor of Jakarta:[4] "One example is Ahok, Governor of DKI [Jakarta], who is always attacked because of his religion, said to be unfit to be governor because he is Christian. But for a governor, there is no relationship between the formal position and his religion!" She then moved on without further discussion, asking students to give examples of behavior that doesn't discriminate based on race. The teacher's choice of concrete example is significant in its focus on the national context, where Christians are a minority, and there is resistance against the prospect of a Christian governor in a Muslim-majority region. Months earlier, during the regional election for governor of North Sulawesi, one of the three candidates (Benny Mamoto) had chosen a Muslim running mate and promoted the slogan "United in Difference" (*Bersatu dalam Perbedaan*) on their campaign fliers. Though the duo was popular in some circles, they did not win the election. The same concern was inevitably raised among Christians: What if something happened to Benny, and then a Muslim would be governing the Protestant-majority province?

The leader of the province-wide Christian club Pelsis spoke often about the situation of Christians as a minority in the national context, and the need for strong Christian leaders from North Sulawesi to have a national impact. Pastor Liow, when talking to me about the mission of the organization, explained that, as Christians, they live in a country where they are considered not just a minority but *kafir* (unbelievers or infidels). Despite being scorned, he claimed, Christians continue to work for the unity of the nation. His sermon for the province-wide meeting in a conference room at the governor's office addressed selected Protestant students from across the province. Although Christians are a majority in North Sulawesi, he said, he wanted them to know that maintaining a Christian identity is not always easy, but they have a calling to be God's blessing for the nation. Though explicitly mentioning the position of Protestants as a local majority, the pastor also encouraged the students to broaden their thinking to the national context, where Christianity is a minority but should still be able to contribute to the nation.

Christian youth in North Sulawesi who might think life is easy are also warned that their status as a local religious majority can entail feeling too comfortable, ultimately leading to a lack of commitment. At the SMA Protestant student retreat, Pak Daniel was passionately revving up his sermon, preparing students to reflect on the sins they would write down on a piece of paper and throw into the bonfire. He relied on the popular topic of sexual deviancy and promiscuity as he encouraged youth to consider all of their wrongdoings. Using the phrase "permissive society" in English, he remarked that "this is a Christian region, but the majority of people are acting against God!" He was drawing on the popular notion that because of living in a Christian-majority area, they have started to lead lackadaisical religious lives.

These instances show how Protestant teachers at SMA and leaders of extracurricular religious clubs shift discourses between a focus on Christians as a majority and as a minority in different contexts and for different effect. An emphasis on Christians as a minority in the national context is used to draw attention to the difficulties that Christians face and as an example of religious discrimination. On the other hand, the status of Christians as a regional majority is typically invoked to argue for increased religious commitment, based on the observation that Christians had become overly complacent.

EMBODIED AND DISCURSIVE DELIBERATIONS

The public high school SMA in North Sulawesi encourages a deepening of religiosity in general and espouses respect for religious diversity in principle, but ultimately establishes a Protestant space that sets the terms for accommodation. This reality must be understood not only in a local sense, but as a response to the national context and for how it parallels the religiosity promoted in public schools in Muslim-majority regions in Indonesia. In some public schools in Java, Qur'anic readings have become part of the daily routine of students, veiling is a requirement for all Muslim girls, and Islamic organizations have a strong involvement in shaping normative understandings of Islamic teachings through their influence on extracurricular activities (Salim, Kailani, and Azekiyah 2011). The practices at these schools in Java demonstrate that the exercise of majoritarian influence has not only taken place in North Sulawesi but is a widespread strategy for control of the public sphere. These findings underscore the importance of examining schools as arenas of deliberation, not only for how they are used by organizations, but also for how perspectives from the public sphere are channeled through them to shape the lifeworlds of Indonesian youth and how they navigate ethical frameworks regarding religiosity and respect for diversity.

This chapter has demonstrated how embodied forms of religious belonging promoted in the school as a space of socialization also create a sense of belonging through the encounter of religious difference. Embodied religious belonging as experienced through space, sound, food, and dress continually shapes the environment at SMA as Protestant, navigated by Muslim students who discursively deliberate about their position as a minority. At the same time, Protestant students and teachers also discursively underscore their position as a minority by invoking a national frame. In doing so, they contextually switch positionality, using a local majority to assert a Protestant environment while emphasizing their position as a minority that continues to face discrimination in other areas of Indonesia. This understanding of religious embodiment and the relationship between self and other that takes shape at SMA is certainly not limited to the confines of the school, but models what is taking place in the city and the region, as a Protestant majority continues to define the terms of religious accommodation and remains concerned about the religious future of the region.

As religious belonging is shaped through discursive and embodied practice, a deliberation of ethical frames about coexistence is also taking place. The unquestioning support for religious diversity in principle represents for many an aspiration toward coexistence in some form. However, the shifting and contextual positionality of Christians also represents deliberation about the limits of coexistence, provoked both by an uncertainty of their current position as a national minority and a perceived insecurity of their current position as a local majority. Accordingly, some assert that it is the Christian fabric of the society itself that has contributed to the religious harmony of which Manadonese are so proud, tying together the region's fate as a Christian-majority province and a religiously harmonious one to promote a majoritarian coexistence.

For a final consideration about religious belonging in terms of majority/minority positioning, I want to share a discussion I had with students that helps to indicate the way that these proposed frameworks for religious belonging are actually deliberated about—and are not determined. Following reports of a church burning in the overwhelmingly Muslim province of Aceh, I asked a group of Muslim students how it impacts them personally when there are church burnings like the one that took place in Aceh, thinking that some of them perhaps faced discrimination from their Christian classmates. Rejecting an exclusively local interpretation—and a majority/minority framework—one student active in Rohis quickly responded that they were certainly impacted personally, as any such conflict is troubling for them because it is troubling for the unity of the nation as a whole.

4 Private Catholic High School
Developing Faith and Character to Develop the Nation

During her high school's morning assembly, tenth grader Alicia walked to the center of the field and took the microphone to practice for an upcoming speech competition among Catholic high school students from North and Central Sulawesi. Standing under the red-and-white Indonesian flag flapping in the breeze, with majestic Mt. Lokon visible in the background, she appealed to her fellow students gathered around her in almost-neat rows. "As the young generation," she said, "it's up to us to realize the dreams of the generations who have come before us." She made a reference to the young nationalists in the Dutch East Indies who took the Youth Pledge (*Sumpah Pemuda*) in 1928 and declared Indonesia one homeland and one nation with one language. To continue this mission, they will need to be faithful, knowledgeable, and take responsibility for their actions, she explained. "Exactly how can we do this?" Alicia asked her fellow students. She paused for effect, and then continued, providing them with the answer: "Without giving up, we have to keep praying!"

Alicia is a student at Lokon St. Nikolaus High School (Lokon), a private boarding school boasting an expansive and well-groomed campus and a prestigious academic reputation. Its boarding program is geared toward character education, and has been able to attract students from various provinces and different ethnic and religious backgrounds. As the school has expanded in size and scope, it has explicitly articulated a project of multicultural education. The multicultural approach is based on a Catholic perspective, which positions Christian principles as fundamentally universal and able to provide a foundation for interethnic and interreligious coexistence on a local and national level.

As a national minority in Indonesia, Christians "have a precarious role in the struggle for shaping the nation" (Schröter 2010, 9). The project of Lokon school, however, is a bold attempt to redefine the relationship between Christian piety, development, and national citizenship. It is also bolstered by a surrounding environment that is majority Christian (though Protestant), and a historical context looking to the high position of Minahasa and of Catholic education in the colonial past. In this chapter, I focus on the ways in which Lokon School, both in its mission and in its daily happenings, recasts ideas about ethnic and religious difference. In doing so, it proposes a more central position for Christians and for the province of North Sulawesi in Indonesia's future, projecting an aspirational coexistence beyond the region by demonstrating the role Christians can play as a religious minority in the national context.

What I refer to as the school's "missionizing for the development of the nation" approaches individual faith and character building as the first step toward producing Christian—not exclusively Catholic—elites from eastern Indonesia who can shape the future of democratic, multiconfessional Indonesia. Influenced by the piety, status, capital, and politics of its founders, the vision of the school aspires to more than the shaping of religious yet atomized individuals. Yet, as the school puts forth its approach for dealing with religious difference, tensions arise between the school's vision and practice, challenging the Catholic universalist lens that advocates for multiculturalism.

RELIGION, DEVELOPMENT, AND THE NATION

The harnessing of religious values to national ones—as is undertaken by Lokon School—is not new, particularly in the context of modern development. For example, Lila Abu-Lughod explains how Egyptians have increasingly seen Islamic values and morals as "leading to the reform and restoration of the good society and nation, not its downfall," challenging previous local assumptions about the relationship between secularism and patriotic nationalism (2005, 175). In a similar vein, Kevin O'Neill has noted how neo-Pentecostal groups in Catholic-majority Guatemala seek to solve national economic problems and fight crime through organizing prayer networks (2009). As religious resurgences and revitalizations have impacted much of the world over the past several decades, ongoing conversations have demonstrated how religion and religious organizations can contribute to a vibrant civil society, as has often been the case in Indonesia (R. W. Hefner 2000). However, this coupling of religious and nationalist values can also lead to exclusivism in redefining the criteria for belonging in the nation (Hansen 1999; Jerryson 2011).

The way in which religious and civic values become linked has consequences for how people reimagine the boundaries and the contours of national communities, as new ethical frameworks emerge in the context of the linkage. Lokon School was launched in the early 2000s, during a historical moment of democratization and decentralization in Indonesia. This involved a changing conceptualization of national center and periphery, and a renewed questioning and eventual reaffirmation of the multiconfessional—rather than Islamic—basis of the nation. These conditions shaped the goals of Lokon's founders, including a renegotiation of the position of the province of North Sulawesi, and the projection of Christianity and national values as mutually reinforcing.

Educational settings are particularly powerful potential sites where states have sought to influence narratives about religious values and orient them toward nationalist and development-focused ends. This process of "functionalization," described by Gregory Starrett in the context of Egypt, transformed how state-filtered discourses on Islam came to be disseminated through the education system, presenting religious values that strategically aligned with state interests (1998, 9). Though initially ignored by scholars and assumed as contradictory to the modernizing impulses of development, religious organizations have increasingly been recognized as important in shaping the field of development. Development projects that engage religious actors, whether linked to the state or not, create entangled moralities as politics and religion, the local and transnational, and the secular and religious all contribute to normative ideas about progress (Bornstein 2003; Fountain, Bush, and Feener 2015).

Development is inherently political in nature, but the reliance on technical expertise that it often entails can transform development initiatives into seemingly mundane and bureaucratic ones. This process of "rendering technical" (Li 2007) often has the consequence of depoliticizing development issues while simultaneously expanding state presence to meet political ends (Ferguson 1990). However, the rise of neoliberal development and its view of markets rather than states as the primary vectors of progress, coupled with an ongoing presence of religious actors in development projects, raises questions about how such projects operate. Could the focus on the individual, put forth as the site of religious transformation, serve to depoliticize, but by rendering ethical (rather than technical)? Is Lokon School, understood as a project of development, converting serious issues into matters of individual faith? I argue that such an interpretation obscures the important—and politically significant—deliberation that is taking place at the school about what it means to bring Christian values and identity to the nation.

Since democratization and decentralization have opened up possibilities for redefining national belonging in Indonesia, new nodes linking religion and development have formed. Daromir Rudnyckyj (2010) argues that the creation of a new spiritual economy has shifted the locus from the state to the individual in neoliberal fashion, as previous state-led development failures are turned into individual problems to be addressed through careful religious self-cultivation. In his ethnography of workers in a privatizing steel corporation in Indonesia, he indicates how individuals learn to apply systems of neoliberal governance in their own lives from spiritual self-help seminars held in the workplace. Spirituality becomes a "site of management, intervention, and manipulation" where religion and neoliberalism are combined to instill an ethic of individual accountability and practice (2010, 146). Though ethical self-work is focused on individual improvement that could align with neoliberal values, it should not be assumed as a necessarily atomizing and individualistic project. Focusing on the broader social implications of Islamic seminars in a different context, James Hoesterey instead examines them as "religio-civic forums through which issues of civic virtue and Muslim citizenship are constituted and contested" (2012, 39). Educational endeavors should be analyzed for their potential to transform individuals as well as their possibilities for defining new modes of belonging, delineated by moral frameworks steeped in both civic and religious values.

In addition to Lokon School's insistence on individual religious transformation as an important step toward national development, the project itself is a forum of deliberation about the relationship between Christian and Indonesian values. The founding of the school represents an effort to prove the contribution that Christians can make to the nation and underscore their commitment to national values. Inspired by a colonial past marked by the conversion of Minahasan people to Christianity and the institutionalization of formal education, the founders propose an answer to the question of what this legacy might have to offer for the Indonesian national future, in part through the contemporary coupling of civic and religious values. In this chapter, after situating the historical missionization and establishment of education, I discuss the vision of Lokon School and its goal to contribute to national development through advocating Catholic-based multicultural education. I also focus on the tensions that arise in this dynamic and meaningful debate, with consequences for how individuals understand the national framework and its approach to plurality.

Looking beyond the intended goals of the school and focusing on everyday life on campus, we can see that there are consequences when its Catholic universalist recasting of difference is put into practice. As a result of an insistence on participating in Catholic ritual traditions and an emphasis on broad moral values extrapolated from Catholic teachings, religious difference is often glossed over both by administrators and students. However, the discourse about inclusion becomes challenged in practice, for example, in attempts to integrate Papuan students—who make up a sizable minority of the student population—into the academic and social life of the school. In lofty discussions about national development taking place at the school, as well as in mundane questions about how to assign students to classes and dormitories, students, teachers, and staff work in many ways to reconcile the multicultural approach of the school with Catholic (and broadly religious) values about respect for diversity. At the same time, the differentiation of Papuan students is justified on a number of different fronts, often in their implicit framing as the recipients of Catholic charity, as the objects—rather than agents—of development.

When considering the educational project of the school and its relation to the national imaginary, it is important to keep in mind that the students at Lokon weave together multiple aspirations as they dream about their futures. Although Alicia's speech clearly echoes the objectives of her school's educational project, along with her own desire to be a faithful Christian who prays regularly, her aspirations are necessarily plural. The mostly upper-middle-class students at Lokon hope to become successful individuals, are interested in expressing their religiosity, want to find a boyfriend or girlfriend, and often also have a desire to participate in and align themselves with a global pop culture through their choice of music and accessories. Lokon students are not singularly focused on the school's vision, yet their concerns and efforts at times do overlap with the approach of the school toward making a difference in Indonesia and contributing to national development. It is not surprising to find this "coexistence of various motivations, aims, and identities that can and often do conflict but do not constitute exclusive opposites," as youth weigh various aspirations and their accompanying moral connotations (Schielke 2009, S29). In other words, some of the goals and desires of the students, including those to be pious and successful individuals, can interact with and reinforce the broader vision of the school, but these same students also have aspirations that may lack commonality with or may even conflict with the kind of subjectivity that the school seeks to cultivate. To give historical perspective to this educational project and the way youth deliberate about national values, it is helpful to examine the shifting geographical conceptualization of Minahasa since colonial times and the historical entanglements of education, missions, and development in the region.

MISSIONIZATION AND THE ESTABLISHMENT OF FORMAL EDUCATION IN MINAHASA

The development of education in the Minahasan region during the Dutch colonial period took place through the establishment of both Protestant and Catholic missions and the expansion of the colonial government that created a need for educated natives to work as colonial officials. The establishment of mission schools put Minahasa on the path to becoming a Christian-majority region, and by the late nineteenth century, Minahasans had the highest levels of literacy and education among those native to the Dutch East Indies. During the colonial period, Minahasa came to be nicknamed the "twelfth province of the Netherlands" because its inhabitants were known for being educated Christians with a taste for European culture and styles of sociability (de Jonge, Parengkuan, and Steenbrink 2008, 430). Due to a set of circumstances including missionization and education, "in the nineteenth century it was still possible for Minahasans to see their homeland, not as a remote outstation of Batavia, but as a discrete Dutch colony in its own right" (Liwe 2010, 45).[1] Today, however, the province of North Sulawesi is consistently lumped in with disparaging geographical conceptions of the "outer islands," referring to islands outside of Java, or as part of an underdeveloped "eastern Indonesia." The contrast between the prominent position of Minahasa in colonial times and its relatively marginal position in post-independence Indonesia provides a historical context for the contemporary discourses of development prevalent in the elite Catholic boarding school.

In Minahasa, intensive efforts by the Dutch Protestant missionary society Nederlandsch Zendeling Genootschap (NZG) led to the establishment of formal educational institutions, a process intertwined with widespread conversion to Protestant Christianity in the mid-nineteenth century. Previous waves of missionaries, starting with Portuguese Jesuit missionaries in the sixteenth century and continuing with Dutch Protestant missionaries after the Dutch East India Company established its presence, had been relatively unsuccessful in converting local populations and were mostly active in coastal areas rather than in the heart of the Minahasan highlands (de Jonge, Parengkuan, and Steenbrink 2008, 419). NZG missionary Joseph Kam, who played a central role in spreading Christianity to Maluku, began sending missionaries, including G. J. Hellendoorn, to North Sulawesi in the 1820s. Before they had set up many schools, missionaries evangelized by inviting children to their homes to learn about Christianity and to witness the daily lives and activities of missionaries and their families. These children were then encouraged to enter schools as they were built and, later, to build schools themselves to spread the gospel. While Hellendoorn effectively increased the number of schools and students, his missions remained limited to Manado and other coastal areas. Even at this early point, the importance of education in missionization was already evident: "The success of the mission was counted in pupils rather than in baptisms" (de Jonge, Parengkuan, and Steenbrink 2008, 421).

Widespread conversion did not occur until German NZG missionaries J. G. Schwarz and J. F. Riedel began their missionary activities in the Minahasan highlands in 1831. This was in the first years of the colonial Cultuurstelsel policy (the compulsory cultivation system), as the Dutch were in the process of consolidating their control over the vast archipelago of the East Indies (de Jonge, Parengkuan, and Steenbrink 2008, 419–422). Mission schools played an important role in helping to imagine a Minahasan identity as well as convincing locals that education was "an avenue to material gain and increased status in the realm of colonial power and indigenous social hierarchy alike" (Swazey 2013, 77). The secondary-level teacher-training schools, some of which used Dutch as the language of instruction, offered a chance for Minahasans to increase their status. However, one of the most remarkable characteristics of these mission schools was that many elementary schools (*sekolah rakyat*) offered basic popular education for both boys and girls from the villages in the highlands of Minahasa. Conversion efforts were highly successful, and 80 percent of the population had converted to Protestant Christianity by the year 1880 (de Jonge, Parengkuan, and Steenbrink 2008, 422).

Mission schools continued to grow even as the Dutch colonial government established schools in Minahasa to train colonial personnel. Minahasans who passed through either of these two educational tracks were sent all over the East Indies, continuing their education, working for the colonial government, or being assigned to missionary posts, commonly among the Karo Batak in Sumatra (Henley 1996, 81). In 1930, the Manado residency recorded the highest rates of schooling anywhere in the East Indies (Henley

1996, 80n30). While there are no literacy statistics for Minahasa alone, the combined literacy rate for Minahasa and Bolaang-Mongondow (two regions that are now part of the province of North Sulawesi) in 1930 was the highest in the Netherlands East Indies, at 39 percent, compared to 5.5 percent literacy rate for Java and Madura (Henley 1996, 80). In 1934, when the schools that had been established by NZG (and had continued to expand under the auspices of the Protestant Church in the Dutch East Indies, Indische Kerk) were transferred to GMIM, the autonomous Minahasan Protestant denomination, there were 220 elementary schools, 20 secondary schools with Malay as the language of instruction, and several elite Dutch-language secondary schools (Lintong 2015, 6). Minahasans' high level of education, linked to their embrace of Christianity and their thirst to emulate European culture and speak Dutch, gave them a high status relative to other ethnic groups in the Netherlands East Indies (Steenbrink 2003, 265).

Although Portuguese Catholics were the first European missionaries in North Sulawesi, by 1660, the Dutch presence there had forced them out, and Dutch Catholic missionaries were banned from entering Minahasa (Heuken 2008, 63). In the 1880s, Catholic missions were finally allowed to enter, despite an official ban on "double missions." At that point, however, the Catholic missionaries faced a majority-Protestant Minahasan population (Van den End and Aritonang 2008, 140). The establishment of Catholic missions in Minahasa in the late nineteenth century was the start of a long period of competition and mutual suspicion between Protestants and Catholics, despite the fact that Protestants have remained a majority and the Catholic population in Minahasa has never been above 5 percent (Steenbrink 2003, 262). Though their numbers have remained small, Catholics have made an impact on Minahasan society, particularly through their educational and health care institutions. As was the case for Protestants in Minahasa, schools became a key site for conversion, and for setting in motion the significant social and cultural change that accompanied it. Teachers played important roles in communities, and schools also functioned as chapels in different mission areas (Steenbrink 2003, 263). One strategy for extending the influence of the church was by catering to elite families in founding Catholic schools with Dutch as the language of instruction. This strategy was effective in attracting students from elite Protestant families, and, into the 1930s, more than half of the children in the prestigious Dutch-language Catholic schools were Protestant (Steenbrink 2003, 273).

In this historical context, Lokon St. Nikolaus High School is drawing on a Catholic legacy in Minahasa and adapting it to contemporary political circumstances. In harnessing this high status of the colonial past, the vision for the future of a democratic, multireligious Indonesia is fundamentally about forming young Christian elites who will have an influence in national politics and raise the profile of the region.

LOKON SCHOOL: VISION AND MISSION

Lokon St. Nikolaus High School is a coeducational boarding school with over four hundred high school students who are housed in dormitories on the school's expansive campus. It is set back from the main road in the lush, green city of Tomohon in the Minahasan highlands. The campus is impressive in its distinctive style: the buildings are modern, functional, and well maintained, and the manicured landscape showcases stunning flowers and trees native to the region. The facilities include classrooms, separate male and female dormitories, a library, dining hall, sport hall, laundry facilities, a swimming pool, and a fully equipped hostel for parents and other guests to stay when visiting. An elegant and sober modern-style chapel was built and consecrated in 2019 to become the primary space for religious rituals and events. The physical campus is a testament to the founders' ability to map their educational vision onto a well-planned physical environment, as well as their access to financial capital. Its quality also speaks to its elite nature in terms of the families able to afford the monthly fees charged for boarding full-time at a school with state-of-the-art facilities.

The school's academic profile has also been cultivated through recruiting teachers and training students who have consistently placed in provincial and national academic and sports competitions. The success of students in academic and extracurricular activities is prominently on material display in the large trophy cases in the school lobby. The school has welcomed numerous guests of honor, including former president Susilo Bambang Yudhoyono, who attended the school's official inauguration ceremony in 2006. The minister of education and culture visited in 2016 for the inauguration of the middle school that shares a campus with the high school. Each of these visits is memorialized by engraved marble plaques near the school's entrance.

The administrators often mention the founders' goal of educating students to be "successful in life," rather than just successful at school and in academic achievements. The boarding aspect of the school is understood as essential to this end, and is portrayed as the primary mechanism for building up students' character. The rhythm of the school is marked by Catholic

FIGURE 4.1 Lokon students participate in the Flag Ceremony (*Upacara Bendera*).

rituals and traditions: morning and evening prayer with dorm mates, a pause for "Hail Mary" over the intercom at noon, and a weekly mass initially held in the sports hall, now relocated to the chapel since its consecration. In addition to religious rituals, the daily realities of sharing a room, the discipline of keeping a strict schedule, and the close monitoring by dormitory staff are also viewed as contributing to the character-building ethos of the school. When representing the school to outsiders, the founders and the principal consistently draw on the boarding aspect of the school as its most valuable attribute, convinced of its effectiveness and proud of the uniqueness of the school as the only Christian boarding school in the region.

Ronald and Mary Korompis, the couple who cofounded the school, are Catholics of Chinese descent from North Sulawesi who have used some of their considerable private capital to implement a number of religious initiatives in the province. The Korompis family funded construction of Prayer Hill (Bukit Doa), with stations of the cross positioned along a path that climbs up Mt. Mahawu in Tomohon. The stunning bronze statues of Jesus Christ are set against a backdrop of lush greenery and jungle ferns, and are made even more impressive by the fog that often sets in as part of this tropical mountain landscape. The mountaintop offers a spectacular view of the city of Tomohon and the boarding school campus, and the site includes a chapel and amphitheater. There is also a retreat center designed for groups of pilgrims or tourists, but is also made available for Lokon students during spiritual retreats. In addition, the Korompis family contributes to local parishes to build churches and to local Catholic charities, including an orphanage that cares for children with mental and physical disabilities. These initiatives are part of a broader vision not only to revitalize Catholic presence in the area, but to contribute to development and tourism in the region in order to raise its position on a national level.

The school is run by a private foundation that works closely with the Catholic Church, but is not officially recognized as a Catholic institution. The teachers are all laypeople of diverse Christian backgrounds (including Catholic, Protestant, and Pentecostal). Though the school is private, most of the employees are civil servants and receive their salary from the provincial government. The foundation overseeing the school includes on its board an influential priest in the region, and another Carmelite priest acts as a spiritual advisor for students and often preaches during morning announcements and celebrates mass at the school. There are also several religious brothers from a local order who work as dormitory staff. There is a strong relationship and pattern of collaboration with local Catholic clergy and institutions, but the school is ultimately independent from them as a private foundation.

Lokon welcomes students of all official religions in Indonesia, and the majority of students who attend are in fact Protestant. However, all students who attend the school, regardless of their professed religion, are required to take Catholic religious education courses and attend daily prayers and the weekly mass. This is a common requirement at private Catholic schools in Indonesia, though such requirements have generally been a source of controversy and debate on a national level for decades due to concerns about proselytization via religious education (Crouch 2014, 20–21). The school positions itself as multicultural based on its policy of accepting students of all religions. At the same time, there is a homogenization of existing religious difference on a surface level through the requirement that everyone participate in the same Catholic religious education classes and attend the same worship sessions.

The administration foregrounds the ethnic and religious diversity of the student body as a positive quality of the school that will serve to educate the future generations of Indonesia in the values of tolerance and respect for diversity. The multicultural aspect of the school developed after the project that was already underway, based on both historical and practical circumstances. Most of the students at the school are from North Sulawesi, but many provinces across Indonesia are represented in the student body. A significant 30 percent of the student population is Papuan because the school's foundation signed an agreement with the foundation of the mining corporation Freeport Indonesia, an affiliate of Freeport-McMoRan, which operates in the province of Central Papua the largest copper and gold mine in the world. The foundation funds a number of scholarships to provide students from the city of Timika and the surrounding area with the opportunity to study at the school. Many other provinces are represented, but the remaining portion of the student body consists primarily of the children of elite Minahasans and ethnic Chinese from North Sulawesi. As a result, the difference in socioeconomic status between Papuans and local students is often stark. The gap generally reinforces perceptions of racial and ethnic difference, discussed in more detail later on in the chapter.

Lokon School started out with Ronald and Mary Korompis, now based in Jakarta, wanting to use their position to revitalize education and contribute back to their local community in North Sulawesi. In a publication entitled *Curriculum Based on Life: Education according to Ronald Korompis,* the school's cofounder explains the vision that he hopes to achieve through the school: "This is the concrete form of my intention to make the children of this nation, especially the children of Minahasans and children from North Sulawesi, mighty in the future and with sufficient capacity to make a positive contribution to our nation and country Indonesia, and to humanity on a global scale" (Ratag and Korompis 2009, 43). The language used to express his intention, he explains in the text, is taken directly from the Bible: "Blessed are those who fear the Lord, who find great delight in his commands. Their children will be mighty in the land; the generation of the upright will be blessed" (Psalm 112:1–2). Korompis continually stresses that the inspiration to found this school came from God. Indeed, Ronald became severely ill in the early 1990s and made a vow to God that if he could live ten more years, he would find a way to make a greater contribution and use his influence to benefit many. Having survived this period of time, and also having experienced dreams in which Jesus appeared to him as a teacher reading the Bible, he was determined to make a contribution through education. Ronald's vision is about bringing education back to its true purpose, which he argues can be done only if we recognize that we are God's creation, are loved by God, and must in return offer love to and be fearful of God (Ratag and Korompis 2009, 2–3).

Ronald and Mary Korompis established the Lokon Educational Foundation in 1997, and in the year 2002, Lokon St. Nikolaus High School began operation with its first cohort of students. In the short time span between the establishment of the foundation and the operation of the school, Indonesia experienced major transitions of democratization and decentralization, during which the multiconfessional basis of the nation was thrown into question. Against this backdrop, the Korompises started the school with the aim of forming young people who are religious, have strong character, and are prepared to shape the future of the country.

As the project continued and the foundation began to seek students beyond North Sulawesi (including in Papua and other provinces), the project expanded into a national and multicultural one. Now, rather than just providing education for local Minahasans, the goal is to provide educational opportunities to students in eastern Indonesia, where schools are generally less well equipped and where there are few prestigious educational institutions compared to Java. With this expansion, the project became focused on restoring the educational prestige of Minahasa while simultaneously making a contribution on a national level. Johanis Ohoitimur MSC, a priest at Lokon's educational foundation, explained to me that "Ronald Korompis was thinking about how to revive education in Tomohon run by the

Catholic Church in this framework of *reformasi,* such that this is double-sided: on one hand, he wants to respond to the needs of Indonesians through education. This is on a national level. On a local level, he wants to return to the heyday of North Sulawesi, which was centered in Tomohon in terms of education."

From this Christian inspiration, the "curriculum based on life" (*kurikulum berbasis kehidupan*) is premised on helping students grow intellectually and spiritually by teaching them to fear God (Ratag and Korompis 2009, 44). It can also be understood as a broadly Christian project rather than exclusively Catholic, although religious ceremonies and prayers at the school are according to Catholic tradition. As a result, Protestantism and Catholicism are often grouped together under the broader umbrella of Christianity to engage in discussions about Christian ethics and Christian contributions to the region and nation. The approach to multiculturalism at the school is not taken from an assumed position of religious neutrality, but with a Christian basis, extrapolating Christian values to demonstrate both their universality and their applicability to the civic realm. In the foreword of Korompis's book, the former governor of North Sulawesi, S. H. Sarundajang, himself Protestant, praises the couple's progressive vision of quality education as well as its intended contribution to Indonesia: "Quality education is not only characterized by the ability of its graduates in the mastery of science and technology, but also in the understanding of religious values and devotion, ethics, aesthetics, and personality, as well as improving physical qualities that can deliver Indonesia towards a nation that is *smart, competitive, modern, cultured, and prosperous*" (Ratag and Korompis 2009, vii, emphasis in original).

The "curriculum based on life" comes from an eclectic mix of educational theories, taking inspiration from a golden age of Catholic education in Europe while also drawing from John Dewey's model of progressive education as an attempt to teach respect for diversity and foster critical thinking and democratic participation. However, while recognizing Dewey's progressive education as a source of inspiration, Korompis rejects its secular humanist foundation, arguing that no matter how good, it will be fragile without a basis in religious principles. While there is faith in the ability of an educational model like Dewey's to drive Indonesia toward progress, there is conviction that if it is done without building character and providing a religious education for students, it will fail.

The evolution of the school's vision and mission demonstrates how the educational project that began as one concerned with restoring Minahasa as an important center of education became more national in scope as it sought to incorporate ethnically and religiously diverse students from across eastern Indonesia.

AVOIDING CORRUPTION, BUILDING INTEGRITY

One of the ways in which Lokon School acts as a forum for deliberating about religious and civic values is through discussions about corruption, primarily understood as individual actions that mark one a personal failure both as a Christian and as an Indonesian citizen. Corruption is a national issue and is considered a major obstacle to national development. For many Indonesians, it is shameful that their country, known for its high levels of religiosity, should also become infamous for its rampant corruption.

The national effort to educate youth against corruption is based on an expectation that stressing religious education and instilling good religious character will guide individuals to reject corruption. In a national news report on March 1, 2016, the vice chair of the Indonesian Corruption Eradication Commission (KPK—Komisi Pemberantasan Korupsi) proclaimed religious education (in any of the official religions) as the basis for integrity and anti-corrupt behavior, as "no religion has ever condoned corrupt behavior" (Republika 2016c). Efforts to cultivate religiosity also focus in this case on the moral crisis that Indonesians view as responsible for the failure of earlier national development projects.

In a regional newspaper report in February 2016 about the launch of his new book, *Educating with the Heart,* Ronald Korompis observed, "Indonesia does not lack smart people, but smart people with good character" (Tribun Manado 2016). Thus, according to this reasoning, individuals must be educated in religious values and effort must be taken to cultivate their character so that they can be a part of a broader moral community who will positively influence the future direction of the Indonesian nation instead of being concerned only with personal gain.

Responding to what has been cast as a national crisis of morality and the rampant problem of corruption, character building is a major theme at Lokon St. Nikolaus High School. Religious values are projected as universal, in harmony with and suitable to serve as the foundation for civic ones. In practice, corruption is discussed in both civic and religious education classes, and is often mentioned by administrators and in teacher-training sessions. The typical message from these lessons is that living one's life according to Christian values and principles will automatically make one a good citizen because Christian ethics are universal and in line with the nationalist ideology. Just as the Prophet Muhammad is portrayed by Muslim self-help gurus in Indonesia as "the ultimate exemplar of civic virtue" (Hoesterey 2012, 40), in Minahasa, Jesus Christ takes on the role. Following the example of Jesus is presented as a path toward becoming a good Indonesian citizen.

During a Catholic religious education course at the school, the teacher Pak George paced dynamically around the classroom as he explained the importance of living based on Christ's example. He asked students to open their Bibles and read aloud: "If we claim to have fellowship with him and yet walk in the darkness, we lie and do not live out the truth" (1 John 1:6). Speaking quickly and enthusiastically, switching between a more formal tone in Indonesian and a conversational one in the local Melayu Manado, Pak George continued his impassioned monologue, connecting the biblical lesson to the moral failings of the nation. He explained to the students that while many claim to be morally upright, they are still falling into "KKN" (corruption, collusion, nepotism), an acronym that emerged in reference to the corrupt practices of the New Order regime.

In the classroom, students tend to echo the dominant national discourse that primarily blames corruption for the lack of development in Indonesia. In Ibu Maria's Catholic religious education classes, she also systematically connects national and political issues to religious teachings, though in her own calm and student-centered teaching style. For their homework, the small class of thirteen students had been asked to prepare short orations on "how to develop Indonesia." After the opening prayer, Ibu Maria read through her list of students in the order in which they would be asked to give their speeches. Those whose names were announced first responded with grimaces, though I could not help but note the absence of audible complaints or appeals to postpone the assignment I had witnessed in other classrooms. Students chatted amongst themselves for a few moments as they were given time to finalize their speech preparations.

From the first student asked to present, corruption emerged as a major theme that was elaborated on throughout the students' speeches. Tying together some of the ideas about corruption from his classmates who presented before him, Rocky spoke about widespread poverty, naming it as a symptom and direct consequence of corruption in a country that is so rich in natural resources. Another student gave a short speech to his peers that summarized the connection between religious and civic values and invoked Pancasila: "We need Pancasila as the foundation of this country, and we need Jesus Christ!"

The prevalent discourses at Lokon School that enlist Christian values to fight against corruption diverge in significant ways from those presented at a Christian leadership training seminar run at the school by the Haggai Institute. The Haggai Institute is an international Protestant mission organization that offers an alternative to a foreign missionary model. It operates by running workshops by local missionaries, who train and encourage other local Christians to spread the gospel in their own communities. Lokon students were on vacation at that time, and so the dormitories were taken over by the administrators, teachers, and dormitory staff who were staying on campus for this five-day intensive training. The Indonesian trainers who ran the sessions at Lokon, mostly ethnic Chinese pastors from Jakarta who are associated with various Protestant denominations, stayed at the hostel on the school's campus. The seminar included a four-segment session on building integrity, elaborating on the topic of corruption from a Christian perspective. Integrity was not presented as a requirement for building a better collective future as Indonesians, but a lack of integrity was portrayed as dangerous in jeopardizing one's credibility when missionizing. Individual integrity was a key part of the training because, when enacted in tandem with the methods taught for evangelizing, it was said to determine one's effectiveness as an ambassador for Christ.

The Protestant pastor who led the Haggai session on integrity, dressed in a suit and tie with dark-framed glasses, stressed that moral corruption always starts small, but very quickly snowballs out of control. He pointed to some actions that for him represented a slippery slope toward corruption: running traffic lights, carrying around knockoff designer bags, and breaking international copyright laws by downloading pirated media. He informed the teachers of their important position as ambassadors for Christ, pointedly asking them, "How are people going to know God if Christians themselves don't have integrity?" The pastor is a convert to Christianity, and he cited his own mother's hesitancy toward Christians based on her experience as a neighborhood tailor with whom Christians often went back on their word after negotiating a price. The message was clear: if you are corrupt, you might prevent others from coming to Christ.

An important distinction between the discourses about morality and anti-corruption from the school administration and those from the Haggai Institute is the school's tendency to connect these issues to the importance of building civic values and forming the future generation of Indonesia. For the Haggai Institute, the importance of these values is clearly for effective missionization, encouraging the implementation of Christian values in one's own life to increase the effectiveness of winning souls for Christ. During the Haggai Institute leadership training, one speaker notified the teachers of their luck in having a captive market to transform, but some of the dormitory staff told me they felt this approach was too extreme. Lucas, a religious brother who is part of the dormitory staff at Lokon, explained to me that evangelization is not as narrow as sharing the Gospel, but, most importantly, it is about serving others and being a witness through one's way of life. Whether they realized it or not, the staff's interpretation of missionization aligns closely with the school's project, also more readily reconcilable with multiconfessional and multiethnic nationalist values. However, as described above, while missionization at Lokon is framed as a project for development that transcends sectarian lines and is beneficial to all, it also transgresses some sensibilities about religious mixing and the provision of religious education by insisting that all students attend Catholic rituals and agree to join Catholic religious education.

INTEGRATING RELIGIOUS DIVERSITY AT LOKON SCHOOL

What are the consequences of this link between religious and civic values for the school's broader emphasis on a multiconfessional citizenship put forward as the key to developing the nation? Even if all religions are supposed to be interchangeable in their ability to fill this role of building character in Indonesian citizens, there is still no guarantee that such educational or training programs aspire to religious pluralism or that they will not ask participants to proclaim their religious belonging over and above national belonging (Hoesterey 2012, 41; Rudnyckyj 2010, 192). At Lokon School, there are tensions between different understandings of how to integrate and respect other religions, ranging from a position of extreme relativism to espousing the universality of Catholic values.

From the perspective of the school's founders, Lokon offers an education that is Catholic but appeals to universal values and teaches students about living with difference. Administrators are proud of the diverse student body they have been able to attract and uphold it as an important learning opportunity for students regarding religious tolerance. They also emphasize their accommodation of diversity in several policies, including allowing students to leave the campus to celebrate non-Christian religious holidays with family. At the same time, all students are required to take Catholic religious education courses and participate in Catholic prayers and rituals at the school regardless of religious backgrounds. There are debates at the national level regarding such policies and their status in relation to the 2003 Education Act, which requires public and private schools to provide students religious education in accordance with their professed religion. Many private Protestant and Catholic schools, including Lokon, request that parents sign a form agreeing that their child will join the Christian religious education classes and worship services at the school (Hoon 2014, 512). Christian schools with a good academic reputation are typically able to attract students from other religious backgrounds, which is often framed by critics in the national debate as explicit proselytization and a violation of rights and respect for other religions.

These tensions and internal contradictions represent one way in which deliberation about the coupling of civic and religious values is ongoing at Lokon. The Catholic education teachers recognize that they are teaching a religiously diverse group of students, and explain that they try to teach about Catholicism through universal values that are relevant to people of all different religions (such as love, peace, justice, etc.). In their delivery of the curriculum, they often touch on the importance of tolerance and respect for diversity. The Carmelite priest who acts as the spiritual director for students explained that Catholicism is a universal teaching, and also supported the school's policy of being respectful and open toward other religions based on the recognition in the Second Vatican Council (Vatican II) that there are seeds of truth in other religions.

While religious difference is relatively homogenized on a surface level when all students participate in the same course, it still forms the basis of students' public identities inside and outside the classroom. In religious education courses, religious tolerance is commonly stressed through the discourse that one should not differentiate or stereotype people based on religion. For example, in one classroom session led by Pak George, he explained that the universal nature of Catholicism instructs us not to differentiate or discriminate, and guides us to respect differences in religion and culture. In the same class session, however, he asked students who are Christian to identify themselves by raising their hands, essentially asking them to publicly proclaim their religious identity.

Another religious education teacher, Ibu Maria, commonly speaks on the topic of tolerance, and earnestly tries to teach students to enact it. While teaching students how to lead worship, she praised a Muslim student for enacting tolerance by learning about and participating in Catholic forms of worship. On several other occasions, she also discussed the importance of respecting difference and the benefits of engaging in dialogue with people of other religions, a topic built into the curriculum. She talked to students about the changes brought about by Vatican II, particularly in how the Catholic Church has become more open (*terbuka*), revising its previous teachings that there is no salvation (*keselamatan*) outside of the church. At the same time, she warned students not to go so far in their attempts at tolerance as to recite the creed of another religion, imposing guidelines on how respect is to be enacted. Ultimately, the discourse of respecting difference at the school is projected through the frame of brotherhood and sisterhood in Christ from a universal Catholic perspective.

A major part of the Catholic religious education curriculum, taken from materials produced by the Conference of Indonesian Bishops, focuses on the importance of interreligious dialogue. The textbook's approach features a theologically based dialogue, under the assumption that one must understand the basic teachings of a religion before entering into meaningful dialogue with its followers. In the classroom, teachers discuss the importance of interreligious dialogue and respect for diversity in terms of religious, nationalist, and humanitarian rationales. In one Catholic religious education class session, Pak George supported such teachings by bringing up nationalist principles, including Pancasila and the national motto, "Unity in Diversity." He also recounted to students the significance of diverse humanity as God's creation, and touted the more receptive position of the church toward those of other religions following Vatican II. In the student presentations about interreligious dialogue that followed, Pak George asked students to find Bible verses about the topic. Students presented a range of supporting verses, including the following, taken from 1 John 4:21: "Anyone who loves God must also love their brother and sister." Another group cited Ephesians 4:32: "Be kind and compassionate to one another, forgiving each other, just as God in Christ forgave you." In sum, in one class period, students were encouraged to think about respect for religious diversity as based on religious, nationalist, and humanitarian values.

Students at Lokon School know that they are not supposed to differentiate or discriminate, and one phrase that students like to use with one another is "Don't be racist!" (*Jangan rasis!*), often as a joke, when someone deploys a remark that could be perceived as differentiating among students in any way. After a volunteer group at the school spent time raising funds for and volunteering at both a Catholic and a Muslim orphanage, I asked one of the Student Council Organization (OSIS—Organisasi Siswa Intra Sekolah) leaders about any differences he had noticed between the two experiences.

The typically confident and articulate young man stumbled as he attempted to respond to my question, which had clearly violated the norm of nondifferentiation he had learned for respecting other religions. Flustered, he finally offered his succinct analysis that everything was the same at the two orphanages except the prayer. He then elaborated on his response, asserting that they had visited both orphanages to serve all people in need, not just people of one religious background.

One striking aspect of the school's approach toward religion is the ongoing endeavor to build a broad Christian—not exclusively Catholic—coalition. Protestantism and Catholicism are officially recognized by the Indonesian government as two separate religions, and are commonly treated as such in social differentiation, which often draws on historical legacies of missionary contests. North Sulawesi has not been immune to this strong distinction, as the arrival of Catholic missions in the already predominantly Protestant region in the late nineteenth century led to a mutual feeling of competition. The school is not officially Catholic, though it adheres to Catholic traditions and has many connections to local Catholic priests and religious orders who collaborate with the school's foundation or work at the school itself in various capacities. This context helps to demonstrate the significance of the institution's ability to draw large numbers of Protestant students and its willingness to host Protestant pastors through events like the Haggai Institute Christian leadership training.

Beyond the administrative decisions taken by the school in collaborating with Protestant organizations, students tend to differentiate little between Protestant and Catholic friends. All students attend the same religious education courses, daily prayers, and weekly masses, so students do not separate based on these activities. On Sundays, students who remain on campus are allowed to leave to attend religious worship. Rather than segregating based on religious belonging, students often remain with mixed Protestant/Catholic friend groups, alternating joining the Catholic mass or the Protestant services together as a group. Their selection of which church to attend on any given Sunday might be based on a number of factors beyond religious belonging, including the worship time, and which restaurants or food stalls they could stop at near the church before returning to the school's campus. Because Protestant students are the majority at the school, this relationship between Protestantism and Catholicism and the general attitude of not distinguishing too starkly between the two are noteworthy.

Among students, although religious belonging is considered public knowledge, it typically does not figure prominently in concerns about whom to eat with at the dining hall or whom they might be assigned to bunk with in the dormitory. On the other hand, racial divisions among the student body are prominent and do clearly impact the social environment of the school.

DEVELOPING PAPUA IN MINAHASA

Another initiative at Lokon that relates to views of development and inclusion of difference brings promising students from Papua to study at the school. Every year, representatives from Lokon go to Timika, Papua, and surrounding areas to administer a selection test and look for promising new students to bring to North Sulawesi to continue their education, funded by scholarships from the Freeport Foundation. While this program is in line with the school's multicultural approach and vision, the implementation of this understanding of multiculturalism based in Catholic universalism struggles with ethnic and racial inclusion in practice. Although religious and racial differences are downplayed in many contexts, Papuan students are consistently marked as other, and ultimately projected as the objects rather than the agents of development.

Papua is a predominantly Protestant province of Indonesia with special autonomy as part of a settlement in which the majority of profits from natural resources are returned to the province rather than channeled to the national government. However, due to a number of factors (including corruption), this settlement has failed to improve access to education and healthcare, which remain at the lowest levels in Indonesia (Bobby Anderson 2013). Since the 1980s, an increasing number of Papuan families have sent their children—particularly for higher education—to North Sulawesi, establishing educational ties between these two Protestant-majority regions of Indonesia (Munro 2018). However, wherever they live as migrants, Papuans are subjected to racist stereotypes and often blamed for drunkenness, violence, and criminal activities.

During the Haggai Christian leadership training for staff and administrators, one trainer who was familiar with the situation at the school sympathized with the teachers, affirming how difficult it must be to work with Papuan students. He recycled common racialized stereotypes about Papuans, imagining out loud that teachers must have to constantly remind them to bathe, wash their clothes, and remain disciplined. As a motivational technique, the trainer invited his captive audience to watch a YouTube video of a talk show interview with a Harvard Business School graduate who founded a program to teach entrepreneurial skills to prisoners and ex-convicts. In the video, the host interviewed rehabilitated convicts who had benefitted from this program and recounted their success stories. The trainer stopped the video and asked his audience: "If she can change these ex-convicts, can we change Papuan students?" Although he was clearly expecting an enthusiastic affirmative, he was met with hesitation, and a preliminary response from one teacher qualifying that "it depends" (*tergantung*). The trainer explained that perhaps Papuan students feel that they do not have a real future, and that it is an opportunity for the school to help change them, and, by extension, change Papua.

Race and ethnicity, like religion, are forms of difference that are explicitly addressed in discourses about the Indonesian nation. They also represent forms of difference that the school tries to teach students about through the experience of living and studying with students of various backgrounds. In this case, national discourses about the acceptance of racial difference dovetail with Christian notions of brotherhood to result in very little tension about the principle of accepting Papuan students. Instead, the tension is between the principle of racial inclusion, easily supported by both civic and religious reasoning, and its actual practice, which is often challenged by the actions of both students and teachers. In practice, Papuan students end up consistently differentiated from other students, and are classed by administrators, teachers, and other students as recipients of charity and the objects of the school's aim toward promoting development.

The founders of the school are ethnic Chinese who are able to flexibly identify as a family with local roots and identifiably Minahasan surnames. While Lokon has attracted mostly local students who are ethnic Minahasan and ethnic Chinese, there are students who come from many other regions and ethnic groups. For most of these students, ethnic difference is something that is clearly publicly recognized and discussed, but easily glossed over by the students' similar upper-middle-class backgrounds that allow them to bond over their high-end smartphones and brand-name accessories. All of the students, Papuans included, conform linguistically to the local Bahasa Manado when speaking among peers. However, for Papuan students, ethnic and racial differences map onto class and cultural differences that are used to reinforce their social distance from other students.

All of the Papuan students at the school are Catholic or Protestant, and therefore share a similar religious profile with the other students. However, unlike other ethnicities at Lokon, Papuan students are consistently grouped together and called "Papuan kids" (*anak Papua*). "Papua" is not an ethnic but a regional identifier, and many of the Papuan students actually come from different ethnic groups from within Papua. However, ethnic distinctions among Papuans are rarely recognized or talked about at the school, and instead their cultural and racial similarity as Papuans is reinforced.

Administrators recall that after launching the program to bring Papuan students to study at the high school level, they ran into difficulties with the gap in academic level compared to students from other regions. To address this concern, the school's foundation decided to put together special courses that Papuan students could take at Lokon School for one year to prepare them to join grade 10 the following year. However, this not only consistently grouped Papuan students together and separated them from other students, it also meant that they were often older than their classmates once they began taking general courses at the high school. This reality did little to challenge the widespread racialized stereotypes that other students held about the lack of intelligence of Papuan students. Administrators have searched for other solutions, and are focusing on bringing younger students to begin studying at Lokon's middle school, which now shares a campus with the high school, in hopes of closing this achievement gap earlier on.

Although the original idea for the school was and still is that it should contribute first to Minahasa, it has expanded its scope. The shift to accept students from other regions was partially for economic reasons, but also in line with the school's expanded vision of providing quality education for eastern Indonesia. However, Papuan students are often assumed to be recipients of charity who might help to make a difference in their own region, but they are not talked about as the "future of the nation" in the same way as other students are. The school, rather than being a site of individual transformation for these students, suddenly becomes a site for bringing them in line with the particular nationalist ideal and its universal Catholic basis and by making them objects of development. In this way, they are similar to the Muslim students described by Jaffe-Walter in her ethnography of a Danish school, who are consistently projected as in need of special guidance because of their inability to think for themselves (2016, 72–73). However, in Indonesia, religion is not cast as the problem but as the solution by providing an understanding of brotherhood that can be used to draw Papuan students closer to the ideal of citizenship put forth by the Catholic school.

One Sunday afternoon, while walking around the campus, I came across a group of Papuan students standing in the grass, stretching and warming up for a karate lesson with an outside instructor. I stopped to ask more about the activity and chat with one of the representatives from the foundation active in recruiting students from Papua. Framing the program within the school's mission, he underscored the importance of serving not only those in North Sulawesi, but those in other areas of eastern Indonesia, preparing them to be local leaders in their regions. He followed this with a qualification. Lokon welcomes these students, he explained, even though their low academic performance drags down the school's overall academic ranking in the region. In spite of this, he explained, the school has embraced this program as an important part of its mission to prepare students to go on to higher education or vocational training. The position of Papuan students was quickly shifted from that of potential leaders to recipients of charity.

The school's viewpoint is clearly a mainstream nationalist one that sees Papua as a region in dire need of development and educational opportunities. In Papua, however, separatist movements calling for independence from Indonesia are still active. Across the country, movements calling attention to racism directed against Papuans have highlighted the discrimination faced on a national scale. While the Papuan students at Lokon School talk about their identity as Indonesian, they are also trying to negotiate their own identities. Some are influenced by the separatist movements, whether they express it by putting symbols on their personal Facebook pages or by pulling a stunt—as one group of students did—by raising the Morning Star flag on the school's grounds.[2] All students who were involved in the flag raising were expelled from the school and sent home, and the rest of the Papuan students were taken for a retreat (*rekoleksi*) to the nearby Prayer Hill. On the school's campus, teachers and dormitory staff discussed the incident among themselves in hushed tones and with shaking heads, adding further weight to its seriousness.

The school counselor confided disapprovingly that sometimes parents call to request that their child not be assigned to share a room with Papuan students. Although the counselor never grants such a request, in practice, Papuan students are often assigned to bunk together in the dormitories. Dormitory staff readily gave examples of cultural differences that made dormitory life challenging, particularly the way in which Papuan students' ideas about sharing are perceived by others as a lack of respect for personal property. Papuan students also typically choose to eat in the cafeteria together and spend their free time together. Without family nearby and only able to go home during summer vacation, they are also the most consistently present on campus, as other students might go home for the weekend or during short holidays. Academically, they are invariably placed together with other students in the social science track (IPS—Ilmu Pengetahuan Sosial), unanimously accepted as less rigorous than the natural science track (IPA—Ilmu Pengetahuan Alam). In practice, racialized differentiation is marked in structured and unstructured social interactions throughout the school, despite the foundation of the Catholic multicultural approach.

While the students at Lokon are all influenced by global pop culture, Papuan students are most likely to be seen wearing trucker hats and listening to Bob Marley or American rap music, rather than watching Korean dramas or listening to Taylor Swift like the rest of their classmates. Matt, a friendly and charismatic Papuan student who is highly proficient in English, has expressed his concern about the future of Papua, where he says corruption is high. His dream is to study politics and go back to be an upright leader there. An effective mediator taking the role of an older brother, he often speaks to the administration on behalf of other Papuan students. Another Papuan student with a much weaker academic record, who was later expelled on behavioral grounds, came up to me one day while I was sitting on one of the leather couches in the lobby of the school library. He nervously asked if I was American, and when I answered in the affirmative, he confided his wish to study in New Orleans, the former location of Freeport-McMoRan's headquarters. His family had been affected by the mine's acquisition of land, and he shared his dream to become successful and reform corporations so that they would not be able to treat people unfairly. Papuan students, like all students at Lokon, have multiple aspirations as they are trying to imagine their future and also navigate the day-to-day life at boarding school.

Civic and religious principles called upon in the school together support ethnic and racial inclusion in an abstract sense, but there is tension between the principle and practice, particularly when Papuan students are consistently positioned as recipients of charity and objects of development. Even so, the effort to educate Papuan students at Lokon does have political implications in its attempt, however tenuous, to incorporate ethnic difference and reinforce a mainstream nationalist understanding of the Indonesian archipelago as naturally including Papua. At the same time, the Papuan students (just like all the other students) are also participating in a global pop culture and trying to navigate what their identity might mean for them personally, and in a national context.

LEARNING CITIZENSHIP THROUGH RELIGIOUS EDUCATION

Overall, Lokon's educational program participates in a broader public discourse that portrays deepening one's own religious commitment (as a member of one of the six recognized national religions) as an essential step toward national progress. Daromir Rudnyckyj argues that discourses such as these signal a shift in Indonesia from the previous "faith in development" during the thirty-two years of the authoritarian New Order era to a new focus on "developing faith" following the 1998–1999 transition to democracy (2010, 3–4). Drawing on his research in a privatizing steel company that began implementing a spiritual training program based on Islamic principles, he claims that this transition entails a growing disillusionment with the nation-state as the principal agent of modernization and development. Furthermore, he argues that the program integrates citizens into a spiritual economy that is founded on mutually reinforcing neoliberal and Islamic principles that interact to produce self-governing subjects. In Lokon's educational project, there is recognition of the importance of individual faith in pushing Indonesia toward progress, but not due to a perceived failure of the nation and its role. Rather, it is an attempt to take action toward shaping the nation as a moral community, bound not only as Indonesian citizens, but also because of their commitment to a religiously founded morality.

An overly technical characterization of New Order national development projects in Indonesia ignores their significant moral component and strong functionalization of religious and moral principles. During the New Order period, missionaries and religiously based organizations often acted as adjuncts of the state in modernization and development programs.

FIGURE 4.2 Students in Catholic religious education at Lokon.

Describing the way in which the Salvation Army missionaries in Central Sulawesi promoted development initiatives during this period, Lorraine Aragon offers one example of a relationship between religious institutions and the government that demonstrates how "religious devotion and economic development have become quietly indexed to one another" (2000, 305). In addition, Robert Hefner has indicated that Rudnyckyj's particular characterization of "faith in development" as relying simply on the state and technical expertise overlooks the New Order's strong emphasis on religious education and the launching of nationalist ethical and moral training programs (2012, 105), discussed in more detail in chapter 2. These analyses indicate that a harnessing of religion and ethics to national development projects is not new, but that changes in the political and religious atmosphere have allowed it to evolve in different ways. Democratization, decentralization, and a broad religious resurgence have made public reflection about the relationship between religion and development more politically possible.

Another important shift that occurred during and after the transition to democracy and relates very strongly to the relationship between religion and development in a national framework is the emergence of "majoritarian intolerance in post-authoritarian Indonesia" (R. W. Hefner 2012, 105–106). Performances of nationalism through religious piety take on particular significance in the current political context of Indonesia, where there is increasing polarization across religious lines and competing frameworks of belonging. At Lokon, the proposed vision of citizenship is based on Catholic and more broadly Christian principles that are cast as universal principles of all religious believers, consistent with national values and understood as holding the key to progress and development for the region and nation. The way this relationship is constructed, far from settled even in the day-to-day activities of Lokon School, has serious consequences for the future of a multiconfessional and multiethnic Indonesia.

In contemporary democratic post-*reformasi* Indonesia, with the reemergence of local identities and increased decentralization following the authoritarian New Order era, the terms of the nation itself and the basis of national cohesion are under negotiation. Efforts of schools like Lokon are part of a broader movement by some educational institutions across Indonesia to respond to threats to the multiconfessional basis of the nation, made painfully clear through the reassertion of ethnic identity, religious identity, exclusivism, and, in some cases, outbreaks of mass violence as a result.

North Sulawesi has been praised by local religious and political leaders as well as national-level politicians for its ability to resist being pulled into the kinds of conflicts that occurred in so many surrounding regions. The discourse of religious harmony (*kerukunan beragama*) has been a major strategy in North Sulawesi to promote "an inclusive cultural identity while re-invoking religious difference through a non-threatening nationalist idiom" (Swazey 2013, 98). In Lokon's educational project, the history of education and Christian missions in North Sulawesi is also used by the founders of Lokon to present the unique position of Christians in the province as an example of this multiconfessional religious citizenship. The form of aspirational coexistence infused in the school's vision turns the educational project and the province into a model for other regions to emulate. The goal to revive education in the region conjures up the historical prominence of Minahasans during colonial times, and the school's intent to contribute to development pledges its commitment to national values.

SPREADING CHRISTIAN VALUES AS CIVIC VALUES FOR MINAHASA AND THE NATION

Born out of the era of decentralization and democratization in Indonesia, Lokon St. Nikolaus High School is promoting an educational program that offers a foundation in Christian values and strong character, understood as a necessary prerequisite for future leaders of the nation. While self-management and discipline are a crucial part of this process of self-transformation, the broader goal here is a national one: to establish a moral community that will have impact on the future of the nation. It is a goal that looks back at the former importance and status of Minahasa and the history of education in the region. Accordingly, Lokon seeks to convince the rest of Indonesia that North Sulawesi has a role to play in the country's future and that it is preparing the kind of leaders required toward this end. Missionization in this sense channels the development of faith through broader ideas about building character and civic values. Consequently, this educational initiative is also an attempt to shape national values, simultaneously emphasizing their overlap with Christian values. As I have shown, there are tensions in how the relationship between religious and civic values is understood and practiced at Lokon School, and the processes through which these are deliberated about and contested are important ones.

This particular school does not downplay but in many ways emphasizes its Catholic and more broadly Christian foundation and provides a space for deliberation about the mutual influence of religious and national values. This approach reflects another vision of the school that was born out of the *reformasi* movement and the transition to democracy. As ethnic and religious violence broke out in several regions across the Indonesian archipelago during this period, the school's founders felt the urgency to educate a new generation so that such ethnic and religious conflicts would not be repeated in the future. Although all the religiously diverse students join Catholic mass and religious education at Lokon, their experience with others at the school is designed as a lesson in multiculturalism and in "universal values" that are taken from Christianity, but also considered important for character building and nation building. Therefore, the nature of the relationship forged between religion and development also has important ramifications for imagining the contours of the nation and how religious and ethnic belonging are envisioned and enacted. As this example from Lokon School demonstrates, deliberations involving students, teachers, and even the school founders have ethical and political consequences for the future of Indonesia.

5

Public Madrasah

Islamic Discipline as the Foundation of Civic Deliberation

Dozens of students and teachers from the public madrasah MAN in Manado excitedly stepped off the buses they had gotten to know well, having spent five hours in them on the previous day to reach their destination in the city of Kotamobagu, North Sulawesi. The students who undertook the journey are all members of an extracurricular religious club at the madrasah supporting Qur'anic recitations and *dakwah* activities intended to increase piety among students. Having spent the entire morning preparing their costumes and practicing performances at the hostel where they stayed the previous night, many of the students were impatient to get the event started as they entered the auditorium of the public madrasah in Kotamobagu. The auditorium had a white tile floor and white walls, immediately directing the eyes to the colorful painted mural behind the stage—it depicted the campus of the madrasah, flanked by scenes of students learning.

The students from MAN had been looking forward to this trip for weeks. They supplemented the funding received for their program from the local Ministry of Religious Affairs by selling snacks and holding a fundraising campaign. The stated goal of the event was *silaturahim,* an Islamic concept focused on establishing familial relationships and strengthening ties with others, which would be achieved by showcasing the religious commitment and artistic talents of students from two public madrasahs in the province. At the event, Qur'anic recitations were performed by both teachers and students, at times their particularly moving expressions leading to a collective exclamation of "Allah!" A group of girls dressed in two-toned green floor-length dresses with black hijabs performed an upbeat yet restrained choreography to an Islamically themed pop song by Swedish-Lebanese singer Maher Zain. One student, dressed in all black and wearing a more enveloping veil than her classmates, gave a persuasive speech about the temptation of premarital sex and the dangers of social media as teachers nodded in agreement and a group of students seemed to mockingly feign outrage, exclaiming *"Astaga!"*[1]

In addition to these religiously themed performances, several student groups gave presentations drawing on nationalist themes. One group from the madrasah in Kotamobagu wore all white, with red-and-white ribbons tied around their wrists, as two lines of students separated by gender stood swaying and gesturing as they sang the nationalist pop ballad "Indonesia Jaya," about defending Pancasila and fighting for the future of the nation. During this song, the chorus of students supported the dominant voices of one boy and girl each singing into a microphone, whose powerful and heartfelt rendition of the song elicited applause and cheers from fellow students. Though perhaps not as flashy as the song performance, a group of three students delivered a speech that wove together Qur'anic verses with quotes from nationalist addresses given by Sukarno, the leader of the struggle for independence and first president of Indonesia. One of the students in the group then gave his own commentary, disparaging conflicts taking place in Indonesia and their violation of the nationalist vision of unity. Emboldened with a bit of applause, he stated, "Unity and togetherness are the key to the successful development of our nation," as he motioned to his classmate to recite Qur'anic verses to support his statement. His ending with the punchy reminder *"Torang Samua Basudara"* (We Are All Brothers) proved successful in engaging attention and drawing applause from teachers and peers.

FIGURE 5.1 Madrasah students perform a nationalist song.

At the event, the seemingly natural weaving of nationalist songs and themes with Qur'anic recitations and other religiously themed dances and persuasive speeches demonstrates the importance given to both religious and civic values, not as exclusive but as intimately intertwined. As the rest of this chapter will show, it also relates to a particular conception of morality put forth by the public madrasah in which students must understand the truth and perfection of Islam in order to be able to act as moral individuals, including engaging in good civic behavior. Islam is understood as the foundation of a moral society, and living in a region where Muslims are a minority requires the school to take on the major task of educating students who may not have a strong background of religious knowledge and who live in an environment that may not provide a strong Islamic influence.

This chapter focuses on MAN, an all-Muslim public high school in the Protestant-majority city of Manado, and on the way that the school's model of moral action aims to provide students with a strong foundation in Islam as the path toward becoming upstanding citizens. It also considers how this model of ethical selfhood and collectivity relates to the coconstruction of deliberation and discipline within this context. Ethical discipline grounded in religious ideas about individual and collective virtues, and enacted through institutions like schools, are fundamental in creating the backdrop against which deliberation takes place (Burchell 1995; Hirschkind 2001, 5). In the particular model put forth by MAN, religious piety is conceived of as not only an individual duty but within the scope of civic responsibility. Although it guides students to have a strong grasp of religious principles and to develop a strong religious selfhood, it is not a deterministic model, as this requirement is one that needs to be met in order for students to then deliberate about precisely how Islamic values are to be implemented.

During my ethnographic investigation of ethical deliberation about belonging in schools, I selected the only public madrasah in Manado, Madrasah Aliyah Negeri Model 1 Manado (referred to here as MAN), as a case study. As I began spending more time there and word about my research interests began to spread, many teachers pulled me aside between classes or after school, wanting to have a chat about the importance of religious harmony in the region and discuss the relation of Islamic teachings to tolerance and religious coexistence. Through my conversations with these teachers and students, and the extensive time I spent in the classroom, it became clear that the goal of the teachers and administrators is primarily to build up students' foundations as pious Muslims, teaching them to understand the truth and perfection of Islam. At the school, students are guided toward deepening their religious practice and internalizing Islamic principles, meant to ultimately allow them to act morally as good individuals and as good citizens. Part of this is about respecting diversity and being prepared to enact tolerance outside of the school as they encounter religious difference in their diverse communities. As a result, teachers often do not feel that material about religious diversity or tolerance needs to be emphasized or addressed more than it already is in the formal curriculum, as students will be able to practice tolerance only if they have a properly grounded understanding of Islamic teachings.

MADRASAHS IN THE NATIONAL AND LOCAL CONTEXT

In Indonesia, madrasahs are modernist institutions of Islamic learning, in contrast with the traditionalist Islamic boarding schools called *pesantren,* and are distinguished in their offering of a general curriculum in addition to a curriculum in the Islamic sciences (Azra, Afrianty, and Hefner 2007, 176). A Madrasah Aliyah Negeri like MAN is a state or public madrasah at the senior secondary level. While some madrasahs, especially private ones affiliated with Islamic organizations like Muhammadiyah, may also act as boarding schools (C.-M. Hefner 2016), state madrasahs typically function as day schools, with students most often living with family while attending school. Following a 1975 national ministerial decree, state madrasah graduates have the option to enroll in general institutions of higher learning or Islamic ones, rather than being restricted to religious institutions as was previously the case (Azra, Afrianty, and Hefner 2007, 186). Madrasahs, though under the auspices of the Ministry of Religious Affairs, have, since 1989, been required to fulfill the national general curriculum standards determined by the Ministry of Education and Culture (Azra, Afrianty, and Hefner 2007, 177). In practice, this means that most madrasahs—like other public and private secondary schools—now utilize the 2013 Curriculum.

In the province of North Sulawesi, there are four public madrasahs at the senior secondary level, though only one of them is located in the city of Manado. A private madrasah in the city of Bitung (40 km east of Manado) changed its status to become a state madrasah in 2015. The other public madrasahs are in the southern area of the province, in Dumoga and Bolaang-Mongondow (150 km south of Manado), which have a higher proportion of Muslim residents. In Manado, there are a handful of private *pesantren* and madrasahs, and several more across Minahasa and in the nearby city of

Bitung, including a *pesantren* in Tomohon affiliated with the *dakwah* organization Hidayatullah (see Rusli 2020). However, most are relatively recent, with the earliest government-registered *pesantren* in Manado dating to the 1970s. Most other Muslim schools in the area were founded in the 1980s and 1990s, concurrent with a growing national interest in and demand for Islamic education (R. W. Hefner 2009, 69). *Pesantren* in Manado today have enrollments in the dozens, compared to MAN, by far the largest Islamic school in Manado, with an enrollment of approximately 1,200 students.

MAN in Manado was established as a state madrasah in 1992, though it had already previously functioned as a teacher-training institute for Islamic education. In 1998, MAN was chosen among a group of thirty-five madrasahs in Indonesia as a "model madrasah," explaining the school's current designation as MAN Model 1 Manado, referred to locally as MAN Model. It is located in a Muslim-majority district (*kecamatan*) in the northern part of Manado. As one crosses the river toward the school from the city center, the increasing prevalence of mosques, halal restaurants, and Muslim clothing boutiques signals this demographic change.

Like most other public and private high schools across Indonesia, MAN has implemented the 2013 Curriculum. Consistent with its increased focus on Islamic education relative to public high schools, MAN requires students to take additional courses in religious education beyond the regular academic subjects. Students at MAN take up to ten hours of religious education per week, significantly more than the mandatory three-hour minimum in public high schools. At the public high school SMA, for example, Muslim students attend one comprehensive course on general Islamic education in addition to religious programming on Friday afternoons. At MAN, students attend various courses on the Qur'an, Islamic jurisprudence, Islamic ethics, and the history of Islam, among others. Compared to students at the public high school, who take classes in approximately thirteen subjects (depending upon their year and educational track), students at the madrasah may have classes in up to seventeen subjects if we take into account all the religious education courses. In order to accommodate the scheduling requirements of the additional subjects, students attend school from 7 a.m. until 3 p.m. from Monday through Thursday, and on Saturday. On Friday, students attend academic classes from 7 a.m. until 12 p.m., followed by Friday prayer and other religious programming. By way of comparison, this makes for approximately 45 hours of class per week at the madrasah, whereas at the public high school SMA, students only attend school from 7 a.m. until 1:30 p.m. from Monday through Friday, for a total of 32.5 hours of class time per week.[2] Many students also stay at the madrasah after school to participate in extracurricular activities or eat snacks and socialize with friends in the cafeteria.

OVERVIEW OF MAN

There are approximately 1,200 students enrolled at the madrasah, all of whom are Muslim. Parents typically decide to enroll their children at the madrasah specifically because it offers an Islamic-based education. MAN does have a good academic reputation, but there are many other general public and private schools that also offer rigorous and competitive academic programs. The students at MAN represent many ethnic groups from the region, including Bolaang-Mongondow and Gorontalo ethnic groups. A significant number of students, many of whom are Javanese, have parents who are originally from other regions in Indonesia who have been relocated to Manado for civil service. Around two hundred of the students stay in dormitories on school grounds, but dormitory life is not considered a major part of character building as it is for local *pesantren* or for the private Lokon School, and the majority of students commute to the school daily.

Students at MAN, though all Muslim, come from a range of religious education backgrounds. Some have attended only Islamic schools, and/or have a strong foundation in religious education from their family or mosque community. Other students have attended public middle schools, or, in some cases, Christian schools. Many religious education teachers view this range of backgrounds as a challenge, because some students come in with a strong grasp of Islamic teachings, while others have received minimal instruction and struggle with basic skills, such as reading the Qur'an.

The teachers are from several different ethnic groups in the region, some having roots in Manado's Kampung Arab (Arab neighborhood) or coming from Kampung Jawa Tondano, a Javanese settlement in Minahasa dating from the nineteenth century. As a state madrasah, the school is not affiliated with any particular Islamic organization. Teachers are involved in local branches of national Islamic organizations, such as the modernist Muhammadiyah and the traditionalist Nahdlatul Ulama (NU), among others. Many of the teachers are graduates of the State Islamic Institute (IAIN) in Manado.

The school campus is organized as several different buildings (classrooms, library, cafeteria, administrative offices, and the school mosque) all around a central courtyard similar to SMA's though lacking a roof. Consequently, students typically avoid the central courtyard during the hottest hours of the day or gather at its edges, seeking shade from roof overhangs or plants as they are able. There is one covered shelter in the courtyard that often functions as a stage or as the location for smaller events during the middle of the day. The classrooms are in two-story buildings on the perimeter of the courtyard. Students have a homeroom class and teacher, and are responsible for decorating the classroom and maintaining its cleanliness on a daily basis. On some occasions, for example, the commemoration of the Youth Pledge (*Sumpah Pemuda*), teachers organize a competition to select the best classroom on the basis of both cleanliness and aesthetic value. There is a cafeteria with several vendors, all of whom sell exclusively halal food, both prepackaged and freshly prepared. There is also a library, which houses government-provided course textbooks shared among classes. Student representatives can be seen going back and forth between the library and their classrooms at the start and end of class periods to pick up and return textbooks for particular academic subjects to be used during the class.

The mosque on school grounds is newly rebuilt, and is now large enough to accommodate students for Friday prayers and for special events at the school, such as the prayers preceding the school's Eid al-Adha (Feast of Sacrifice) celebration. The principal of the madrasah, Ibu Hesty, had started a program several years earlier to supplement government funds for the mosque renovations. The program, called the 1,000 Rupiah per Day Infaq Movement asked students to bring 1,000 rupiah (US$0.07) to the school every day as *infaq*, a particular kind of Islamic charity intended for the betterment of society, to donate toward the mosque. Each morning, the homeroom student leader circulated among students in the class to collect the money and give it directly to the school treasurer to be recorded and kept safely. In 2016, the mosque had already been rebuilt, but students continued to bring money daily in order to contribute to the construction of a dedicated area for performing ablutions (*tempat wudhu*) adjacent to the mosque. The religion teacher Ibu Rahma understands this requirement for donating on a daily basis as a facet of character education at the school. Students typically come to school with pocket money (*uang jajan*) from their parents, usually to buy snacks and/or lunch. Donating requires them to go through the daily practice of setting aside a portion for the purpose of charity, also giving a recurring reminder of the need to contribute to society with no expectation of return.

FIGURE 5.2 Newly refurbished mosque at MAN.

At MAN, students have the option of a variety of extracurricular activities. Some of the extracurricular activities are religiously focused, described in more detail below. However, there are also a number of general clubs and after-school activities. These offer concrete ways for MAN students to pursue sports or academic interests, and in doing so, meet students from other schools in Manado. Because students at the school are all Muslim, these extracurricular activities represent one of the potential arenas of interaction with students from different religious backgrounds. Participating in activities like scouting (*pramuka*), marching band, science and math Olympiads, and sports, gives students and teachers the opportunity to engage with people of different religious backgrounds through school-sponsored activities.

MODELS OF MORAL ACTION BASED IN ISLAM

In line with the school's role as a madrasah, designated to pass on religious knowledge and practice, and in conjunction with national concerns about declining morality and a need for character education, MAN teachers and administrators take seriously their duty to cultivate piety among students. Their efforts acquire particular significance in an environment where Muslims are the local minority, and it cannot be assumed that students will be steeped in Islamic traditions outside of the school. Furthermore, in Indonesia, having a strong religious background is typically seen as protection from radicalization, as those who have a proper understanding of the Qur'an are less likely to be lured by extremist interpretations. One poster at the school indexed this conviction through the caption "Education is a weapon that has the power to change the world."

Consistent with both the focus of the 2013 Curriculum and the Islamic identity of the school, teachers at MAN claim character education as the central component of their educational approach. The general consensus is that in order to be effective, the character education must be based in Islamic principles. Overall, there is a positioning of religion as the foundation for morality that is similar to that of Lokon's cofounder, who argues that a progressive education model should be implemented with a religious foundation. The head of the Ministry of Religious Affairs regional office, a former English teacher at MAN, agrees with this perspective. During the Eid al-Adha celebration at MAN, he paid a visit to the school to eat with the teachers. When I asked him what the biggest challenge is for education in Indonesia today, he responded that it is character education, and that it must be implemented with religious education as the basis.

It is, of course, not surprising that teachers at a religious school aim to give students a strong religious foundation. Rather than overlooking this reality as banal, I propose to look deeper at the particular model of moral action promoted by the school: the way that teachers seek to cultivate religiosity, and the intended impact of this religious practice. The encouragement of religious practice is not an end in and of itself, but is an essential step toward students achieving moral selfhood and being fully capable of engaging in deliberation about the future of society. This model positions Islam as the important basis of moral action, without which students will be unable to act as moral individuals and moral citizens. This approach is not unique to this madrasah, as some of the notions of religious and civic values being part of moral selfhood parallel the efforts at character education with a religious foundation taking place at Lokon and even in public schools. However, particular elements and conceptions of moral selfhood are drawn from the specificities of Islamic tradition concerned with the moral transformation that happens as individuals encounter the perfection and truth of Islam through religious practices such as prayer and recitation.

Teachers at MAN often voice perspectives that align with the importance of Islamic values as the basis for character building. The Islamic jurisprudence (*fiqh*) teacher Ibu Vita, who has taught at MAN for ten years, described her teaching goal as illuminating aspects of Islamic law in a holistic way, such that it would have a moral impact on students and improve their character. As an example, she pointed to the involvement of students in the distribution of meat following the sacrifice on Eid al-Adha. That year, students had raised enough money to purchase three of the seven cows that were sacrificed in the school's courtyard during the celebration. After the animals were slaughtered, the meat was redistributed to economically disadvantaged neighborhoods near the school, as well as to officers and workers at the nearby police station. Through this experience and lesson in Islamic values, she explained, students can learn how to maintain a good relationship with God (*habluminallah*) and with the broader society (*habluminannas*). These two relationships are seen as interdependent, in that one must focus on deepening religiosity and becoming closer to God in order to fully understand and respect the diversity of humankind. Ibu Vita cited from Surah Al-Hujurat (Q 49:13), "O Humanity! Indeed, We created you from a male and female, and made you into peoples and tribes so that you may get to know one another," saying that she works to "plant" (*tanamkan*) verses like this for her students and to encourage them to pray regularly. While she feels strongly about the need to build character, she expressed that doing so depends on students having concrete knowledge about Islamic law and ethics, which they must master in order to implement it in their lives.

At an in-house training on executing the 2013 Curriculum, one session focused on employing an Islamic scientific approach in teaching. The speaker, from the regional Ministry of Religious Affairs, attempted to empower teachers to see the potential for integrating an Islamic perspective in all subjects. She spoke about the need to teach students to be scientific and critical, and also the need to realize the religious aspects of all subjects, particularly through the use of prayer to start lessons. As she implemented a mock lesson with the teachers pretending to be students, she wove together educational methodologies like student-centered learning with her step-by-step Islamic scientific approach. The speaker had eagerly jumped in to explain her PowerPoint slides before realizing that she had forgotten to start the lesson with a prayer, as she had instructed the teachers to do in their own classrooms. Before moving forward with her next slide, she asked the group of teachers to say *"bismillah"* (in the name of God), along with her.

The environment of the school is concerned with instilling religious values, particularly as a minority religion in the region, with the assumption that a strong religious grounding will provide students with the necessary ability to enact these social competencies inside and outside the school. On the whole, students are encouraged to partake in religious activities in hopes that they will integrate religious discipline and Islamic values into their daily routines for the rest of their lives. According to the perspective of teachers and administrators, it is the development of spiritual competency that allows students to enact social competencies such as honesty, cooperation, and respect for others. In addition to the daily prayers and recitation discussed below, boys are required to attend Friday prayer at the school mosque, while girls attend a religious sermon or participate in a religious activity in the multipurpose room. Throughout the school year, the school also puts on events for religious holidays. For example, during the fasting month of Ramadan, the school hosts an *iftar* dinner, inviting teachers, students, and their families to come to break the fast together as a group. Also, several extracurricular groups, like the one that raised money to support their trip to Kotamobagu, involve religious activities. While the administration is supportive of many kinds of extracurricular activities, they particularly admire students' participation in religious clubs and the contribution of these students to maintaining the Islamic identity of the school.

RELIGIOUS PRACTICE AS THE PATH TO MORAL SELFHOOD

As a major mechanism for demonstrating existing religious commitment, but also for inculcating piety and participating in the cultivation of moral selfhood, daily prayers are the single most common religious practice that teachers stress as essential for a properly Islamic character education. Students are encouraged to go to the school mosque to perform the daily prayers that fall during the school day. As the class period ends and the midday call to prayer sounds, teachers walk around their classrooms and the school campus, corralling students to make sure that they are headed toward the mosque to pray, rather than to socialize or buy food at the cafeteria, for example. When Ibu Indah, the Islamic ethics teacher, first introduced the concept of *akhlak* (encompassing ideas of virtue, morality, and character) to students in her class, one of the first things she mentioned was the importance of daily prayers as the basis for "maintaining good character and morals" (*menjaga akhlak yang baik*). In my discussions with Ibu Indah, she detailed her dual approach to Islamic education in giving students knowledge (*ilmu pengetahuan*) about Islam and in shaping their character (*akhlak*). She explained that the performance of prayer (*sholat*) integrates these together, helping students learn how to implement religious values.

Drawing on Islamic understandings of the performance of prayer, the encouragement of the practice is understood to "create moral selves, not merely because the practices are mandated or recommended by Islam, but also because they are thought to lead to moral dispositions more broadly" (Simon 2014, 172). It is in this way, as Ibu Indah explains, that the knowledge of Islam can effectively shape students' moral selves through the mediation of the ritual practice of prayer. Her colleague Ibu Rahma, who teaches a course on the Qur'an and hadith, similarly positions daily prayers as central in building moral selfhood. When I asked her about her pedagogical approach to character building, she unequivocally stated that the main way is to get students to fulfill their "obligation to pray" (*perintah sholat*).

Teachers do at times emphasize the emotional or subjective experience of performing daily prayers, focusing on the transformative potential of the practice itself on one's state of mind and attitude, as well as the potential for longer-term effects. However, teachers also turn it into a practice to be monitored and evaluated for the purposes of grading, using both moral and bureaucratic authority to discourage students from forgoing it. For many teachers—not only religious education teachers but also those who teach subjects like chemistry or English—the behavioral grade (*nilai sikap*) they are required to submit for each student and factor into all academic grades amounts to whether or not the student is diligent in performing their prayers. Teachers at the madrasah at times admitted exasperation about the effort it takes to get students to perform this most basic religious requirement. Ibu Rahma explained that her approach to behavioral grades is based on many factors, including a student's attitude in class and behavior outside of class, but most importantly, whether they regularly perform their prayers. Ibu Rahma can often be seen walking around the campus at prayer time, scolding students who are not heading toward the mosque, in a manner that is firm yet also humorous in its purposefully over-the-top display. She also monitors her homeroom students, for whom she has a soft spot, more closely in their religious practice, as she feels she has an important duty toward ensuring their religious upbringing. At the end of one class period, as the call to prayer resonated throughout the classroom, she instructed her homeroom students to finish up their tasks and then head toward the mosque for prayer. One boy proclaimed to the class that he was on his period and thus could not go pray, clearly stalling by citing the normative prohibitions against performing *sholat* while menstruating. His male classmates erupted in laughter at his failed excuse as Ibu Rahma shooed them all out of the classroom in the direction of the mosque.

Students at MAN certainly understand the expectation surrounding daily prayer, and often discuss it in religious education class, acknowledging its importance. In the debates for student council (OSIS) president, candidates were asked by teachers what kind of initiatives they might start at the school. One candidate said that she would like to start a program where friends encourage one another to go as a group to pray in the school mosque. She was more specific than other candidates who said in a rather vague manner that they would promote religious activities at the school. Despite understanding its importance and requirement for grades, many students admitted to avoiding their prayers, even when asked by teachers. While teaching Islamic ethics to one of the classes where students were often praised by teachers for their diligence, Ibu Indah asked students, "How many of you have already done your *subuh* [dawn prayer]?" When only four students raised their hands, she exclaimed, *"Astaghfirullah!* Only four people?" She clearly felt compelled to launch into a mini-sermon: "There's no excuse for this! If you say that no one woke you up, that's an excuse from 'back when' [*jaman dulu*], because now you have a cell phone, alarm, and you're already adults! *Subuh* is the beginning of our day. We hope the day will go smoothly, but if we don't pray at the beginning . . . if we don't start our day with prayer, how can it?" While students clearly recognized the importance of praying, they also didn't want to be seen as diligent about prayers just to get a good grade, as this indicated that students were overeager to please teachers. Having such desires could also be construed as holding the wrong intentions (*niat*) for performing worship, which could have not only social but religious consequences in terms of how their actions will be judged by God. It is clear that teachers encourage students to practice discipline through prayers, with the idea that they will be shaped by this pious practice, ideally developing into moral individuals. Adequate discipline is assumed to be a prerequisite for deliberation, as students must have a foundational knowledge of Islam and be sufficiently pious to deliberate about the application of Islamic principles in the broader multireligious society, for example.

Qur'anic recitation is another religious practice that is seen as essential toward moral cultivation, and is encouraged and practiced at the school on a daily basis. Each morning, students spend fifteen minutes for group Qur'anic recitation (Tadarus Al-Qur'an), with their classmates and homeroom teacher. Once a twelfth-grade class has successfully read through the entire Qur'an together, the school holds a special event—Khataman Al-Qur'an—where students recite passages from the Qur'an and collectively say a prayer that they have learned, before taking part in a feast. On the day of the celebration for one twelfth-grade class, Ibu Rahma came to the school offices and warmly grabbed my arm, inviting me to join the other teachers in the auditorium too. The floor had been covered in red carpets to allow all the students and teachers to more comfortably sit on the floor during the event. Some students from the class, who had been chosen to perform the recitation for the event, were featured prominently in the front row, each holding a Qur'an, with other students from the class sitting behind them. Teachers sat in a row facing the students reciting. Just to the side, there was a long table, every inch of which was covered with dishes brought by students and teachers for a celebratory feast to follow. The variation in ability among those who had been chosen to recite was clear, as some spoke skillfully and seemingly effortlessly, while others stumbled, were corrected, and asked by teachers to repeat the correct pronunciation before continuing.

At the Khataman Al-Qur'an event, Pak Sudirman, who teaches the history of Islam, gave a speech to encourage the students to continue reading the Qur'an and to share their knowledge by teaching peers and younger children how to do so. He also pushed students to keep deepening their own knowledge by learning not only how to read the Qur'an, but also understanding its interpretation. He commented on the difference in skill level among students, expressing his hope that all students—not just those who were the most skilled at recitation—were participating in the morning readings, giving all a chance to improve. However, referring to the expectation of spiritual rewards for the practice, he reminded students that "whether you

FIGURE 5.3 MAN students take turns reciting for the Khataman Al-Qur'an event.

are reading or listening to the Holy Qur'an, you still get the same reward." Pak Sudirman encouraged the students to continue reading the Qur'an after they graduate from the school, possibly by inviting their friends to go to the campus mosque. He paused briefly, qualifying that if they attended the local state university, maybe they should have the event at the village mosque, hinting at the reality that the state university is majority Christian. "If you go to IAIN, everyone is Muslim, so you can invite everyone to the mosque!"

Students and teachers also spoke about the perfection of the Qur'an that could be experienced through reciting or listening to verses. Once, as I was sitting in the back of the classroom, after a class period ended and students began chatting amongst themselves, one student began playing an audio file on his phone of Qur'anic recitation, eagerly smiling and offering me his headphones to listen. As the students were aware that I was not Muslim, actions such as this were not uncommon, as many were hoping that I would have an emotional response and feel a "compelling pull" (Gade 2004, 4), experiencing the affective facets of Islamic piety as they did. Indeed, in Ibu Rahma's class on the Qur'an and hadith, she spoke often of the amazing beauty and perfection of the Qur'an that could be both analyzed scientifically and experienced through emotion. In-between the material of the official lesson, she told about a former student confused by his upbringing in a religiously mixed household. She proclaimed that he ultimately became committed to Islam, having been moved by hearing his diligent mother's beautiful recitations fill their household.

Teachers at MAN also seek to provide space for peer learning, as students can encourage and guide one another to grow in their faith. Ibu Rahma feels strongly that the Islamic character of the school should involve students motivating one another to study through Qur'anic recitation. During one class session, she asked each student to speak in front of the class about how their habits of reading the Qur'an have changed since they began attending MAN. In their speeches, many students claimed to be inspired by their fellow classmate Nurhayati, gifted in Qur'anic recitation and memorization. Her classmate Ayu said that Nurhayati was inspiring in the way that she used her free time to memorize the Qur'an, and how she put religious interests above her own. When Manado was experiencing a water shortage and there was no water at the school for *wudhu* (ablutions), Ayu observed that most of the students simply stayed in their classrooms and played on their smartphones instead of praying. Ayu admired Nurhayati's dedication, and had witnessed her leaving the school to find a nearby mosque where she could pray, even risking being late for her next class to do so. Even though

Nurhayati was often mentioned as a role model, she also faced teasing from her fellow students, who saw her as something of a teacher's pet and made disparaging remarks that she only did her prayers for the sake of getting good grades.

DELIBERATING ABOUT RELIGIOUS DIFFERENCE

Providing students with a strong foundation of religious values and practice is undertaken to give them a model of moral action that will allow them to act as proper Muslims, family members, and citizens. Within this model, there are significant ramifications for how religious difference is discussed in the school and the approach the school takes in attempting to ensure that students are tolerant and value religious diversity. In a region where Muslims are a minority, students often come up with questions about how Islamic principles apply in a religiously plural society, seeking to deliberate about the practical and logistical aspects. Teachers continually reframe these discussions, bringing them back to abstract and clear-cut principles and moral codes, primarily concerned with socializing students into the certainties provided by Islamic teachings. The teachers at MAN are not distinguishing between the ideal of proper Islamic selfhood and an imperfect application of these rules, but are socializing students into a particular model of moral action. Teachers are certain that if they can help students to apprehend the truth, purity, and totality of Islam, fully inscribed on an individual's selfhood through prayer and Qur'anic recitation, then students will be equipped to live as Muslims in a religiously diverse society.

Therefore, the additional time students spend in religious education at the madrasah, compared to the public high school, does not necessarily mean there is additional class time spent on religious diversity or interreligious relations, though there are aspects of the curriculum that do approach these topics. For example, the tenth-grade curriculum on the Qur'an and hadith addresses the importance of respect for all in a broad sense, and the twelfth-grade curriculum specifically addresses the importance of respecting non-Muslims. In the civic education classroom at the madrasah, the topic of diversity still emerges primarily through the frames of Pancasila and human rights. These discussions, like the one recounted in the introduction of this the book, remain largely abstract and concentrate on formalistic concepts of national stability and perceptions of Indonesia in the international arena.

Although the topics of diversity and coexistence rarely come up directly in the classroom, many of the teachers are proud of the region for its reputation as a place of interreligious harmony. They are readily able to point to structural factors in society that contribute to the peaceful situation, as well as cite Islamic principles in support of coexistence for a plural society. For example, several religious education teachers drew on Islamic teachings to explain that in addition to building a strong vertical relationship with God, it is also important to build a strong horizontal relationship with people in society, regardless of their religious and ethnic background. In her discussions with me, the civic education teacher Ibu Aisyah pointed to the importance of tolerance and respect for diversity, grounded in the Pancasila ideology and supported by the Islamic principle of *silaturahim*. She believes that the relatively high level of tolerance in Manado and the ability to avoid conflict are the result of the culture of mutual assistance and also a government and local leaders who take care to address any potential provocations.

Not only religious and civic education teachers, but also several science and math teachers enjoyed discussing these topics with me, often seeking me out in the library or the teachers' lounge, where I tended to spend time in between classes. A science teacher recited a verse from the Qur'an that had also been mentioned by students at the public high school SMA: "To you be your religion, and to me my religion." For her, the verse provides a basis for tolerance and acceptance in a religiously diverse society. However, the teachers' enthusiasm for these topics does not necessarily mean that they are explicitly addressed in the classroom as part of the formal curriculum or informal class discussions.

Yet students in the school are clearly trying to navigate how to carry out their own religious requirements in a plural society, and on this front, there were several instances of attempted deliberation. I witnessed several classroom discussions in which students wrestled with the question of how certain Islamic principles and directives apply to non-Muslims or can be carried out in a religiously diverse setting. In these cases, the intent of providing a strong foundation in Islamic principles by the teachers meant that students' concerns and questions were often brushed aside as peripheral, treated as minor details in relation to the importance of understanding the teachings underlying the moral principles themselves. Later in the chapter, I also discuss assumptions about the space outside the school as a place for students to learn and practice tolerance, while the space inside the school should be about instilling a strong Islamic foundation. As a result, students often attempted to answer the questions among themselves, but struggled in their estimation of how these Islamic principles might apply in a plural society, especially when Muslims are a religious minority locally.

In Ibu Indah's tenth-grade class on Islamic ethics, a group of students gave a presentation on how to avoid various "spiritual illnesses" (*penyakit iman*), based on material from the textbook. They warned their classmates about the potential dangers of what was referred to in Arabic as *"hubbu ad dunya,"* and in Indonesian as *"cinta dunia,"* or attachment to worldly matters, which could lead one to neglect their duties toward God. The first question for the group, posed by a fellow student, was whether these potential sicknesses must be avoided just by Muslims (*umat Muslim*) or by everyone (*umat manusia*). The students in the group, required to respond, discussed it for a few moments, talking over one another in disagreement about whether or not non-Muslims should be responsible for avoiding corrupting ideologies like hedonism and materialism. Finally, Irwan, one of the students in the group, stood up and exclaimed loudly, "Unbelievers' hearts are already locked!" implying they are already beyond hope. Without any real response to the statement, the group moved on to answer the next question. Ibu Indah was supervising the discussion but did not weigh in on this particular question or the student's response, as she did for the next question about the acceptable parameters for saving money without falling victim to such moral corruption. In such situations, students are trying to figure out the ethical requirements of Islam, as well as to whom its principles apply. However, teachers tend to see these concerns as much more peripheral, and are focused on making sure that students have a clear understanding of the principles themselves.

A similar situation arose in Ibu Vita's eleventh-grade class on Islamic jurisprudence (*fiqh*). She had also employed the student-centered group-learning and presentation method encouraged by the 2013 Curriculum. The topic of the day was *zina,* pre- or extramarital sex, and the groups were given selected articles about current events related to *zina* to read and discuss. Ibu Vita directed them to investigate why *zina* is forbidden in Islam, identify its negative consequences, and give suggestions for how to avoid it. Ibu Vita stepped out of the classroom while the groups read and discussed their assignment. I joined a group of five girls where one appointed herself the recorder for the group and began to write down the main points to be covered in their presentation. One of the other group members started by dictating that Allah dislikes and forbids "that act" (*perbuatan itu*) between men and women who aren't married. After more than a half hour, the teacher had still not returned, but the class leader (*ketua kelas*) took charge, announcing that the groups would begin their presentations so that they would all be able to present within the remaining class time. While each group stood at the front of the classroom and shared their findings, the remaining groups that had not yet presented mostly did not pay attention. Instead, they continued to talk amongst themselves, preparing for their own presentations in front of the class.

In my group, as other groups presented, the girls continued working on a statement on what must be done to avoid *zina*. The student sitting next to the group recorder began to read aloud as the recorder was writing: "As Muslims, women must cover their *aurat* and stay away from forbidden things," but another student stopped her mid-sentence.[3] Her peer brought up the question: Is it just Muslims (*umat Islam*) that have to do this, or is it humans (*manusia*)? The girls looked at one another, unsure of which statement was correct. Another group member chimed in, suggesting that it is something required from everyone, not just Muslims, and the other students in the group backed her interpretation and nodded in agreement. Ibu Vita had returned by the time my group was asked to present, so the group stood in a line at the front of the classroom as their spokesperson read their conclusion that humans must take care to cover their *aurat*. Without further discussion, Ibu Vita invited the class to applaud their group presentation, and moved on to have students read verses in the Qur'an that specifically address *zina*.

Once again, students were curious about the application of these moral precepts. They were deliberating about what carrying out Islamic norms and directives means in a religiously plural society, coming up with different answers about how to address the coexisting or contending moral systems they see present in society. Even when Ibu Indah explicitly referred to differences in punishments for *zina* based on man-made Indonesian laws versus Islamic law, they were only used as contrasting examples, rather than a discussion of how they might logistically function in a society like Indonesia, where the legal system is not based on Islamic law. Teachers tend to see such questions as largely irrelevant to their task of making sure that students understand, for example, the danger of *zina* and the potential punishment, rather than being concerned with who has to follow these specific rules. In this way, teachers reinforce the model of moral action in which students are introduced to the clear-cut moral codes before considering their specific and contextual interpretations, particularly in terms of their implementation in a religiously plural society and a multiconfessional state.

Speaking with Ibu Vita, who agrees that interreligious tolerance is high in Manado, I asked her which kinds of teachings and policies from the school can continue to support this reality. In her opinion, activities like the daily Qur'anic recitation that encourage religious values in addition to lessons that talk about peace will give students the character they need to uphold interreligious harmony in the region. However, the school does not provide only abstract principles with no model for outsider interaction or engagement. Through the organization of school activities and extracurricular opportunities for students, the school administration does give some models for community engagement. For example, to celebrate the anniversary of the school's founding, MAN organized a volleyball competition for boys and girls. They invited a girls' team from a nearby *pesantren,* boys' and girls' teams from SMA, and boys' and girls' teams from a nearby Christian high school. For the event, students and teachers gathered around the courtyard after school to watch the games, cheering on their teams before heading home for the day.

THE MADRASAH AND THE "OUTSIDE" WORLD

Because of the religious identity of the school and the minority status of Islam in the region, MAN takes on an important position toward character building based in Islam, offering a foundation in Islamic values and teaching, and encouraging a commitment to religious practice like prayer and Qur'anic recitation. The strong basis in religious values emphasized within the school is understood to equip students to properly enact these values outside the school. The diverse environment outside the school is therefore seen as having the potential to teach students about tolerance and living in a plural society firsthand. At the same time, the space outside the school is conceived of as a potential threat, not only because it could be a source of temptation but also because it is assumed to be an environment that is more likely to test students' religious commitment than reinforce it. While this is perhaps exacerbated by the reality of living in a Christian-majority region, it also reflects more general anxieties about proper engagement with the secular world and all that it entails, including orientation toward material things in a capitalist society, ways to use the internet, and how to interact with non-Muslims. The concerns of teachers are therefore based not only on the local specificities but also on narratives about the moral degradation of the young generation, which they have been called on to change.

In Ibu Indah's course on Islamic ethics, she teaches about the role of the family, the school, and society in contributing to Islamic education and the formation of good character in a lesson that provides a rather nuanced understanding of socialization into a religious tradition, tying together individuals with interpersonal relationships, institutions, and Islamic tradition. Ibu Indah had printed out pictures of various scenes and asked a couple of students to describe them and explain whether they represent good or bad character (*akhlak baik atau buruk*). Then, she asked groups to present their interpretation of the environment surrounding the school. One group of students pointed out that the family is an important influence that teaches how to be good, in addition to the examples provided by teachers at the school. The outside environment, including religious leaders, community leaders, and events at the mosque, they explained, can also play a role in character building. After students got into a minor debate about whether or not it is okay for parents to use harsh disciplinary methods to influence their children's moral foundation, the lesson ended. As I walked out of the classroom with Ibu Indah toward the teachers' lounge, she reflected on the students' interpretation of the lesson. She was concerned that though the students were not wrong, they did seem to assume that society always has good influences. Hopefully most students have a positive home environment that will reinforce the principles of an Islamic education, she reasoned, but the influences of society are often negative, and students need to know how to protect themselves.

Unlike traditionalist *pesantren,* which are often in a more rural, enclosed, and controlled boarding school environment, the public madrasah is in an urban setting where students are commuting back and forth from the school, encountering myriad influences and being required to navigate family and social life and all the questions they entail. A nearby *pesantren,* though also in an urban environment, takes the approach of keeping students inside the boarding school as much as possible, shielding them from all the potentially negative and un-Islamic influences in the surrounding area. Although teachers at MAN are concerned about immoral influences outside the school, they still feel that if they succeed in giving students an education grounded in Islamic values and practice, these principles will help students to thrive as they go out in the world. This attitude is closely aligned with that of some Islamic boarding schools in Java as described by Claire-Marie Hefner, not in opposition to the model of the *pesantren* but positioning themselves as "mediators of an integration into mainstream culture and into the nation's prosperous, new Muslim middle class" (2019, 487–488). This approach also has parallels among Hasidic Jewish communities in urban New York City, where elaborate socialization structures within the school and family attempt to teach young Hasidic women how to navigate the moral challenges of the secular world to benefit the greater good and serve their religious community (Fader 2009, 172).

As teachers work to guide students in their moral socialization, stressing religious ritual as a means of grounding oneself in Islamic values and principles, they hope to shape ethical subjects (their students) able to transcend all the potentially negative influences of the outside world. In his detailed ethnographic description of how Minangkabau in Sumatra become Muslim subjects through performance of daily prayer, Simon outlines the perfection that interaction with God can bring: "God is the perfect influence, existing at once as an 'outside' power and a reflection of one's own deepest moral core" (2014, 175). MAN teachers lead students to embrace the purity and truth of Islam as guidance for interacting with the outside world, confident that a commitment to religious practice will allow students to transcend any potentially negative influences they may face beyond the school. At the same time, teachers are also anxious that students might not be fully prepared or spiritually grounded enough to encounter these challenges.

MOBILE PHONES AND MORAL UNCERTAINTY

Across many different schools in North Sulawesi, principals and teachers are consistently concerned about the impact of mobile phones (referred to as "HP" in Indonesian, short for "handphone") on students' moral characters. Internet access is associated with a plethora of potential negative influences, but specifically with the capability to instantly obtain pornographic images and videos. Using the internet to view sexual content was by far the biggest concern of educators with regards to how students might use their phones, much more so than how students might use social media or communicate with others. At the same time, in many of these schools, textbook collections are incomplete and libraries do not always have necessary materials, making smartphones logistically useful for students to access information they need in class. As I describe in more detail below, MAN's approach to regulating HP use represents somewhat of a middle ground compared to other schools. There is no school-wide policy on the use of phones, so each teacher has their own guidelines in their classroom. The same principle of moral action guiding the general approach of the school also applied to cell phones: focus primarily on teaching a grounding in Islamic principles, and students should be able to properly navigate smartphone and internet usage as pious and upright Muslims.

At Lokon School, as in other educational settings, concerns about mobile phone usage relate primarily to pornography. However, teachers and dormitory staff now also focus on the dangers of bullying via social media, and the competition and jealousy over or theft of expensive smartphones. Because many students at Lokon come from privileged families, high-end smartphones are commonplace at the school. Until the year 2014, students at Lokon were forbidden to use their cell phones during the school day and were asked to leave them with their belongings in the dormitory. Then, the principal reversed the policy, with the argument that the school should help students to learn how to use technology like cell phones in a positive and productive way. In religious education courses, Ibu Maria has integrated lessons about having a critical attitude toward the media in general, to warn students about blindly trusting what is written online and on social media, and to encourage them to fully investigate what they read before believing or sharing it. She also tries to get students to think about how they can use things like Facebook status updates to be constructive, for example, writing a post to thank and praise God rather than being negative or engaging in destructive behavior like bullying. This approach to teaching students how to appropriately use media in their daily lives is regularly tested. At one point in time, many students downloaded an application that allowed them to chat anonymously, a social experiment that quickly and perhaps predictably devolved into unbridled bullying. Once the dormitory staff had figured out what was going on and notified the administration, students were collectively reprimanded during morning announcements for misusing their smartphones.

In contrast, the policies at a local all-boys *pesantren* are strict, requiring all students to hand over their cell phones to administration for safekeeping. They are allowed to use their phones during set times to call parents or to use the internet, but can only do so in monitored settings. A religious teacher at the *pesantren* said that this policy alone has led to major character changes in his students. Some children arrived there with the bad habits of downloading pornographic pictures or videos, and some parents had explicitly enrolled their children at this school to help them overcome this immorality. The religious teacher claims that the *pesantren*'s dedication to highly disciplined religious education, alongside the strict policy regarding cell phones, has enabled a major moral turnaround for many students. He recounted several cases of parents returning to pick up their children at the end of the semester and being overcome with joy at the positive changes they recognized in them.

At MAN, there is no unified policy regarding the use of mobile phones. As mentioned above, they are often used in the classroom for learning purposes. The school even has a Wi-Fi network installed that students can pay a small daily fee to use. Some teachers implement their own restrictions in the classroom to minimize or forbid HP usage. On the other hand, many allow cell phone use in the classroom, with guidance grounded in general Islamic values rather than explicit rules and regulations. During a religious education lesson about respecting teachers and parents, Ibu Indah used the behavior of some youth with their cell phones as a negative example. She informed students that it was disrespectful to look at your HP or play games on it during class, not to mention that it would be impossible to gain anything from the lesson. She scolded students who switch off their phones to avoid being reached or tracked by their parents. She also gave a short extemporaneous sermon on the dangers of having pornographic images on one's cell phone: "If you have pornographic pictures saved on your HP . . . you will not have good fortune [*rejeki*] if you have 'strange' pictures, pornographic pictures. If you have them, please erase them, okay? Try some introspection. If you have them, please erase them, okay? HPs are not for that—what are they for? They're for sending messages, taking pictures, calling people."

Ibu Rahma creates a WhatsApp group for her homeroom class each year so that she can easily communicate with her students and be available to answer their questions. She also uses it to extend her influence to students' home lives by sending them spiritual as well as practical reminders. It also allows her to stay in touch with students after they graduate. In Ibu Rahma's class discussion about character (*akhlak*) according to Islamic teachings, she asked students for examples of good and bad *akhlak*. The class leader, a confident and articulate boy, suggested that if he got a new HP and reacted by bragging and showing off to his friends, he would be encouraging jealousy in his friends, an example of bad character. Ibu Rahma then directed students to look for verses about good and bad character so they can better understand the Qur'anic injunctions on the subject.

Overall, the policies regarding the usage of smartphones at MAN represent a sort of middle ground. Phones are not banned, as at the local *pesantren*, where concerns about pornography dominate the attempt to get students to eliminate smartphones from their daily activities and rituals. Neither are they clearly encouraged and integrated into the curriculum, as they are at Lokon, where students encounter lessons in the religious education classroom about maintaining a critical attitude toward what one reads on the internet. The approach at MAN is based on providing a general spiritually grounded basis in moral action that will give students all the guidance they need to navigate their daily lives outside of the madrasah, whether in interacting with non-Muslims or in logging on to social media to catch up with friends.

UNDER THE INFLUENCE: DRUGS AND ALCOHOL

Educators in North Sulawesi are concerned about the negative social influences that might drive students to start experimenting with drugs and alcohol. In Manado, alcohol is more readily available compared to many Muslim-majority regions of Indonesia. Locally produced palm wine (Manado: *saguer*) and moonshine (Manado: *cap tikus*), but also beer and imported hard liquor, are relatively easily procured. Alcoholism and public drunkenness had become such a public nuisance over a period of several years that the North Sulawesi police started a public campaign to discourage drinking, called "Stop Drinking!" (Manado: *Brenti Jo Bagate*). Cigarettes are also relatively easy to get, even for teenagers, especially as general rates of smoking in Indonesia are high. At MAN, as well as in the other educational contexts described below, religious education and the religious viewpoint on drug and alcohol abuse are embraced as the mainstream approach toward discouraging youth from drinking, smoking, or experimenting with drugs. This remains true even as Islam and Christianity clearly diverge on their perspectives toward alcohol.

The Museum of Minahasan Art and Culture, which teaches students about Minahasan history, traditional music, weaving, and other forms of cultural heritage, is a popular field trip spot for high schools. This explains the recent installment of an Anti-Drug House (Wale Anti-Narkoba), an exhibit to teach students about the negative effects of drug use. As students walk in, they are greeted by a graveyard scene with a coffin and a plastic skeleton hanging from the ceiling. On the coffin, there is a poster with an eerie font quoting a United States Drug Enforcement Administration agent about how doing drugs ruins one's life. The décor is decidedly macabre, unabashedly aiming to scare the students away from using drugs, despite the tour guide's explanation that this exhibit is not meant to frighten them, only to show them the truth about drugs. In addition to posters about the physical impacts of doing drugs and lists of celebrities who have died from overdose, the exhibit has posters summarizing religious teachings on drugs. One of these, "Drugs from a Religious Perspective," demonstrates how religious teachings from the six official religions in Indonesia universally condemn the use of drugs. In this case, any differences—notably concerning religious stances on the allowance or prohibition of alcohol—are glossed over as superficial. Visitors can read a fatwa from the Indonesian Council of Ulama regarding drug use and browse a letter written by the Conference of Indonesian Bishops on the same topic.

The approach of MAN teachers toward anti–drug and alcohol education fits within the mainstream approach toward drug resistance education, though it is more focused on the deterrence that a strong religious background can impart than on employing a fear-based pedagogy. At MAN, teachers feel strongly that teaching Islamic values is the best way to discourage drug and alcohol use. Ibu Rahma previously taught Islamic education at a public school in Manado, where she knew students were experimenting with alcohol and drugs. At MAN, she explained, she has not yet seen these same issues come up and feels strongly that the Islamic environment of MAN and increased time for religious education helps to shape a feeling of togetherness (*kebersamaan*), such that students do not feel the need or the pressure to turn to drugs.

In the course on Islamic ethics at the madrasah, there is material about alcohol (*minuman keras*) from an Islamic perspective, and Ibu Vita considers it a component of character building in her course. When she brought up the topic with me in conversation, I remarked that students might wonder why alcohol is forbidden according to Islam, but not according to Christianity. In fact, a Muslim student at the public school had admitted her confusion and disdain to me after seeing some of her Christian neighbors drinking and having raucous gatherings for all of their events, including funerals. Instead of taking a more socially based comparative approach, the curriculum takes a scientific perspective, explaining all of alcohol's negative health impacts on the body to reveal the wisdom of Islamic teachings on the subject. In addition, Ibu Vita explained, students are also presented with the potential negative social consequences of alcohol in terms of the kinds of detrimental social encounters that drinking encourages, which are also contrary to Islamic values.

As teachers guide students through various teachings about drugs and alcohol, once again, they draw students back to Islamic values that provide a clear path for moral action, in this case further justified and proved through scientific studies. Here, teachers focus on explaining the Islamic reasoning as to why drugs and alcohol are considered haram, pointing to the wisdom of Islam that goes beyond human understanding and, if trusted, can guide students to live an upright and fulfilling life. Once again, giving students a strong foundation in Islamic values is meant to provide them with everything they need to flourish in the outside world despite its negative influences.

TO BIRTHDAY PARTY OR NOT?

Making decisions about birthday parties is not as clear-cut as the abstinence conversations about drugs and alcohol, and provides interesting insight into how teachers at MAN consider the appropriateness of birthday parties in terms of religious and social expectations. Birthday parties are extremely popular among Christians and Muslims in Manado, and are typically designed as religiously themed celebrations that include some element of prayer and/or religious worship. Considering birthday parties from a Muslim perspective in Manado, there are several issues, as more strictly modernist Muslims might oppose birthday parties, even those that integrate religious elements, because they are seen as an unacceptable ritual innovation that is not supported by Islamic teachings. There is also a question about whether or not it is acceptable to attend birthday parties in general, and in particular those held by one's Christian neighbors. At a typical birthday celebration, Protestant youth begin with a worship session, including readings from the Bible, prayers, and hymns, before offering a feast. Muslim youth begin birthday celebrations with Qur'anic recitation and prayers.

For most students and teachers, throwing or attending Muslim birthday parties is considered mainstream, particularly as the gatherings are framed as religious events. Several teachers at MAN held birthday parties for their own children, making sure to post pictures of the gatherings on social media with eye-catching decorations and copious amounts of food—a staple for all celebrations in Manado. Students at MAN who held birthday parties often invited their homeroom teacher in addition to their classmates and friends. For students, birthday parties are not only a fun way to spend time with friends and family but also a status symbol. Birthday parties for students at MAN are typically more modest in terms of gift giving compared to those for students of Lokon or other elite private schools, where it is not unheard of to receive a motorbike or even a car for what is referred to (in English) as a "sweet seventeen" gift.

While the mainstream opinion of Muslim birthday parties among teachers at MAN is that the celebrations are appropriate and fun, remaining grounded in religious values while encouraging a kind of togetherness, this was not necessarily the view of all teachers. For some strict modernist Muslims, the popularity of birthday parties represented an un-Islamic innovation. Pak Binyamin, one of the vice principals at the school, maintained that the celebration of birthdays is not in line with Islamic culture, as it has no basis in the Qur'an. According to his perspective, even gatherings that purport to be Islamic can still have spiritually dangerous influences that students must learn to identify and avoid, though it may go against popular practice. For some religious education teachers like Ibu Rahma, attending birthday parties hosted by her Christian neighbors is not problematic at all, but represents an important form of social solidarity. As long as she remains quiet and does not participate in the worship songs and rituals, she has no problem in partaking in other aspects of the ceremony, including the food provided specifically for Muslim guests. However, many students still express uncertainty about how to navigate such unfamiliar rituals and situations as Muslims.

In addition to making decisions about whether to have and/or attend Muslim birthday parties, Muslim teachers and students have to make decisions about attending celebrations held by their Christian friends and neighbors. The question of whether or not it is okay for Muslims to attend religious rituals of other religions as long as they do not participate looms large, and is further compounded by the fact that attending will put them in close proximity to food that is considered haram. If they have invited Muslim friends and neighbors, Christians typically make available a table with food prepared separately and containing no pork, typically referred to as "national food." Muslim students from the public high school, who likely have more invitations to Christian birthday parties than students at MAN because of their numerous Christian classmates, still have mixed feelings about attending these occasions. One Muslim student from SMA sees the provisioning of halal food at Christian birthday parties as a clear enactment of tolerance, one that he returns by being quiet and respectful during any worship session that might take place before guests dig into the food. Another Muslim student from SMA felt uncomfortable attending birthday parties because they put him in such close proximity to food that is haram, even if there was a separate table of food for Muslim guests. Food and its relation to sociality and religious plurality are discussed in more detail in the following chapter, as food figures largely in concerns about interreligious interactions, especially from a Muslim perspective.

RELIGIOUS FOUNDATIONS FOR CIVIC PARTICIPATION

At MAN, the largest Muslim school and only public madrasah in Manado, teachers strive to leave students with a strong foundation in Muslim values and religious practice that will become a model for moral action as they go out into the world. Religious discipline is taken as the route toward shaping upright and tolerant citizens. Therefore, teachers continually underscore daily prayers and Qur'anic recitation as the most important aspect of character formation. As students deliberate about the significance of Islamic requirements and their application in a plural society, or about using mobile phones and attending birthday parties, teachers bring them back to concrete moral principles found by embracing the truth and perfection of Islam, rather than getting into the messy details and imperfections of everyday life.

Importantly, this approach does not directly juxtapose ideal and practice. Instead, it creates a model of ethical self and society making based on Islamic principles. First of all, revealing the specificities of this model is important because this ideology about education is influential far beyond this one particular madrasah. Upon first witnessing it, I puzzled over the teachers' seeming avoidance of answering students' questions, wondering if it related to a dogmatic view of religion that does not want to admit flexibility or talk about application. In other words, I assumed that teachers pointed back to the ideal simply because they did not want to get into the potential flexibility or contextual interpretations of Islamic ethics. However, it became clear that pointing back to the certainty and guidance that Islam provides, realized through Islamic practices, is in itself a model of moral action. The discipline and religious grounding are a necessary prerequisite for students to engage in deliberation about how to coexist in a plural society and apply Islamic precepts to their daily lives in this context.

The ramifications of the approach to education taken at the madrasah should also be used to question assumptions about the way that deliberation occurs. In chapter 3, insights from the public high school demonstrated how embodied and discursive deliberations about religious belonging both impact the way that interreligious relations play out at the school and shape ideas about accommodation and coexistence. The case of the madrasah further illuminates aspects about the different ways that deliberation can occur. In putting forth a clear and Islamically grounded model for ethical self-making, the students, teachers, and administrators also participate in deliberation about the realization not only of good individual Muslims and citizens, but of a just and tolerant society. Notably, the way toward doing so highlighted at the madrasah requires not a retreat from religion, as many liberal models would assume as the first step toward religious coexistence. Rather, it requires a full embrace of and commitment to Islamic principles. Understanding the self and the processes of ethical self-making have ramifications for the model of coexistence put forth and deliberated in the public sphere.

The preceding two chapters have demonstrated how schools become loci of deliberation about ethical frameworks for approaching religious difference. At the religiously mixed public high school SMA, policies toward religion tend to encourage an embodied religious belonging that establishes a majoritarian Protestant influence, despite discursive attempts to extoll the value of respect for religious diversity. At Lokon private school, a self-consciously multicultural approach is projected through the universality of Catholic teachings by teachers and administrators. While students at Lokon remain wary of mentioning difference, the ethnic, cultural, and class differences of Papuan students emerge as a challenge to this approach as the only forms of difference that are openly mentioned, discussed, and reinforced. Finally, focusing on the public madrasah in Manado in this chapter has further elaborated the way in which discipline can relate to deliberation in the process of shaping citizen-believers. Discipline, in this case a religiously based discipline, has a major role in molding students' foundational selves that are only then seen as fit to engage in deliberation about religious plurality and difference.

6

Interreligious Exchange
A Pedagogical Project of Ethics across Borders

I sat in one of the pews near the back of the chapel early one Wednesday morning at the Sacred Heart Catholic Seminary near Manado. Fabila, a university student at the State Islamic Institute (IAIN) of Manado, sat next to me in her green university blazer, her black *jilbab* neatly pinned, her eyes open wide as she observed the ritual of Catholic mass for the first time. Scattered around the chapel were several *frater* (seminarians) of the Sacred Heart religious congregation (MSC), their superiors, a few laypeople, and a group of university students. That particular morning, the mass was celebrated in English, and Fabila turned to me each time a page or hymn number was announced as we juggled the hymn and prayer books meant to help us follow the ritual.

The presiding priest began to distribute the communion, and the seminarians, all dressed in simple white robes, walked toward the front of the chapel to partake. As each pew started to file out, Fabila looked at me, her eyes suddenly filled with worry as she whispered, "Are we supposed to go?" I smiled at her and responded, "Let's just wait here together."

Fabila was one eager participant in a weeklong interreligious university exchange program (*pertukaran mahasiswa lintas agama*), an interreligious initiative involving dozens of university students and coordinated among several religious institutions of higher education in Manado and Tomohon. This program allows university students aspiring to become religious leaders or religious education teachers to spend a week at a different religiously affiliated university, attending and observing religious rituals, activities, and classes at their host university. As students like Fabila participate in the program, they are required to reflect on their own religious beliefs and requirements, for example, whether it is acceptable for a Muslim to attend Catholic mass. These events also encourage them to think not only of the religious beliefs and requirements of others, but of their social responsibilities in a multireligious group, like the way Fabila considered whether she could remain an observer without offending her Catholic hosts. These situations require ethical navigation and reflection, encouraging dialogue among participants while building up personal relationships among students of different religions. On the last day of the program, I chatted more with Fabila, whose smile and enthusiasm for the program had only continued to grow. "I had only ever been friends with Muslims," she explained, admitting that she had only heard negative things about Christians in her Muslim-majority village in Bolaang-Mongondow, the southern part of the province. She said that now, having experienced and having been exposed to much more positive thinking about religious difference, these kinds of remarks would go in one ear and out the other.

This chapter focuses on the interreligious exchange program as a pedagogical project of "ethics across borders" (Mair and Evans 2015) in understanding how individuals seek to engage one another across religious traditions and forge an ethical framework for living together in difference. Examining the case as one of building ethics across borders is intentional in its focus on specific strategies for dealing with religious difference, though it also addresses the same broader issue examined throughout the book about the possibilities for forging an ethics of belonging through deliberation.

In analyzing the kinds of ethical deliberation and dialogue that participants engage in both during and following the program, I argue that the interreligious exchange program entails simultaneous processes of commensuration and incommensuration, which Mair and Evans observe is commonly the case in attempts to build up an ethics across borders (2015, 215). While they engage in commensuration, or bringing "values into a relation vis-à-vis one another in such a way that they can both be compared and contrasted" on a social level, participants also engage in incommensuration, or production of difference in such a way that religions are rendered incomparable on a theological level (2015, 214). The process of incommensuration allows the students involved to discuss similarities among religions without endangering their own truth claims, whereas the process of commensuration allows them to discuss differences while reinforcing a shared commitment to religious coexistence with acceptance of a normative pluralism in their definitions. An analysis of these simultaneous processes allows for a view on how religious borders are not fixed but are continuously being both fortified and chipped away in social interactions. Furthermore, in this case, both processes are central for making an ethics across borders thinkable.

The program calls on participants to question their understanding of religious others by asking them to reflect on ethical principles about religious borders not through a discussion of dogma, but through what one priest involved in the program referred to as a "life dialogue" (*dialog kehidupan*). These religious boundaries are not only sites of ethical but also political entanglement as participants face up to their own religious beliefs and requirements, in addition to confronting politically charged cultural expectations of themselves and religious others. Though the term "dialogue" seems to imply that this all happens on a discursive level, ethnographic insights show that religious belonging and difference are also expressed and experienced in embodied forms, where religious selves and beliefs are not abstractable from the individual subjectivities and bodies in which they are grounded. Overall, participants attempt to build up a normative expectation of religious coexistence through a common experience, rather than imposing a singular framework for approaching religious difference.

BACKGROUND

The interreligious exchange program discussed in this chapter, referred to informally as *pertukaran mahasiswa* (university student exchange), has been taking place since 1978. It started as an ecumenical initiative between the mainline Protestant GMIM-affiliated university in Tomohon (UKIT—Universitas Kristen Indonesia Tomohon) and the Catholic seminary (STF-SP—Sekolah Tinggi Filsafat—Seminari Pineleng) near Manado (Renwarin 2015, 45). The program later expanded to include students from the Pentecostal theological school STT (Sekolah Tinggi Teologi) Parakletos, the state-run Protestant institute STAKN (Sekolah Tinggi Agama Kristen Negeri) Manado, and most recently the State Islamic Institute IAIN Manado. The participating universities, all of which have programs to train religious leaders and teachers, support students in planning and implementing this annual exchange. Institutes send a small group of students to each of the other participating universities. Student committees organize lodging, meals, and activities for the guest participants over the course of one week. During this week, guest students "live in" at one host campus, participating in collective activities, observing religious rituals, and attending courses on campus with their hosts.

There are other programs for interreligious dialogue across Indonesia, including in Java, where the Interfaith School (Sekolah Lintas Iman) has been running since 1991. However, the Interfaith School is primarily coordinated by the NGO Institut DIAN/Interfidei and includes a formal curriculum as well as organized reflection, typically over the course of a summer semester (Zemmrich 2020, 153). In contrast, the exchange program in Manado is only one week in duration and is largely student organized and run, without a formal curriculum.

One goal of the exchange program is to get youth to begin a lifelong process of dialogue with those from different religious communities, so that as future religious leaders they will be motivated to continue building relationships with other religious leaders and communities. Rather than focusing on a theologically based or even exclusively religious dialogue, the objective of the exchange program is to build up trust as an initial step toward dialogue, mostly by allowing participants to spend time together in daily activities and observe religious rituals. During the exchange program that took place in 2015, I was hosted at the Sacred Heart Catholic Seminary with Protestant and Muslim students from three different institutions. At the seminary, guests stayed in dormitory rooms across several different units that acted as the main groups of activity. Visiting young men were spread out, each sharing a room with one of the seminarians, while the young women were put together in pairs in empty rooms. All participants were required to take part in early-morning religious activities: either attending prayer with their assigned unit or a collective mass with all seminarians. We ate together at designated times in the campus cafeteria and joined the seminarians in their classes at the main university campus up the road. We also participated in field trips, some of which were religious in nature, including going to the cathedral in Manado and visiting Carmelite nuns. Students also organized other excursions during free time that were purely recreational, such as exploring and taking pictures at a waterfall near the campus. After the exchange program, I visited each of the university campuses to interview student participants, and remained in touch with many of them over social media and continued to meet some in person. For the 2016 group of participants, three participants agreed to write daily journal entries about their experiences, which they entrusted to me after the exchange program.

In addition to its importance as a pedagogical project related to a consideration of ethical boundaries around religious difference, this exchange program is also a potential example of building up what Zainal Abidin Bagir (2011) has called *pluralisme kewargaan* (civic pluralism), a particular normative frame that moves beyond toleration to require more active engagement. Rather than seeking to push religion to be an exclusively private matter, this

FIGURE 6.1 Muslim and Protestant exchange program participants pose with Catholic seminarians in a chapel at the Sacred Heart Seminary.

perspective recognizes the potentially public role of religion. It also moves away from understandings of pluralism as based exclusively in theology—often mobilized in Indonesia as the basis for a rejection of pluralism on principle—focusing instead on the sociopolitical dimensions of religion in building up dialogue. The "life dialogue" that is the focus of the program is not intended to take religion out of the question—indeed, religious identity is recognized as integral for these students who want to become religious leaders and teachers. It is the experience of spending time together, getting to know one another, and observing different religious rituals that is important in building up dialogue and engagement that goes beyond theological or dogmatic questions.

In this chapter, the focus is on the ways in which the exchange program leads to reflection about religious boundaries as participants deliberate about how to recognize and respect difference while carrying out their own religious requirements. Shared experience can be an important mechanism for engaging across established boundaries, making it possible to set aside irreconcilable differences (Seligman and Weller 2012, 162), and acting as a strategy for incommensuration. The religious boundaries considered by participants, at times ethically fraught, are also shaped by political discourse, normative calls for religious tolerance, and current frameworks for coexistence. When discussing the ethical considerations of the participants and deliberations about boundaries, I take care to link them to broader frameworks dealing with religious difference in the region, many of which are circulated through schools.

DISCOURSES ABOUT DIVERSITY AND RELIGIOUS BOUNDARIES

As demonstrated throughout the previous chapters, the educational system emphasizes the need for curricular material about respecting diversity, a measure responding to the prevalence of violent religious and ethnic conflicts and general intolerance in society. These particular frameworks for coexistence, though vague in their exhortations to "respect and value difference," clearly remain premised on an assumption that differences—especially religious differences—must be preserved. In the context of the classroom, calls for tolerance are often framed in terms of the importance of knowing about other religions or other ethnic groups so that one can respect the boundaries of the communities. The commensuration of religions, for example, when teachers discuss the ways in which all religions advocate peace and harmony, is often accompanied by a conviction that one must know the limits of other religions, engaging in a fortification of religious boundaries in order to not endanger the distinctiveness of the communities.

Discourses about diversity circulating in Manado tend to emphasize the beauty of difference and the need to maintain it, supported by metaphors of gardens made more beautiful with a variety of colors compared to boring monochromatic ones. Johan, a Protestant university student who participated in the interreligious exchange program, likened religions to puzzle pieces of different colors. "When the puzzle is put together," he explained to me, "we can see that the puzzle is beautiful; it gives a beautiful image." Johan, who aspires to become a Protestant pastor, chose to spend a week with Muslim students at IAIN because his entire extended family is Muslim and he wanted to know more about their religion. Johan's metaphor in some ways accomplishes commensuration, by viewing each religion as a distinct entity in a kind of celebration of difference, where they come together to achieve something greater than each could individually.

While discourses on diversity may imply the integrity of religious boundaries in the abstract, the practical approaches to socializing allow for an understanding of how individuals implement these ideas in their daily lives. Johan's willingness to participate in a weeklong exchange program among Muslims would certainly be criticized by some for encouraging too much religious mixing. Interreligious socializing is often accompanied by the specter of religious conversion, which manifests as a concern that religious boundaries may become blurred and will not be maintained. For those who participated in the program, it was a process in building interreligious connections. Yet for many, the decision to participate did not simply provide an answer to ethical questions about how to relate to others—instead, it opened the door to numerous decisions about how to navigate one's own religious identity and commitment while respectfully engaging with others. Even those who were enthusiastic about joining the program described themselves as nervous (*gugup*), awkward (*canggung*), or uncomfortable (*tidak nyaman*) at the beginning, unsure how to act.

At the opening ceremony for the program, a reinforcement of boundaries was used to diffuse tension about the prospect of interreligious mixing. Fears of proselytization and conversion often implicitly permeate interreligious encounters. Students knew that as a part of the program they would be required to attend religious rituals outside of their own faith backgrounds, which is often discouraged or considered an inappropriate boundary crossing and a form of unacceptable syncretic pluralism. One speaker at the opening ceremony, a Muslim professor from IAIN, shared his view of religious difference from what he described as a social science perspective. In his understanding, religious belonging is as simple as "environmental influence" from one's family. Taking himself as an example, he said that his parents always brought him to the mosque as a child, and by five years of age, he would have been able to tell you that his God was Allah. Children have the same God as their parents, he clarified, so it doesn't mean that what he learned at the mosque was wrong; it means that he had a different social environment from others.

In this case, the professor emphasized religious boundaries, though his doing so from a "social science" rather than a theological perspective allowed for a particular kind of boundary emphasis. He described religious difference as a product of the social environment of one religious group. In the context of the exchange program, discussing religion as a product of one's social environment had the potential to diffuse tension because it reinforced lines between specific religious communities on a social (not dogmatic) level, without rendering conflicting theological claims as problematic. Emphasizing the permanent nature of the borders allowed for a temporary crossing, and for some a temporary relief from anxiety about the possibility for religious conversion that often emerges in situations of religious mixing.

The ability to be religiously tolerant is often assumed to be a question of the depth of one's own religious training and commitment, yet also potentially learned from experience in interreligious settings. This perspective, similar to that expressed in the approach at the public madrasah MAN, is also made clear in the reflections of Pak Umar, the head of an all-girls *pesantren* for high school students in Manado. He began by voicing his concern about the lack of religious knowledge among his own students, related to his estimate that as many as 30 percent of them come from religiously mixed families. He lamented that many of the students arrive with only a superficial understanding of Islam, having received the majority of their education from either public or Christian institutions. Pak Umar explained his conviction that educating students about tolerance happens through a strong grasp of religious values, and that schools contribute through providing students with a solid religious foundation they might not have previously received.

At the same time, Pak Umar claimed that many students—like those coming from religiously mixed families—already have firsthand experience in tolerance. He drew on the practical importance of being exposed to religious others in order to learn about tolerance, still maintaining that religious values imparted at school lay the foundation for the way students approach and respond to religious difference. While these understandings may appear contradictory, they work to balance the concerns of conversion by looking positively at interreligious interactions and simultaneously maintaining the importance of a strong religious belonging for strengthening individual identities and borders, so that individuals will not be confused by such encounters. Overall, he advocated for the importance of schools in teaching youth boundaries and providing the unshakeable foundation necessary when navigating religious difference.

Pak Umar asserted that in learning how to implement tolerance, youth should understand that religious mixing is okay for social events, but not for religious ones. He made clear that youth should respect other religions but understand the limits of religious boundaries. However, as he reflected on his own experiences in a religiously diverse neighborhood, he struggled to define the boundaries so clearly. When his Christian neighbors are preparing a funeral or another ceremony, he always donates money, qualifying his action by explaining that it is a social gesture of care, and not to support their religious activities. In practice, it does directly contribute to his neighbors' ability to hold what are necessarily religiously based funerals or celebrations. For Pak Umar, however, efforts to parse out the religious from the social proved important in his own ethical deliberations about the extent of religious boundaries and the best way to respect them.

Like Pak Umar's experience in a religiously mixed neighborhood, for exchange program participants, the experience in a religiously mixed group also leads to ethical deliberations about the limits of religious boundaries and possibilities for coexistence. Many students do not participate in the program precisely because they deem the kind of religious mixing taking place as surpassing the limits of acceptable interreligious interactions. Others are simply not interested or perceive it as too much of a burden, since they must continue to complete assignments from their own classes and make up work missed while they are away at the program. Those who do participate, however, engage in a constant renegotiation of boundaries through this shared experience. Their strategies often involve processes of incommensuration on a theological level, an elaboration of incommensurable difference that allows for more open discussions without endangering truth claims or bringing religious boundaries into question. Yet, importantly, they also involve commensuration on a social level, shaped by their common experience as participants in the program and as university students in Manado.

POLITICAL AND RELIGIOUS ENTANGLEMENTS

As students show up at their respective locations for the week of the exchange program and begin interacting, the boundaries they encounter are cast as religious, yet these religious boundaries and the ethical deliberations that take place in their shadows are entangled with political discourse. Paying attention to the ways in which individuals are not starting the program on equal grounds—despite discourses of commensuration that seek to project this image—underscores how power dynamics impact this pedagogical project. While nearly all of the student participants indicated a desire to learn about other religions as a motivation for joining the program, only Muslim students indicated that they joined the program in order to help educate others about Islam and challenge others' ostensibly negative opinions of their religion. This reality relates directly to ideas about Muslim belonging and the powerful influence of discourses about a majoritarian coexistence that emerges in Manado, in tension with discourses and practices of aspirational coexistence.

While all students certainly arrive with preconceived notions about how others will look or act, Muslim students actively prepare themselves to encounter and dismantle the negative assumptions about Muslims that are implied in the local manifestations of majoritarian coexistence. It is commonly assumed that Christians in the region are those who guarantee tolerance and coexistence, grounded in an essentialized characterization of Christianity as a religion based in love. Accordingly, Muslims are assumed to be the group that is tolerated, setting up a particular power relation in which they are also positioned as inferior (Brown 2006, 13). This does not mean that the tolerance of Muslims is not evaluated, but rather that it is not evaluated on the same terms. Muslims are often assessed as tolerant when they accept the terms of the implicitly Christian public sphere. On the other hand, Muslims who are perceived to adhere too closely to religious requirements are often viewed as radical and intolerant by the Christian majority, who wield this as proof that Muslims do not value religious harmony. Muslims who do not accept the terms of this majoritarian coexistence are therefore projected as outsiders to the region, which implicitly contributes to stereotypes that Muslims may pose a threat to this balance of religious harmony.

Iskandar, a Muslim student who reflected on his participation in the program several years prior, recalled the tense atmosphere from the outset of the exchange program. He felt that the Christian participants were eyeing their Muslim peers, wondering, "Could they be terrorists? Are they holding a bomb now?" Over the course of several days, he recounted that as everyone became more open, the tension slowly dissolved away. For Iskandar, this was not understood as the result of a mutual process of communication and shared experience; rather, it was a conscious effort on the part of Muslim students to communicate more about their religion in a way that allowed Christian students to realize that Islam was not everything they had heard in the media or been told by their Christian friends—particularly, that it was not a violent religion.

For some Muslim students like Iskandar, participating in the program represented an opportunity to not only communicate about Islam with their Christian peers, but to act as examples for their Muslim friends. Several of Iskandar's Muslim friends did not agree with his decision to join the exchange program, as they were worried about guarding their own faith and being subject to Christian proselytizing. "My more fanatical friends don't want to go outside," he said—meaning outside of a Muslim environment—but Iskandar saw this as a necessary step to further strengthen tolerance and enable communication. Iskandar felt that in order to not bring his faith into question, he also had to justify himself to his Muslim peers and convince them that participation in the program was not against Islamic teachings.

This conception that all religious groups are coming together on equal grounds through a process of commensuration is challenged not only by political discourse and the projections of majoritarian coexistence, but also by religious requirements, which differ across the religious groups in the context of the exchange program. Muslim requirements regarding the consumption of halal food, which are the focus of the next section, ended up being a major point of concern among Muslim participants around which significant deliberation occurred, particularly among Muslim students themselves. Concerns furthermore disproportionately impacted Muslim women, who had to take particular care in maintaining gendered propriety while staying in a seminary that typically only houses men, for example. Desy, a young woman staying at the seminary, had gotten to know the seminarians quite well, and they were all spending time sharing stories and getting to know one another. She was shocked, however, when they said they would like to get to know her even better and asked her to take off her *jilbab*, an action that the seminarians apparently saw as a natural progression of trust and friendship. As she was telling me what had happened, one of her male classmates chimed in to explain that the seminarians' request came from a place of curiosity. Desy said she approached their request as an opportunity to stay strong in her faith, explaining to the seminarians that she only takes off her headscarf when she is with her own family.

Finally, several Muslim students reported feeling particularly moved by instances when they perceived their religious requirements were adequately accommodated by others, whereas Christian participants (both Catholic and Protestant) tended to speak more generally about the celebration of difference and a recognition of the beauty of differences. Effendi was surprised when a priest at the Catholic seminary had asked him whether Catholicism or Islam "protects women more" (*lebih melindungi perempuan*). Effendi hesitated, saying that he did not know. The priest responded that Islam is actually more protective of women because it allows for the possibility of divorce. Effendi was surprised by this recognition, and also appreciative of the spirit of the exchange program that allowed a follow-up discussion from participants about whether it is more important for religions to uphold and protect the sanctity of marriage or to allow divorce. Eri, who also stayed at the Catholic seminary, said that her most memorable experience during the exchange program was during a worship session in which she was asked to give a sermon based in Islamic teachings. "I felt so amazed because for the first time, I was asked to give a sermon in front of those outside of my environment, with a different understanding," she remembered. If it had been among her Muslim peers, she qualified, it would have been just ordinary (*biasa-biasa saja*), but the invitation from the priests and seminarians and the opportunity it presented her during this exchange program made it an unforgettable experience.

CROSSING BOUNDARIES AT THE TABLE

For many exchange program participants, the experience of sitting around a table together and sharing a meal played a major role in cultivating a sense of togetherness and commonality. Several noted that the atmosphere during communal meals was more relaxed (*santai*), comfortable (*nyaman*), and ultimately conducive to chatting and getting to know one another. For Eunike, a Protestant student staying at the Catholic seminary, common meals in the cafeteria were a highlight because they provided an opportunity for casual discussions and joking that made the experience joyous. Fabila felt the same way; as someone whose family members often eat at different times of the day and usually in front of the television, she was surprised at how emotionally moved she was at this experience of eating together at the seminary. This does not mean that meals were only lighthearted or superficial in nature. Indeed, it was precisely the relaxed atmosphere that diffused tension and ultimately fostered a space for participants to informally ask questions to one another.

The exchange program underscores the fact that food plays such an important role in defining embodied religious belonging, particularly in Muslim-Christian interactions. The act of eating together is also one in which participants cannot simply bracket out their religious identities. The process of building up an ethic across borders is again shaped by religious entanglements and identities, which are also necessarily linked to political discourses about belonging. One of the most commonly voiced concerns among Muslim participants in the exchange program was the practical question of how to eat with Christians while adhering to religious requirements about the consumption of halal food. This is just one example of how the initial decision to participate in the exchange program is only the beginning in a progression of ethical questions about how to participate in and engage with an interreligious group while faithfully following one's own religious requirements. These interactions are certainly shaped by political discourses, including common discourses among Muslims in Indonesia about the potential dangers of eating with Christians, whose invitations to eat together are often construed as suspicious and possibly even having an underlying motive to trick Muslims into eating pork. As one Muslim participant expressed, it was challenging to enter "an environment where we can't eat haphazardly." Desy also found herself constantly questioning the cleanliness of her plate and wondering whether the food served on it was actually permissible.

When speaking about their experience after the program, several Muslim students described the process of adopting a more open (*terbuka*) attitude toward food over the course of several days. Raihan recounted his own experience as follows: "The first day, I would eat only one or two spoons and would feel full. The next day, I thought, I can't keep going on like this. In the morning I was already hungry because the previous day I hadn't eaten much. I still held back. At lunch I did the same. But in the evening, I went back twice for more rice. So, I already found a strategy to cross these boundaries [*melewati batas-batas*]." Desy, who had become fixated on the cleanliness of the dishes, also started out by barely eating at each meal. Eventually, she decided to eat the food served to her, but would pray before doing so, asking Allah to "make everything halal" (*halalkan semua*). Others reported feeling less anxious after the organizing committee, made up of students from each of the campuses, had reassured Muslim students that their hosts would not offer them any food considered haram.

These interactions are also shaped by a common projection of Christian gestures of hospitality and toleration of Muslims as the foundation of religious coexistence in Manado. Such discourses about Christian-Muslim religious difference often emerge through the trope of food, as it has the potential to create an atmosphere of sociability and togetherness while also setting religious difference in relief. Many Manadonese have remarked to me that the popular vegetable porridge dish *tinutuan* is an apt metaphor for the pluralistic nature of the city, its diverse makeup reflected in the mixture of pumpkin, rice, corn, and greens, each of which maintains its own qualities but becomes more delicious when put together with the others. It can be eaten by both Muslims and Christians, and is made from ingredients typically grown in the Minahasan highlands. Indeed, this conception of multiculturalism is not far from the aspirational coexistence expressed by many students who participated in the exchange program: an idea of celebrating diversity as something beautiful, and having the ability to create something even more remarkable than its individual parts by coming together.

BELONGING AT THE TABLE

However, understanding the possibilities for coexistence through an examination of food also connects to a framework that projects majoritarian coexistence as uniquely guaranteed through the goodwill of Christians. Before continuing the examination of the interreligious exchange program, I turn to several relevant discussions encountered in secondary schools as well as in the public sphere. During a session at a teachers' Christian leadership seminar run by the international Protestant organization Haggai Institute at Lokon School, teachers eagerly posed questions about Islam and interacting with Muslims to a Protestant trainer after he gave a presentation about Jesus from the perspective of the Qur'an. One of the young Protestant teachers at the school, clearly distressed, confessed that her Muslim neighbor had attended a celebration at her house and had inadvertently eaten a dish with pork in it. The teacher admitted feeling deeply ashamed about what had happened and was seeking advice about whether or not she should broach the subject with her neighbor and apologize. The other teachers sitting around her consulted with one another, sympathizing with the gravity of her dilemma, and came to the agreement that she should just leave the situation alone. Based on his understanding of Islam, one teacher offered, it is not wrong for Muslims to eat pork if they are unaware it is in their food. The trainer, however, jumped into the conversation, asking why the young teacher felt so ashamed, provocatively suggesting that perhaps her neighbor even enjoyed eating the dish. The trainer then upheld the teacher's concern as a self-congratulatory example, exclaiming, "Look how tolerant Christians are!" He contrasted her behavior in interacting with her Muslim neighbors with an account of how he had been treated by Muslims in Manado who aggressively questioned him about the authenticity of the Bible.

While some of the trainer's statements were perceived as extreme by the teachers, others still echoed common statements about Muslims as tolerant when they accept the implicitly Christian-dominant public sphere. In this case, tolerance is not necessarily seen as uniquely guaranteed by the Christian majority, but by Manadonese Muslims as qualitatively different from other Muslims in being less fanatical. For example, a GMIM-affiliated Protestant pastor involved in interreligious dialogues explained to me in an interview that interreligious tolerance in Manado is decreasing, citing changing food practices as one piece of evidence for his case. He voiced his assumptions about Muslim encroachment, weaving together a narrative that linked increasing intolerance toward Muslims as a direct response to

Muslim disregard for Minahasan cultural practices. He recounted that at Minahasan parties in the past, the traditional roast pig (*babi putar*) was prominently displayed, and that Muslim neighbors typically had no qualms about attending the parties and simply eating other dishes. Now, he claimed, dominant cultural norms dictate that it is polite to keep the roast pig inside the house so that it is not as visible and is more clearly separate from the rest of the food. As anecdotal evidence, all of the events I attended continued to prominently display the roast pig as a centerpiece of the meal, and guests crowded around it with their utensils, scrambling to get a piece as soon as the end of the prayer signaled the beginning of the meal. Christian-hosted events with Muslim guests do typically have a separate table of food, clearly set aside from the main buffet.

In the Catholic religious education class at Lokon School, teacher Pak George discussed Muslim eating practices after a student group presented about Islam for a lesson about interreligious dialogue. A girl in the class asked the presenting group, "Why do Muslims have to eat halal food?" Competing with the loud din of the classroom, Pak George demanded the students' attention, shouting, "Listen!" Upon repeating the question, he rephrased it, asking instead, "Why can't Muslims eat pork?" When the presenting group of students looked at each other in confusion and had difficulty answering the question, the teacher offered a personal anecdote related to the topic. He had once invited a friend out to eat, without realizing that the friend was Muslim. At the restaurant, Pak George ordered *brenebon* (pork and kidney bean soup) and pork *satay*, forgetting to ask his friend whether or not he could eat them. However, his Muslim friend ate the dishes anyway and explained to Pak George that some Muslims eat pork, and others do not. Ending his story, Pak George asserted, "Some moderate Muslims do eat pork." Anecdotes like this are meant to emphasize the tolerant nature of Muslims in Manado, as opposed to a conceptualization of tolerance as uniquely guaranteed by the Christian majority. Yet, they also imply that Muslims in Manado are tolerant when they accept the dominantly Christian public sphere, including its cuisine.

It is common for Minahasan Christians to equate halal food to food without pork, unaware of the specific requirements that must be met for food to be properly considered halal. Many Muslim participants in the interreligious exchange programs are aware of the tendency. Iskandar, who had been using the program as a platform to educate Christian participants about Islam, also taught his hosts about this topic. He was staying as a guest at the Protestant university in Tomohon, and his hosts proudly declared that they had slaughtered the chicken they were eating at dinner themselves, and they were therefore certain that it was halal. Iskandar, who did not personally see any issue with eating the chicken, still thought it important to explain the criteria for halal food to his hosts. He clarified that the requirements for halal certification are not just about contamination with pork, but also govern the method of slaughtering an animal and require accompanying prayer.

While many Muslim participants in the exchange program were concerned about the provenance of the food served to them, several also expressed feeling touched by Christians in the program paying attention to their needs and making the effort to procure food for them. I spoke with Ita, who had joined the exchange program at the Catholic seminary the previous year and continues to regularly visit when there are public events or special occasions. She said that she noticed how the seminarians were always looking out for her, separating dishes that she couldn't eat from the rest of the food lest they be mixed up, explicitly telling her, "Please, don't eat this," to make sure there was no ambiguity about which dishes contained pork.

Bahruddin, a Muslim student who also stayed at the seminary, shared a memorable experience at a Christian birthday party in Bitung he had been invited to by one of the seminarians on a free afternoon during the exchange program. Before arriving at the party, he was reassured that there would be other Muslims as well, and that there would be a specially prepared meal for

FIGURE 6.2 Exchange program participants eat in the cafeteria among seminarians.

them. Still, upon arriving, Bahruddin saw the roast pig and could not shake the feeling that his food also contained this meat. He calmed himself down, reassuring himself that he was eating food that was separate and had been carefully prepared for Muslim guests. The seminarians had checked for him, and were also eating the same dishes, opting not to eat pork in front of him, demonstrating their intent to accommodate Bahruddin's needs and making sure he was comfortable.

As it began to get late, Bahruddin and the seminarians decided to leave the party and make their way back to Manado. To show respect, they first approached the parents of the child celebrating the birthday, the hosts of the party, to shake hands with them. Bahruddin followed suit, not thinking anything of it at first. However, after shaking hands, Bahruddin realized that the father had just finished eating pork and had not yet washed his hands. As soon as they left the gathering, one of the seminarians, Marsel, looked concerned and asked Bahruddin if everything was okay: "You just touched his hand, right?" Bahruddin, though concerned, brushed it off and said he was okay. But Marsel took a cup of water and washed Bahruddin's hands, a moment that has remained with Bahruddin as a touching demonstration of tolerance from Marsel.

FORTIFYING AND ERASING RELIGIOUS BOUNDARIES

In the midst of these processes of commensuration and incommensuration, perceptions of religious boundaries are simultaneously fortified and erased for the participants in the interreligious exchange program. This outcome also draws attention to the way in which the program allows for normative pluralism in terms of how individual participants understand religious coexistence and belonging. Rather than imposing one particular vision through a curriculum, it leaves room for interpretation and negotiation regarding how to approach and accommodate religious others. Thus, as participants expressed their ideas about religious difference, tolerance, and belonging, they did not converge on one particular understanding. Participants continued to express respect for difference in terms of both maintaining and ignoring religious boundaries.

In general, youth in Manado often express the importance of respecting boundaries in interactions with people of different religious backgrounds. Those who espouse this point of view often feel it is necessary to have a basic understanding of different religions to be able to properly respect those who follow them. This perspective is certainly present at the exchange program. Paulus, a Catholic seminarian who spent a week at the Protestant university in Tomohon, articulated this approach and the importance of maintaining difference in interreligious interactions: "In togetherness in the atmosphere of another religion, we can enjoy togetherness if we are able to accept the diversity (*keberagaman*) among religions. If we only let go of or lose religion, and we act as if we are all the same, or only search for similarities when together, it will be difficult to enjoy togetherness." According to Paulus, it is important to focus on identifying and celebrating differences rather than attempting to downplay or ignore them. In his conceptualization, real togetherness is possible only through the recognition of difference. In what can be considered an articulation of aspirational coexistence by Paulus, this concept of togetherness, *kebersamaan,* puts value on the community and communal order over and above individually oriented rights or freedoms.

Some participants distinguished qualitatively in terms of what kinds of boundaries must be emphasized or maintained in interreligious interactions. Rhena, a Muslim student, explained that she had previously seen religious boundaries as something to be avoided. However, now, she felt that the program had given her the wisdom that she needed to not only open up to accept differences, but to make those who were different feel comfortable if they were among her community. She noted no longer feeling afraid of these differences. In other words, while for Rhena religious boundaries still existed, there was a shift in how she perceived them: while she had initially seen them as a self-imposed obstacle for interaction, they now became an opportunity to respect and to accommodate others' needs.

A student from the state Protestant university recounted how the conversations about religious dogma had actually helped him to understand basic tenets of different religions, which he felt might be important for him to explain to his own congregation as a future religious leader. He felt adamant that religious leaders must have knowledge about other religious groups, "so that, once in the community, we can explain that difference must be celebrated, not used as a wall to create conflict." He distinguishes between that notion of religious difference and one that might lead to misunderstanding or even conflict, and identifies knowledge about other religions as an important step toward recognizing and maintaining difference without turning it into an obstacle for interaction.

Yet, participants also express other viewpoints that work to erase religious boundaries, like the suggestion that Islam and Christianity both worship God, they just have "different rituals of worship" (*tata ibadah berbeda*).

This was one phrase that stuck out to a Muslim participant in the program when he heard it formulated this way by a Catholic seminarian. He liked this phrase and relayed it to me as a perspective that he had adopted from the program. Some students also felt that it was important that in certain situations they were all treated the same, for example, as university students. They appreciated circumstances relevant to social commensuration when they were not viewed as others but were welcomed into an atmosphere of solidarity and togetherness.

However, some participants experienced this feeling of similarity and solidarity in different ways. For example, one Muslim student expressed that through his increasing engagement with Christians, he perceived an atmosphere of kinship that approximated the kind of togetherness he experienced as a student in an Islamic boarding school. He reported perceiving others as if they were not from different religious backgrounds, feeling that he could even recognize the spirit of Islam among them. In this case, the erasing of religious boundaries that takes place is accomplished through the universalization of Islam, which other participants (especially Protestant and Catholic ones) might not accept or appreciate. Overall, this student's experience helps to underscore the significant variation in ideas about religious difference and religious coexistence that participants cultivate during the program.

CONTEXTUAL ETHICAL VALUES

In his study of interreligious dialogue among youth in Java, Zemmrich suggests that participants felt moved by their experience to abandon universal truth claims based in religion in favor of "universal truth claim on a meta-level," whereby participants subscribed to embrace peaceful relationships in pursuit of a common good (2020, 165). This is based on participants stating that they no longer thought of other faith traditions as either right (*benar*) or wrong (*salah*), but instead focused on respect for others and the truth claims of their religions. However, in this interreligious exchange program in Manado, ethical deliberation about interreligious interactions did not lead to a simple upholding of religious coexistence over religiously specific truth claims. In this case study, it becomes clear that the process of incommensuration was crucial in allowing participants to engage with one another and discuss their similarities and commonalities without calling into question any particular truth claims. Along with processes of commensuration on a social level, where religious differences manifest through eating habits or rituals of prayer, the program enables individuals to build up an ethics across borders without concerns about endangering religious truth claims they (or other participants) espouse. In other words, participants are not simply trading a previous embrace of universalism for a new relativist perspective, but are engaging in incommensuration on a theological level that enables them to also engage in commensuration on a social level.

Participants in the exchange program in Manado did discuss how the program led them to reflect on religions as "right" or "wrong," often discussing it as a shift in perspective. Gracia, a student from the Protestant university UKIT who studied at the Islamic university in Manado expressed this shift as follows:

> I thought my religion was right. But after joining the exchange program and studying, it's clear that religious pluralism has already become an actuality in North Sulawesi. So, to live within this plural society, we cannot view our religion as the most right [*yang paling benar*] and other religions as wrong [*salah*]. We have to open ourselves up, that I am right according to my faith, and they also feel right in their faith. My professor has said that we cannot judge others from our own perspective [*kacamata*], only from the perspective of that religious understanding. If not, we're going to judge all religions as wrong. Therefore, in the exchange program we learn to understand the foundation of religious teachings so we can understand, and from this understanding can engender a behavior of respect . . . So, we have to begin with ourselves to say that we are all different but we are all right.

Another student, a Catholic seminarian who stayed at the Protestant University discussed this issue of what is true (*benar*), similarly using the idea of *kacamata,* perspective, or literally "eyeglasses." At times, he felt bothered by some of the material encountered in the courses on the Protestant campus, which explained aspects of theology in a different manner from Catholic teachings, prompting him to want to speak up and question them. However, he said, in a situation like this, "I am still working to take off my glasses [*melepaskan kacamata saya*] when studying another religion." The metaphor of glasses that both of these participants use helps to underscore the importance of perspective as well as context. While there is a realization that a relativist perspective can be essential in building up an ethics across borders, the metaphor of glasses also aptly demonstrates that it is not necessarily a perspective that one needs to espouse with one's coreligionists, or at all times. It is a position that, in this case, makes interreligious understanding possible through building up incommensurability specifically in the context of interreligious encounters.

During the exchange program, participants found ways of expressing a kind of social commensuration, using phrases such as "we are all humans who were created by God," and "we all worship God, we just have a different way of doing so." As participants had already worked to establish a kind of theological incommensurability and to assuage any concerns about proselytizing or conversion that could result from religious mixing, phrases such as these helped them to establish a kind of commonality that could be leveraged as a basis for mutual respect. In this sense, it is similar to what anthropologist Nicholas Evans observed at more formalistic peace symposia held by Ahmadis in India, where participants expressed the equality of all religions, engaging in commensuration of religious traditions (Mair and Evans 2015, 215). The exchange program participants' affirmations of equality were contextual, based on shared aspiration toward interreligious understanding, and also dependent on simultaneous processes of incommensuration so as not to bring certain systems of value into direct comparison with one another. Such phrases used toward social commensuration may also be based on or related to real theological principles the participants believe in, even though they might be worded in a more general or religiously neutral way so as to be applicable to all.

These strategies in interreligious dialogue also demonstrate how ethical positions are not necessarily absolute or mutually exclusive, but can be contextual. An interreligious experience like the exchange program may cause one to deliberate about ethical values, realizing that mutual communication and respect are important in maintaining coexistence. But this does not necessarily mean that participants have embraced these values over and above other truth claims that have effectively been rendered incommensurable in the setting of these specific interreligious interactions.

Toward the end of my research, I asked students at each of the high schools where I conducted fieldwork to complete a short exercise in class, requesting that they each write about an experience they had had with someone from a different religious background. One student at the madrasah wrote about an occurrence in which someone came up to her and gave her a Christmas card, and she smiled and simply accepted it as a gesture of respect. She wrote: "The lesson that I can take from my own experience is that no matter whether a person is Christian, Buddhist, or Hindu, we still need to value them. We must value every religion." A few lines further down, she added a personal message for me: "Islam is the true [*benar*] religion, I want Mrs. Erika [*sic*] to convert to Islam. Hehe :D." She knows that she is supposed to respect all religions, but she also believes that Islam is the one true religion, and is expressing her concern for me by sending me this message, as well as her friendliness through the addition of an emoticon. These messages do not seem to be conflicting for her, as each corresponds to a specific context where these statements make sense.

MOVING OUTSIDE OF THE EXCHANGE PROGRAM

Although many students do have a positive experience during the exchange program, it can be difficult to explain or justify their new perspectives to family members or to friends back on their own campus who did not join the program. The participants' behavior can be perceived as transgressive, dangerously flirting with religious boundaries that are better kept solid and untouched. Furthermore, participants in this group are self-selected. Students who take part are those who aspire to become religious leaders or teachers, and therefore typically have a strong sense of religious identity. In addition, they are interested in seeking out knowledge about other religions and engaging in interreligious dialogue. Many students do not want to participate because it is a demanding program that takes time and energy in addition to the studies they are completing on their own campus. Others have concerns about the kind of interreligious mixing that the program entails and choose not to join.

A few weeks after the religious exchange program, a Muslim student from IAIN named Hera posted a photo on her Facebook page without any caption. In the photo, she posed with a Muslim classmate inside a Catholic church, each of them on either side of a crucifix by the altar, with one of the seminarians kneeling below it. Many friends from the exchange program "liked" her status, and some of her Muslim friends started to post positive comments or reactions, asking where the photo was taken. After receiving her first negative comment from a Muslim man saying that her photo was wrong because "the background doesn't fit" (*begrounnya gak pas*), Hera shot back: "Oh, so it's forbidden to take a picture there according to the Qur'an?," ending her comment with a smile emoji.

A few more short but positive comments from friends followed, saying things like "great" (*mantap*), before another negative comment from a Muslim man identifying himself as her senior by referring to her as *dek* (younger sibling/peer) warned her that posing next to symbols from a different religion could lead to slander (*fitnah*). Still ready to defend herself, Hera wrote, "Just look at Al-Kafirun in the Qur'an[1] and so on ... So why is it wrong,?! The most important thing is that I continue to keep my faith [*akidah*]. Oh, yeah—slandered by whom? Hmm ..." As Hera was clearly not deterred in her willingness to defend her position, the commenter countered that a good Muslim woman would have accepted his advice rather than trying to start a debate using Qur'anic evidence, outright accusing her of being arrogant (*angkuh*). Another young woman whom I recognized as a former exchange participant jumped in to defend Hera, saying that she wasn't being arrogant. Hera commented once again, expressing her expectation that this man, as her senior, would have understood better than her. Then, as if to prove her superior status, she proclaimed, "I've joined the exchange program." As additional comments came in, she posted again to thank those who responded positively.

I bring up this social media post because it draws attention to the possibilities and also the challenges of applying new approaches toward religious difference outside of the context of the program itself, where participants have engaged in normative work in establishing an ethics across borders. This interaction, captured in a photo and displayed on social media, is then viewed outside of the context of the processes of commensuration and incommensuration that shaped its possibility. Many participants who feel that the experience is transformative also report having difficulty explaining this to outsiders who have not been through the same program. While Hera started to defend her own position with references to the Qur'an and reassurances that she had not acted in contradiction to her own faith, she then fell back on the explanation that she had joined this exchange program, leaving this as a source of authority and an explanation in and of itself, which others were not so quick to accept.

Finally, I bring up one more example of another interreligious dialogue event among university students to once again highlight the challenges in explaining the results of their interreligious deliberations beyond the context of the program or the dialogue itself. A group of approximately twenty-five university students already active in interfaith initiatives invited a few local professors and religious leaders to speak at and help facilitate an interreligious dialogue. This gathering was spurred by events elsewhere in Indonesia—the destruction of a church in Aceh Singkil and a mosque in Tolikara, Papua, in 2015. Several local organizations acted quickly to increase interreligious dialogue and communication in the region.

As participants spoke about the current events, they tended to couple together these two incidents as a larger systemic problem of growing religious intolerance in Indonesia, rather than fixate only on the destruction of the church, as many Christian organizations in North Sulawesi had tended to do. Yet, the students struggled to come up with an action plan for reducing religious intolerance and the destruction of houses of worship. Although activism was encouraged and an invited speaker called on all the participants to be "provocateurs for peace," the main call for action was to continue participation in interreligious dialogues and to invite friends to join.

These challenges do not necessarily mean that the ethical positions developed through such initiatives end with the exchange program or interreligious dialogue. Going back to the very definition of education as "deliberation" (Varenne 2007), the focus is on the social activity of discussing something that happened and making decisions about something to happen in the future. In other words, the ethical deliberations that have taken place, even if difficult to explain or advance outside of that specific context, have not ended with the program. Indeed, they have likely impacted how the participants approach belonging and coexistence, which should not be overlooked. But moving outside of these environments does require individuals and groups to mobilize normative and organizational mechanisms to advance their ethico-political positions, taking into account the social resonances and consequences that these particular perspectives may have on a broader public level.

7

Going Public
Scaling Deliberation about Belonging

This chapter considers how interpersonal ethics of coexistence might relate to the public debates taking place in North Sulawesi about religion and belonging. Instead of focusing specifically on schools and educational institutions, the focus is on two major groups of organizations: interreligious organizations and self-described *adat* (traditional) organizations. The public debates about religious coexistence and belonging pick up the familiar threads discussed in schools, as interreligious organizations make claims about the importance of guarding the religious harmony that is considered so precious in North Sulawesi, projecting an aspirational coexistence. At the same time, some *adat* organizations project this religious harmony primarily as a reality guaranteed by the Christian majority and called into question by "outsiders." Going beyond an examination of how schools become the objects of political debate, this book has sought to investigate how schools articulate with or become disjointed from debates in the public sphere about religious belonging, national belonging, and the accommodation of difference by channeling, boosting, and/or redirecting the kinds of ethical normativities and reasoning encountered there.

These organizations and the actors that represent them engage in normative work relevant to perspectives on religious plurality, like the educational institutions and programs discussed previously. The analysis in this chapter follows the "public reasoning" (Bowen 2010, 6) deployed in these debates, as actors advance particular positions in public settings, aiming to provide justifications that will resonate with individuals. The positions advocated do not simply rest on intellectual reasoning, but on the moral frameworks that undergird these possibilities for belonging. An analysis of responses to major incidents that sparked public discussion about religion and national belonging reveals a strong tension between a commitment to religious harmony as the basis for a regional identity and the desire to secure the province's future as a Christian stronghold with majoritarian influence in the public sphere. In some positions advocated by particular mass organizations, the limits of inclusivity come into stark relief when the future status of Christians as a majority in the province or the rights of Christians in other regions are perceived as threatened.

This chapter focuses specifically on interreligious organizations and *adat* organizations in Manado, particularly in terms of understanding how frameworks for coexistence are disseminated and move across various scales. A concern with how normative discourses are "scaled up" relates to the way in which associations can extend the influence of their values beyond their circle of membership, the kind of normative work involved therein, and the associated ethical framework of plurality promoted (R. W. Hefner 2021, 12). Focusing on the role these organizations play does not simply provide context for what is taking place in schools, but also highlights how debates about belonging and the ethical perspectives driving these positions become mobilized across scales and find broad resonance. It is also for this reason that the chapter comes at the end of the book: to outline how the kinds of deliberations taking place in school map against the broader public ethical debates in the region.

MANADONESE, MINAHASAN

As identities and possibilities for belonging are put forth and contested in the public sphere, they also relate to historical shifts in the formation of ethnic and religious identity in addition to political changes that have reorganized territories and demographic realities. The construction of "Minahasa" as a category, later mobilized to encompass a regional and ethnic identity, is related to a colonial organization of territory and interethnic alliances (Henley 1996). These processes were also intimately entangled with the Christianization of the region, as Dutch missionaries promoted a concept of Christian brotherhood as the basis for the unity of several subethnic groups under a Minahasan umbrella (Swazey 2013, 13). Denni Pinontoan points out that a Minahasan cultural identity based on genealogy and Christianity does not always neatly map onto Minahasa as an ethnic category and identity (2018, 108). This history, particularly the relationship to Christian identity, becomes salient as various groups claim to act in accordance with Minahasan ethnic *adat* (tradition), with very little consensus about what constitutes the basis of this ethnic tradition.

Furthermore, the redrawing of territories and administrative boundaries in the more recent past has also impacted the entanglement of political and religious identities and subjectivities. Decentralization, undertaken in tandem with democratization from the late 1990s to the early 2000s, was partially carried out through a redrawing of administrative territories as a strategy for encouraging local autonomy in governmental structure as well as gaining access to additional resources. Before this reconfiguration of administrative units, the province of North Sulawesi also included the Muslim-majority Gorontalo regency, meaning that at that time the proportion of Christians and the proportion of Muslims in the province were nearly equal (Jacobsen 2004, 74). In January 2001, Gorontalo became its own province, shifting the demographic dynamics of North Sulawesi and making Minahasans the clear dominant ethnic group and Christians the largest religious group in the province.

Another campaign, which officially began in 2010, has promoted the separation of Bolaang-Mongondow, comprising four regencies and the city of Kotamobagu, as its own province. While the outcome of the campaign remains uncertain, it is noteworthy that this would lead to a parallel shift in demographics as the split from Gorontalo. It would lead to a clear reestablishment of a Christian and Minahasan dominance in the province. The main push in this campaign has come from Bolaang-Mongondow, which has advocated for greater autonomy and access to provincial resources that many argue have been funneled to Manado and the northern part of the province. Importantly, these campaigns for separation are nearly always discussed in terms of politics and access to resources, and often qualified with the statement that they have nothing to do with religion. Yet, in the entanglement of political and religious identities and the demographic shifts entailed in the process, it becomes complicated to try to extricate religion and claim its irrelevance. As will become clearer below, there are several groups that are actively reframing the relevance of religious identity in North Sulawesi.

Nono Sumampouw (2015) has critiqued existing descriptions of social identity in Manado that privilege historical accounts of ethnic identity, and he warns against assumptions about religious harmony as an immutable cultural trait. He instead elaborates on the emergence of an overarching contemporary Manadonese identity that does not depend exclusively on religious or ethnic affiliation. He draws attention to major social divisions visible in the geographical organization of the city, as Muslim settlers from various ethnic groups (Gorontalo, Javanese, Bugis) and ethnic Sangihe

Christians are often grouped together in the northern part of the city, with fewer public resources. On the other hand, the southern area of Manado is primarily populated by Minahasan Christians, who, he argues, make clear their position as the rightful owners (*pemilik sah*) of the region in their ample allocation of space for Christian worship (Sumampouw 2015, 13). Yet, in addition to these processes of social differentiation, he also highlights simultaneous practices of building up a common identity through the discourse of *"Torang Samua Basudara"* (We Are All Brothers). In this approach, he draws our attention to broad processes of social commensuration and incommensuration, where individuals perhaps come together with general aspirations related to coexistence, but are also shaped by complex social and cultural divisions. While these divisions do not fall strictly along ethnic or religious lines, they do contribute to a projection of Minahasan Christians as the hosts and other groups as settlers, migrants, or newcomers.

In this book, I have moved between a discussion of the city of Manado and of the province of North Sulawesi not necessarily in terms of a scalar hierarchy, but depending instead upon a local understanding of Minahasa and Manado as interchangeable identifiers. In terms of public identities, individuals may identify themselves as *"orang Manado"* (Manadonese), adopting a regional identifier rather than using the ethnic identifier *"orang Minahasa"* (Minahasan), particularly when presenting themselves in a national context (Renwarin 2006, 16). A Manadonese identity is also shaped by the popular regional language, referred to as Bahasa Manado—a lingua franca based in Malay—as "an indicator of localness, one based in the melding of diverse histories and trajectories of trade and movement that cannot be bound geographically" (Swazey 2013, 68). Significantly, this language is spoken by Christians and Muslims in the region and across various ethnic groups. Some of my interlocutors discussed an identity of *"orang Manado"* as having the potential to be more inclusive, as it connotes a loose regional affiliation without necessarily pointing to a specific ethnic or religious identity. Yet, as mentioned above, in its most common usage, Manadonese is typically understood as interchangeable with Minahasan.

INTERRELIGIOUS ORGANIZATIONS AND COMMUNICATION

In public deliberations about the ethics and politics of belonging, interreligious organizations do play an important role in coordination and communication among various religious groups in North Sulawesi. When I spoke with religious and community leaders about religious coexistence in Manado, interlocutors consistently brought up the practical importance of interreligious institutions as providing a public forum, as well as their symbolic importance in projecting religious harmony as a normative value, promoting aspirational coexistence. Compared to other regions, such as the Muslim-majority West Sumatra, it has been suggested that leaders in North Sulawesi have a more expansive definition of religious freedom, moving beyond an idea about individual or minority rights to worship to also encompass broad support for religious diversity (Salim, Simbuka, and Luntajo 2016, 615). While the existence of interreligious forums does not guarantee tolerance, it does provide institutional support for interreligious communication about social issues. These organizations typically call meetings in response to any local or national event that could potentially heighten religious tensions or motivate religious conflict. They also maintain communication channels among various religious communities as one important mechanism for dampening the spread of rumors or hoaxes, and to continually remind religious congregations not to be provoked by local, national, or international events.

The Committee for Interreligious Cooperation (BKSAUA—Badan Kerja Sama Antar Umat Beragama), tasked with acting as an independent advisor on social and religious issues, was founded in North Sulawesi in 1969 by Governor H. V. Worang (Pomalingo 2004, 64). The history of this organization is significant because it was a locally driven initiative that predates similar national structures and initiatives. The hierarchical structure of the BKSAUA includes representatives of five major religions[1] for each village (*desa*), subdistrict (*kecamatan*), city (*kota*), district (*kabupaten*), and province. Fadjar Thufail has importantly indicated that despite the establishment of this expansive network of representatives, the size and power of the mainline Protestant church (GMIM) have enabled Protestants to continue to set the tone for interreligious relations in the province (2012, 363). In the year 2000, the BKSAUA was given the status of an official advisory board for the governor (Swazey 2013, 115). The organization holds a council at the provincial level every month, and holds a council at all levels of the organization every three months, with the aim of carrying out social dialogue to address any situations that have the potential to heighten interreligious tensions or develop into a conflict.

The Interreligious Harmony Forum (FKUB) is a government-established and government-mandated interreligious body that today exists in

North Sulawesi alongside the BKSAUA. Joint ministerial decisions from the minister of religion and the minister of home affairs in 2006 mandated the creation of the FKUB in each province, with forums on both the provincial and city/district levels. The organization allocates representatives from each of the six officially recognized religions based on the proportion of religious followers in the population. The FKUB's main role, in addition to providing a general forum for dialogue and communication, is to give recommendations to local governments on the allocation of building permits for houses of worship. This is a significant role, as houses of worship often become a focal point of practical public discussions about managing religious plurality, and can turn into flash points for religious conflict. The same sense of urgency that led to the government-mandated creation of the FKUB also gave momentum to educators to include material in their lessons about religious tolerance and belonging more explicitly, and to develop interfaith educational programs both through and outside of state channels.

Both the FKUB and BKSAUA currently act as mediators between the government and religious communities in Manado, as well as promoting dialogue among various religious groups. They are geared toward mediating social issues, rather than engaging in theologically driven dialogue. When local

FIGURE 7.1 Governor Olly Dondokambey inducts new members into the FKUB in 2016.

or national issues have the potential to incite conflict, representatives make official statements reminding the public and their particular congregations not to be provoked by these issues and to allow legal action to be carried out by the proper authorities. Yet, the GMIM's size and influence continue to allow it to wield its power within (as well as outside of) these organizations. In the year 2015, the positions of chairperson in both the BKSAUA and the FKUB were held by GMIM pastors. Many religious leaders acknowledged this as an implicit rule or expected pattern because the province is majority Christian and GMIM is the largest denomination.

Critics of these interreligious organizations, including, most vocally, those who do want to further realize aspirational coexistence, often claim that their function is primarily ceremonial, lacking substance and concrete action items. It cannot be assumed that religious communities will necessarily follow and agree with what their elite representatives say and do as members of these organizations, which challenges these institutions' abilities to negotiate public conflicts in a way that would be accepted as legitimate by all major public actors. In the early 2000s, during the outbreaks of violence in nearby provinces, the BKSAUA in North Sulawesi was perceived as insufficient for maintaining religious harmony in the region, and the organization JAJAK, an informal network of journalists and activists working with religious communities, formed at this time with the goal of maintaining peace in the region (Thufail 2012, 365). However, as Thufail points out, the realm of government-affiliated bureaucracy is not the only one in which deliberation about the religious and cultural politics takes place. As refugees from Maluku arrived in Manado and concern about infiltration from radical Islamic groups spread, national movements of *adat* revivalism took root locally as another public forum for renegotiating the relationship between culture and religion and the politics of belonging and coexistence (Thufail 2012, 370).

ADAT ORGANIZATIONS: RENEGOTIATION OF RELIGIOUS AND ETHNIC IDENTITY

At a coffee shop in Manado down the street from the headquarters of the Milisi Waraney,[2] I sat down with one of the organization's nine commanders (*panglima*), a key advisor, and several other representatives. Milisi Waraney was founded as an exclusively Protestant Christian militia in 2002. Like many former paramilitary groups or militias in Manado, it has rebranded itself as an *adat* organization. Its emergence is linked to two broader trends in democratizing and decentralizing post–New Order Indonesia: the *adat* revival (Henley and Davidson 2008) and the proliferation of religious and ethnic militias that are legally registered as societal organizations (*organisasi masyarakat*) (Wilson and Nugroho 2012). Although these organizations are not officially affiliated with the state, in postcolonial Southeast Asia, displays of power by such nonstate organizations or militias are often able to implicate state authority through their entanglements with local government structures and leaders (Kingsley and Telle 2016).

In the early 2000s, as ethnic and religious conflicts broke out in nearby regions, several paramilitary organizations formed in North Sulawesi. At the time, there was significant fear that these religious conflicts could spread to the region. In particular, concern that radical Islamist organizations such as Laskar Jihad (active in the Maluku conflict) or Abu Sayaaf (based in the southern Philippines) might infiltrate North Sulawesi and incite violence triggered the formation of local militias (Jacobsen 2004, 84). Brigade Manguni, which later became Brigade Manguni Indonesia (BMI), was formed at the Kongres Minahasa Raya in 2001, with the stated aim of protecting Minahasan land (*tanah Minahasa*) in anticipation of the possibility that violent conflicts might spill over. This gave momentum for the creation of several similar organizations, including Milisi Waraney, Militia Christi, and Legium Christum (Pinontoan 2018, 112). Many of the organizations formed at that time have since disbanded. But many new ones have also been created, and those still in existence, like Milisi Waraney and Brigade Manguni, have rebranded themselves in the context of the *adat* movement (Swazey 2013, 174).

The Milisi Waraney commander, who kept on his dark Prada sunglasses for the duration of our discussion, explained that the goal of their organization was to guard against threats from outside and inside the region. He added that while other similar local organizations, such as Brigade Manguni Indonesia, are "mixed" (*campur*)—referring to the fact that members from different religious backgrounds are allowed—Milisi Waraney is "pure" (*murni*) because it allows only Protestant members. When I inquired about the relationship between Christianity and Minahasan *adat,* the advisor quickly jumped in to state matter-of-factly that none of the Minahasan ancestors became *walisongo*.[3] By this statement, he meant that most Minahasans did not become Muslim but instead converted to Protestant Christianity, a transition that was widespread in the late nineteenth century. Some contemporary Minahasan *adat* organizations perform traditional rituals involving offerings and spirit possession, despite the disapproval and resistance from the indigenous Protestant GMIM. The Milisi Waraney advisor began sharing anecdotes about some members who had the ability to perform traditional rituals involving spirit possession, but the *panglima* was clearly bothered. He reached into his polka-dot V-neck shirt to pull out a large silver crucifix necklace and expressed his disapproval of participating in these pre-Christian Minahasan rituals. Grasping the crucifix necklace, he proclaimed: "Once you have this, you cannot be defeated."

My discussion with those involved in Milisi Waraney demonstrates an entanglement of Minahasan *adat* and Protestant Christianity that exists within many of the major self-labeled *adat* organizations active in North Sulawesi today. Although the organization's commander and advisor were at odds about the performance of *adat* rituals and their relevance for the organization, they both agreed on an unquestioned link between Minahasan identity and Christianity. I argue that the flexibility of the concept of *adat* among these organizations in North Sulawesi has ultimately allowed for a reinforcement of the link between ethnic Minahasan and Christian identity.[4] In these circles, *adat* is not heavily discursivized and is often glossed as "protecting the homeland" (*menjaga tanah adat*), which leaves room for the implicit assumption that the Minahasan homeland is a Christian place. Some *adat* groups have organized around the preservation of cultural artifacts and mythology, others reinterpret traditional rituals from a monotheistic Christian lens, and others still foreground Christianity as now having the true status of local tradition in Minahasa. Local rituals of spirit possession and ancestor worship performed by ritual leaders (Manado: *tona'as*) were largely suppressed by missionaries during the colonial period, and the mainstream teachings of the GMIM today similarly cast these traditions as against Christian teachings (Thufail 2012, 366). Stronger objections and claims that traditional rituals are equivalent to satanic practices are also not uncommon. An extensive range of positions on *adat* is found among contemporary organizations in North Sulawesi, yet the framing used across the board ultimately contributes to a reinforcement of the link between Christianity and *adat*, mobilizing identity politics with ramifications for belonging in the region.

ADAT FOR PROTECTION OF THE (CHRISTIAN) MINAHASAN HOMELAND

The flexibility and ambiguity in the definition of *adat* among these organizations allow for *adat* to become mobilized in terms of identity politics, linking Minahasan and Christian identity. Many organizations with strength and influence often take a religious tone and use religious symbols in their logos. For example, Milisi Waraney's symbol includes an owl, a sacred bird in Minahasan tradition, superimposed on a large blue Star of David, with a small red cross above the owl's head. The star and cross, both understood as Christian religious symbols in the Minahasan context, provide a visual reinforcement of the linkage between Minahasan and Christian identity when featured with the image of an owl.

In considering the stakes of such mobilizations of religious identity, it is instructive to take account of the salience that religion took on in the 1999–2000 conflict in North Maluku, from which many refugees fled to Manado. Christopher Duncan (2013) demonstrates how, despite other factors—economic, political—that may have been initially the most important in triggering violence, ultimately, the conflict was primarily experienced by North Moluccans as a religious conflict. The use of symbols such as colored headbands to elicit a sense of religious solidarity and the circulation of a disputed letter that painted the conflict in religious terms and referred to alleged actions of members of the Christian militia Laskar Kristus were effective in pushing a religious narrative that eventually dominated the conflict (Duncan 2013, 57–58).

Since their inception, *adat* organizations in Manado have mostly increased in size, number, and local influence. Despite their appeal to religious symbols, some of the organizations' members are stereotyped as drunken motorcycle gangsters (*preman*). Groups have sought to change negative perceptions through their claims of dedication to principles like religious freedom and harmony, their sponsorship of public debates, and the inclusion of women within their ranks. Other organizations, like Panji Yosua (referring to the biblical figure Joshua), have sought more official links. Panji Yosua is directly affiliated with the GMIM, though their focus is defined more specifically as a neighborhood security force that monitors religiosity and morality among church members (Pinontoan 2018, 114). While the scope of the organization is perhaps more defined and limited than that of other organizations, its official connection to the church provides a sense of both institutional and religious legitimacy.

Adat organizations do not limit themselves to a local or regional scope in their goal to protect North Sulawesi, but also underscore a further link to Christianity through their goal of protecting Christians throughout Indonesia, often leveraging their position as a local majority in order to respond to national events. In the early 2000s, some of the militias did participate in conflicts in nearby provinces. For example, Brigade Manguni troops went to Poso (Central Sulawesi) with the intent of supporting Christians there and protecting them against Laskar Jihad, an Islamist militia that was active there (Bakker 2016, 256). As they transitioned toward becoming *adat* organizations (rather than militias), the groups have focused more on protesting national events, such as church burnings in other provinces, or, as was the case in 2017, protesting the blasphemy case brought against the Christian and ethnic Chinese governor of Jakarta.

Under the scope of protecting the Minahasan homeland, *adat* organizations often do articulate a goal of maintaining religious harmony in the region, acting upon this principle by offering services as security personnel during religious celebrations, especially those of Muslims. In 2001, Legium Christum, an *adat* organization drawing primarily Catholic members, offered to provide security for Eid celebrations among the Muslim community. This offer was based on concerns about potential retaliations for Christmas church bombings a few months earlier in Jakarta (Jacobsen 2004, 86). BMI also often takes on similar roles, for example, leading the *takbiran* procession down one of the major streets in Manado in celebration of Eid as a means of providing security (Sumampouw 2015, 54). However, in doing so, these organizations are also potentially reinforcing a conception that Muslims' protection depends on the goodwill of the Christian Minahasan majority.

The influence of groups like BMI and Milisi Waraney is bolstered by their strong ties to local politicians. Although they are not official or public political links, they often involve financial patronage of particular individuals rather than parties. Bakker has drawn attention to the way in which BMI's extensive network and links to political structure has ultimately created ties to local government representatives, who can be spotted at organizational events (2016, 257). Because of the ability of these organizations to mobilize thousands, they are core support groups for particular candidates during election time. While the actual impact of *adat* organizations on the regional elections across Indonesia in December 2015 may have been minimal (Jaffrey and Ali-Fauzi 2016), they have still been able to exercise significant influence in the public sphere on issues related to plural coexistence. Although they have been involved in an ambiguous deployment of *adat*, their public reasoning positions them as defenders of religious harmony, making it difficult for other groups to speak directly against their stated agendas.

Strengthening the link between Minahasan *adat* and Christianity and conflating Minahasan ethnic identity with religious affiliation have the effect of positioning Muslims as outsiders. In doing so, the *adat* organizations reinforce the common conception that religious harmony in the region is guaranteed exclusively by the Christian majority. However, many of the *adat* organizations define their role as simply "protecting the Minahasan homeland" and lack a framework for addressing diversity and social complexity. Most groups do still continue to define their social mission in terms of protecting the region from outside threats, particularly hard-line Muslim organizations. For example, both BMI and Milisi Waraney justify their existence by referring to the need to protect the region from groups like the Islamic Defenders Front (FPI—Front Pembela Islam), a hard-line Muslim organization known for its vigilante-style violence (Wilson 2008; Bamualim 2011) that was eventually disbanded by the government in 2020 on the grounds that its ideology conflicted with Pancasila. BMI also held a "show of force" demonstration in Manado in April 2015 to denounce ISIS (Islamic State of Iraq and Syria) and to show BMI's readiness to protect the region from terrorism. Local opinion on these groups varies greatly, and while some praise their existence as the reason why the FPI has not been able to establish itself in North Sulawesi, others privately remark that the groups amount to nothing more than the Christian version of the FPI.

ADAT AND IDENTITY POLITICS

In its numerous manifestations across Indonesia, one of the notable characteristics of the contemporary *adat* revival has been the flexibility and paradoxical nature of the concept of *adat* itself, deployed in ways that are "by turns progressive and reactionary, emancipating and authoritarian, idealistic and manipulative" (Henley and Davidson 2008, 835). In Manado, *adat* politics have become increasingly visible in the public sphere during the post-Suharto era, and have emerged in locally specific ways based on the strong association between Minahasan *adat* and Christianity. The simultaneously inclusive and exclusive claims put forth by various *adat* organizations indicate the unresolved ambiguity of what actually constitutes *adat* from the perspective of the organizations and their actors.

While in some post-conflict regions in Indonesia *adat* has been considered as a potential basis for reconciliation, contemporary mobilizations of *adat* in the public sphere in Manado have tended toward exclusivism. In this case, it is interesting to compare the current deployment of *adat* in North Sulawesi, a province that has remained peaceful since the early 2000s, to nearby provinces like Maluku and North Maluku, where violent conflicts broke out and evolved to take on a religious frame and narrative, pitting Muslims against Christians. Birgit Bräuchler, who has written about post-conflict rebuilding in Maluku (2009), has argued that *adat* and the village alliance system it enshrines provided an integrative push necessary for reconciliation even as other measures, such as a legal reconciliation, failed. Though she recognizes the exclusivist potential of *adat* as a concept, she argues that its flexible, dynamic character can contribute to overcoming religious difference (Bräuchler 2009, 888). Christopher Duncan, in his research on the conflict in North Maluku, has noted that the religious framing of the conflict itself has led to a tendency of some local organizations to seek reconciliation and the prevention of future violence through the promotion of an *adat*-based identity, "one that forefronted cultural identities rather than religious ones" (2013, 15). In the search for cultural practices that have historically supported coexistence in these post-conflict regions, the potential of *adat* is clear. The main questions being asked focus not on the nature of *adat* itself, but on its possible effectiveness in overcoming other kinds of social divisions.

In North Sulawesi, there is an ongoing public debate about Minahasan *adat* and religious identity that is proving extremely significant for the future of the region and its ability to accommodate plurality. To be sure, the range of actors mobilizing in the name of *adat* is large, with numerous understandings of what *adat* might mean, and different methods of mobilization on its behalf. Local intellectuals have elaborated the potential for traditional Minahasan values like mutual cooperation (Manado: *mapalus*) and the more recent collective nod to aspirational coexistence through the Manadonese slogan *"Torang Samua Basudara"* to form the basis for a dialogue in the public sphere that normatively affirms pluralism (Sumampouw 2015; Pinontoan 2018). Kelli Swazey has argued that the contemporary movements focused on rediscovering Minahasan *adat* have opened up a space for its conceptual separation from Christianity, and the potential to reshape regional notions of Minahasan ethnic identity and regional belonging to be more inclusive (2013, 24). For example, prominent GMIM pastor and BKSAUA chairman Richard Siwu explained in an interview that the Minahasan ethnic group was formed through the uniting of different sub-ethnic groups, which he sees as providing a framework that can be further developed to accommodate diversity. Reiner Emyot Ointoe, an active Muslim intellectual and cultural observer, sees the historical coexistence between Minahasans and the Muslim Javanese who were exiled to North Sulawesi by the Dutch colonial government[5] as providing a potential strategy of coexistence that can be used to avoid what he describes as a sectarian bent present in North Sulawesi today. In other words, there are movements in Manado attempting to harness the integrative potential of *adat,* seeking out local cultural frameworks that could help to respond to the challenges of living in a religiously plural society.

On the other hand, many of the *adat* organizations that have been visible and vocal in the public sphere actually have very little consensus on what constitutes Minahasan *adat.* They define their organizations' goals in reference to national ideologies and principles, such as Pancasila and religious freedom. Such principles are effective in mobilizing followers and legitimizing these organizations in the public eye. However, as a result of their concern with the place of Christians and the religious freedom of Christians in the country, their actions tend to reinforce the link between Christianity and Minahasan *adat,* and may ultimately threaten the position of local Muslims. Many organizations, in their aim to reclaim and protect the Minahasan homeland, position Minahasan people (Manado: *tou Minahasa*) as the owners of that land with the right to welcome or refuse others (Pinontoan 2018, 105). In addition, Sven Kosel has remarked in regard to Minahasan *adat* organizations that "paradoxically, the ethnically and religiously exclusive ways chosen to make a plea for pluralism tend to undermine tolerance and alienate minorities within the province" (2010, 292). In looking out for Christian interests and attempting to ensure the government continues to guarantee religious freedom, these groups often advance exclusivist claims that ultimately threaten local religious minorities and local religious harmony.

RELIGIOUS THEME PARK: WHICH FRAMEWORK FOR BELONGING?

Plans revived by the mayor of Manado in 2015 for a religious theme park (*taman wisata religi*) in the city aimed to build a monument to enshrine its commitment to religious harmony and aspirational coexistence. Yet, public contestations regarding these plans have ultimately exposed tensions among existing public conceptions of coexistence, leading to public deliberations about belonging. These public debates have involved interreligious and *adat* organizations, with each one leaning on their existing networks and structure to promote and circulate different ethical positions about religious difference and belonging. Debates about the allocation of land and acquisition of permits for houses of worship are highly sensitive and quickly become national issues, so it is not surprising that this case has become a point of debate among Manadonese. Furthermore, in Manado, the Christian majority are set on maintaining the landscape and territory as recognizably Christian, so it can live up to its nickname, City of a Thousand Churches (*Kota Seribu Gereja*). The escalation of debates about this religious theme park and the vision of belonging entailed are turning into a test of the inclusive belonging that Manadonese claim as a defining value of the region.

Importantly, this religious theme park would not be the first in the region. In Minahasa Regency, the Hill of Love (Bukit Kasih) symbolizes an embrace of religious harmony through five miniature houses of worship built on the slope of a volcano. The project was undertaken by North Sulawesi governor A. J. Sondakh in 2002, in conjunction with the network JAJAK and with support from religious leaders and interreligious organizations. Bukit Kasih has since fallen into a state of disrepair and is no longer a popular destination for recreation, yet proud residents continue to mention it as a physical materialization of the religious harmony that is an important value for Manadonese. The sentiment behind the Hill of Love and of the proposed religious theme park in Manado remains popular in its public affirmation of what most people in Manado see as an integral part of their identity: peace, "a norm believed by the activists of Minahasan culture to have lasted for centuries and constitute the core value of Minahasan identity and subjectivity" (Thufail 2012, 366).

The proposed location for the religious theme park in Manado is a neighborhood formerly known as Kampung Texas. In the early 2000s, the neighborhood mostly housed Muslims from Gorontalo who either worked at the nearby market, Pasar 45, or ran mobile food stalls. In 2005, Mayor Jimmy Rimba Rogi began a project to clear the neighborhood, evicting those who had settled on what was officially government-owned land and tearing down the buildings there, except the Al-Khairiyah mosque, which has stood there since the 1970s. The work was apparently undertaken with plans for a religious theme park in mind, and with the intention that other houses of worship would be built next to the existing mosque. However, the project was temporarily abandoned by the succeeding mayors. As Weichart points out regarding earlier cases of dispersing (primarily Muslim) food sellers in Bitung, North Sulawesi, in 2002, they became scapegoats for local social and economic issues, seen as representative of the problems posed by "outsiders" and galvanizing religious divisions (2004, 70).

In 2015, Mayor Vicky Lumentut indicated he would continue with the long-held plans to build a religious theme park on government-owned land to celebrate the religious harmony of Manado, on the site where the mosque still stands. After the plan was announced, uncertainty remained about whether there would be enough space to fit the miniature houses of worship for the six official religions on the existing plot. The mayor had been trying to revive the project since 2012 by requesting the required permits, but it had stalled due to competing claims over the land from mosque officials. In early 2015, as plans were set to move forward, tensions rose again over allegations that the mosque had been renovated and expanded beyond its previous dimensions, and without the proper permits.

The public debates that have emerged in the context of the religious theme park have involved the BKSAUA and FKUB, interreligious organizations charged with helping to find a solution and to avoid conflict. In this context, they appeal to a normative frame of an aspirational coexistence, calling for a form of mutual recognition and belonging. At the same time, the event also prompted the formation of an alliance of existing *adat* organizations called Aliansi Makapetor, standing for Minahasans Who Care about Tolerance" (Masyarakat Kawanua yang Peduli Toleransi) (Pinontoan 2018, 114). Protests triggered by the events employed a majoritarian frame of belonging that continually projects Muslims as outsiders to the province, despite the *adat* organizations' claims of prioritizing the maintenance of local religious harmony. In doing so, they pushed a version of belonging that requires recognition and acceptance of the majoritarian Christian influence in the public sphere.

In March 2015, the mayor met with representatives from the BKSAUA and FKUB to try to come up with a suitable solution for the theme park. They produced a new plan that would maintain the mosque building, but make use of its ground floor for a library for all religions. A multistory tower built next to the mosque would accord a floor to each additional official religion, and one floor for the interreligious organizations to use as a meeting space. A couple of weeks later, Aliansi Makapetor called for protests at the regional parliament building in Manado, shouting the Minahasan war cry *"I Yayat U Santi!"*[6] until they were received by parliamentary representatives. Members of the *adat* alliance made their demands clear, calling for the land to be used for its "intended function," referring to the initial plans for the religious theme park, and for all construction of buildings without proper permits to stop, clearly referencing the mosque and its alleged expansion. The rally coordinator threatened that the group would take matters into its own hands and stop construction of any buildings in the province without proper permits if the government did not take action. The group reassembled for a demonstration and an *adat* ritual several days later, and the police took action to prevent the group from advancing toward the plot of land.

Accelerated meetings with the provincial FKUB, BKSAUA, and the Manado branch of the Indonesian Council of Ulama (MUI—Majelis Ulama Indonesia) led to a decision to move forward with the multistory religious tower. Following an official groundbreaking ceremony for the tower in June 2015, Aliansi Makapetor renewed their protests, and their leader, Decky Joice Tumar, spoke at a press conference. He was later quoted in the local press clarifying that "our presence is not intended to cause conflict or bring up issues related to SARA, but to keep such things from happening," reiterating that the organization was dedicated to protecting religious harmony in Manado from those who try to destabilize it. However, the alliance called for realization of the original theme park plans and for "destruction of the building that is not in accordance with the theme park design," referring implicitly to the mosque. The mayor's office responded by reiterating the symbolism of the park, and the fact that the first stone had been laid one week earlier by religious leaders from the BKSAUA and FKUB. The mayor continued, "I appeal to the entire community of Manado so that we continue to maintain togetherness and harmony in this city so that the image of *Torang Samua Basudara* is maintained properly." However, the mayor ultimately made the decision to temporarily suspend construction of the multireligious tower, pending further discussion with the regional parliament and the police.

Interreligious organizations continued to mediate discussions between the government, local religious communities, and groups like the Aliansi Makapetor. The head of MUI Manado cited the incident as a test of Manado's religious harmony, but one that, as a result of their intense communication with and support from the government, they were able to effectively moderate. The MUI became involved in discussions with government officials and the FKUB and BKSAUA to clarify the situation and find a reasonable solution. However, Aliansi Makapetor organized more demonstrations with hundreds of protestors in October 2016. The *adat* representatives condemned "illegal buildings" that were impeding progress on the religious theme park. The ambiguous reference to illegal buildings left the local media speculating as to whether they were referring to the Al-Khairiyah mosque or the small, unregistered food stalls that had started to pop up on the perimeter of the land intended for the park. The sudden revival of the debate about the religious theme park at this time was influenced by national political events, specifically the accusations of blasphemy leveled against Jakarta's governor Ahok and the sectarian religious and political displays triggered by the incident.

The case of the theme park began to attract national attention. A decision reached by the local government in conjunction with the interreligious bodies of the city and province was strongly rejected by *adat* organizations through highly visible protests and statements. In November 2016, the Indonesian National Commission on Human Rights (Komnas HAM) came to Manado to meet with the mayor and representatives from several *adat* organizations to work toward a consensus about the future of the religious theme park and the Al-Khairiyah mosque.

PUBLIC DEBATES ABOUT BELONGING

The public debates that emerged over the religious theme park demonstrate the existence of a hegemonic normative frame that requires actors to signal agreement with the broad principle of religious harmony in order to be allowed to contribute to the public sphere. Yet, certain groups, particularly *adat* organizations, may be pursuing practical ends that ultimately challenge these dominant ethical norms, advancing instead a majoritarianism that relies on Christians maintaining their religious prominence and influence in the public domain.

Adat organizations react to what they understand as threats against or failures to uphold national principles by other groups. For example, in the event of a church burning in another province, they respond with a conception of religious coexistence as a zero-sum game. They leverage the position of Christians as a local majority, demonstrating regional dominance and justifying their actions as being in defense of national principles. The religious theme park debate, which relates to the allocation of space to various religious groups, also links to local assumptions about public space as implicitly Christian and to strong efforts to maintain a recognizably Christian public religiosity. Religious harmony in this sense is cast as the toleration of Muslims on a Christian land, and becomes used as a bargaining chip when the rights of Christians elsewhere in the nation are perceived as threatened.

The *adat* organizations that have become vocal in the public sphere around issues of belonging importantly engage in public reasoning that appeals to national ideologies and values. They position themselves as defenders of Pancasila in their claimed prevention of Islamist and anti-Pancasila groups in the region. They also project themselves as protecting religious freedom as they speak out on behalf of Indonesian Christians in other provinces who are local minorities. It is significant that these are the same values used as the justification and foundation for an aspirational religious coexistence based in mutual recognition and dialogue. However, the values are recast through an ambiguous though ultimately exclusivist frame of *adat* that has emerged in North Sulawesi, one that has not shied away from identity politics and acts out of a defensive concern about the future of the province and its Christian identity, in addition to the place and treatment of Christians in Indonesia more broadly.

The engagement of interreligious organizations and *adat* organizations in the public debate about the religious theme park helps to demonstrate the importance of putting forth ethical frames that can move across scales and resonate with public ethical culture. It is in this sense that the two major frames of belonging—the aspirational and the majoritarian—become clearly contested. In the context of these two frames, it becomes clear that the question at SMA about how to allocate space for worship and the reframing of citizenship taking place at Lokon School are also debates about the way in which belonging is conceived. Organizations and institutions are important for providing the possibility to expand these ethical deliberations and perspectives, making them public, and allowing them to be mobilized across scales. Institutions, whether schools or *adat* organizations, have particular infrastructures of communication that can be highly effective in disseminating various discourses about citizenship and plurality. Yet, the extent to which particular discourses gain traction depends not only on the potential infrastructures of communication but also on the extent to which the discourses promoted resonate with the public's personal experiences and concerns.

Mechanisms for scaling are important in explaining how some frameworks for belonging have become prominent in the public sphere. *Adat* organizations promote a Minahasan identity strongly linked to Christianity and have the ability to draw a large number of members or informal supporters by projecting their goals through a nationalist lens that ultimately reinforces local exclusion. Religious communities and interreligious organizations also play an important role in scaling as they provide the narrative of these major social debates, and religious leaders play a significant public role in responding to them. Yet, as this book has sought to make clear, consequential debate about belonging is also taking place through educational institutions, which represent both arenas for deliberation and potential avenues of scaling for the perspectives put forth. The case studies in the earlier chapters have shown how the transmission of these messages about national belonging and religious identity becomes localized within the context of Manado, and also constitutes public deliberation about the contours and conditions of belonging.

CONTESTED BELONGING

In North Sulawesi, there is a strong normative discourse of religious tolerance, which is used by the government and civil society actors in the public sphere. The appeals to coexistence are given shape by varied ethical currents, some of which look to religious and nationalist principles to support a working model of aspirational coexistence. However, a more exclusive frame put forth by many *adat* organizations positions ethnic Minahasans as insiders whose Christian religion is projected as the element that guarantees the peace of the region. The same discourse implicitly positions Muslims as outsiders whose loyalty to nationalist principles is suspect. The debate taking place about the nature of Minahasan *adat* and its relation to Christianity demonstrates vividly the tension between the desire to maintain the reputation of the area for its relatively peaceful interreligious relations and the push to guarantee the Christian-majority influence of the province in the future. Some well-known religious figures in the community have sought to develop the integrative potential that *adat* could serve in supporting some measure of religious coexistence in the region. Most *adat* organizations, however, look to national principles of religious freedom to advocate for the position of Christians within the national framework, pushing an exclusivist version of *adat* that has the potential to endanger local religious relations.

Each of these frames puts forth not merely a political position but also an ethical one, involving a particular perspective on how to approach religious difference. While they both claim to act in the name of maintaining religious harmony and coexistence, their understandings of how to ensure coexistence diverge. When it comes to the question of how these ethical perspectives become scaled, the role that institutions play is brought into focus. However, the frames of belonging that resonate are not necessarily those that are brought forth by highly institutionalized structures like schools or interreligious organizations. In the case of traditional organizations, an ambiguous frame of *adat* and the mobilization of identity politics have also been essential for these sometimes loose and fluid structures to gain such legitimacy and agency in the public sphere.

8

Conclusion
Pluralized Ethics for a Plural Society

In January 2018, my social media connections in Manado were abuzz in response to an incident involving a public school, a controversial Muslim preacher (*ustad*), and a Minahasan *adat* organization. The student Islamic organization Rohis at one public high school in Manado had organized an event and distributed flyers for a public seminar with the English title "Change Now for the Better Future." The advertised speaker was Felix Siauw, an ethnic Chinese Indonesian who was raised Catholic but converted to Islam while at university. Siauw, a popular preacher influential among Muslim youth, is as well known for his social media savvy and casual hipster style as for the radical views and teachings he promotes (Hew 2018). The main issue of contention was the *ustad*'s links to Hizbut Tahrir Indonesia (HTI), an Islamist organization that was outlawed by the administration of President Joko Widodo in 2017 on the grounds of its conflicting with Pancasila principles and challenging the legitimacy of the Indonesian state through its aim to establish a transnational caliphate. The event's flyer was circulated on Facebook by Aliansi Makapetor, accompanied by a strongly worded statement rejecting the presence of any representatives of radical organizations in Minahasa: "As indigenous Minahasans who hold fast to the four foundational pillars of our nation, we reject the presence of those who clearly bring a RADICAL understanding under the auspices of HTI (Hizbur Tahrir Indonesia) as well as other radical organizations that have been declared as forbidden organizations according to the Indonesian government, in MINAHASA."

The group, identifying themselves in ethnic terms as indigenous Minahasans (*masyarakat adat Minahasa*), added nationalist hashtags to the post, vowing support for Pancasila as the foundation of the Indonesian nation. As *adat* organizations called for protests, information about the event also spread in Muslim circles, and the local branch of traditionalist Nahdlatul

Ulama's youth organization Ansor began to organize their own protests against the event as well, underscoring their moderate views and reminding the public of their distance from Islamist groups like HTI. One North Sulawesi FKUB member saw the calls for protests on social media and immediately set up a meeting with religious leaders, actors from the provincial government, Islamic organizations, and the Islamic education teacher and representatives from the public high school that had planned the event. At the meeting, the groups ultimately came to the decision that the best course of action would be to revoke the invitation to the preacher and cancel the event.

The incident brings attention to the fact that schools can and do become highly intertwined in the broader public debates about religion, nation, and difference. This occurrence also highlights once again the contested frames of belonging in North Sulawesi. A Minahasan *adat* alliance sought to carve out its role as the protector of the (implicitly Christian) Minahasan homeland, claiming to champion nationalist values and to protect the region from outside threats, namely, radical Islamic organizations. Yet there were also clear official channels that were engaged by local religious leaders, highlighting the importance of infrastructure for interreligious communication, moderation, and attempts to champion aspirational coexistence. The meeting assembled quickly by FKUB members working with religious leaders and organizations was ultimately successful in defusing the situation, with all parties reportedly agreeing to cancel the invitation to the controversial preacher.

Schools often become caught up in debates about the role of religion in the public sphere and the mobilization of religious identities in expressions of belonging. In this case, concerns figured about radical teachings reaching impressionable young minds, but groups also sought to control the articulation of visions of nation and belonging presented to youth as normative. As this book has demonstrated, however, it is not only public debates about schools but also the deliberation taking place within them that has ramifications for negotiating the ethics of belonging.

ASPIRATIONAL AND MAJORITARIAN COEXISTENCE IN MANADO

This book has mapped the tensions between two contested ethical frames of belonging in Manado that emerge in deliberations on public and interpersonal scales. On the one hand, there is strong promotion of aspirational coexistence as normative, wherein belonging is guaranteed by mutual recognition and dialogue, and justified in reference to nationalist principles as well as citizens' respective religious doctrines. This vision of belonging is promoted in many ways in the schools discussed, such as through the national civic education curriculum, and also negotiated through local frames of pride in the region's status and the hopes of Manado not only contributing to national development but shaping its future by serving as an exemplar for the rest of the country. Aspirational coexistence is decidedly put forth as normative, clear through the repeated injunctions to respect and value difference heard in different contexts within and beyond schools. Yet, it is also challenged by a majoritarian coexistence, or the idea that the peaceful coexistence in the region is guaranteed by Christians as the majority. The projection of Christians as the hosts and owners of the land—and, consequently, of Muslims as settlers (*pendatang*)—implies belonging as something guaranteed by the goodwill of the majority. In turn, the terms of this relationship can be called into question and used as leverage when national principles are perceived as threatened, or the precarious position of Christians elsewhere in Indonesia is thrown into the spotlight.

In public debates, tensions between these two frames of coexistence come to the surface, as seen in the local debates about building a religious theme park in Manado. They also emerge in responses to national events, as they did in protests against the trial and imprisonment of Ahok, the ethnic Chinese Christian who lost his reelection bid as the governor of Jakarta, as he became embroiled in controversy over and was ultimately charged with blasphemy against Islam. In the classrooms of the public school in Manado, Ahok had been positively regarded as an example of the way people of all religions can play a prominent role in the country's politics. His fall, indicative of the strong influence of conservative Islamic groups on the level of national politics, led many Christians in Manado to question their role and participation in the national project of Indonesia. These public debates relate to the very fabric of the national project, as individuals consider varied frames of belonging and their mediation of religious, ethnic, and national identity.

Notions of belonging are also deliberated on a daily basis in schools, not just as political questions, but as ethical questions about how to approach difference. I have asserted the importance of attending to the kinds of deliberation taking place in schools, for example, students at the public school SMA imagining their majority or minority status and positioning themselves relative to their classmates from different religious backgrounds. Or the teachers at MAN proposing a specific model of Islamically grounded ethical self-making, with consequences for how one should strive toward being a good and tolerant citizen, able to deliberate about what this means in a plural society. Deliberation is also clearly taking place at Lokon, as the founders and the administration seek to position the school as an example of the contribution that Christians can make toward the future of Indonesia.

PLURALITY AND BELONGING AMID A "CONSERVATIVE TURN"

As mentioned in the introduction, scholars and cultural observers have recently drawn attention to what has been called an ongoing "conservative turn" in Indonesian Islam (Van Bruinessen 2013), raising concerns about the future of democracy as well as the status of religious minorities in Indonesia. In political terms, an increased reliance on identity politics has at times meant encouraging sectarianism by exaggerating the internal agreement among Muslims and projecting a stark and essentialized difference from other religious groups, mobilized for political ends. These tendencies have overlapped and coincided with a surge of Islamic populism, at times working toward markedly conservative and anti-pluralist aims (Hadiz 2018, 569). Ahok's political downfall is an apt example, as highly coordinated mass protests certainly gave the impression that Islamic conservatism and populist tendencies were becoming increasingly vocal and influential, if not mainstream. At the same time, there are indications that there remains broad support for a pluralist "civil Islam" in this ongoing negotiation between Islam and citizenship in Indonesia (R. W. Hefner 2019, 390).

The ethnographic analysis throughout the preceding chapters has demonstrated the importance of situating these observed developments within broader political and ethical debates about belonging. The tendency toward intolerance with regards to religious minorities is not an exclusive feature of a conservative turn within Islam, but can also be seen in other Indonesian religious contexts, including in North Sulawesi. The tension between aspirational coexistence and a more exclusivist majoritarian manifestation of belonging as they emerge in Manado and North Sulawesi are linked to concerns about what is perceived as the increasingly threatened position of Christians on the national stage, resulting in different strategies. The case of North Sulawesi, where the majority/minority dynamics between

Muslims and Christians are flipped compared to the nation overall, provides an important perspective on responses to these trends in a region where Christians have some leverage as a local majority, yet are also hyperaware of their minority status on the national level. However, viewing this as a uniquely political issue provides only a partial account. The politics are entangled with ethical questions related to religious identity, belonging, and coexistence.

In politically focused discussions on identity politics, there is often an emphasis on how starkly drawn religious boundaries are, with the assumption that interpersonal interactions with religiously different others will break down barriers and increase tolerance toward religious groups more broadly. Yet, as a focus on interpersonal interactions (particularly in chapter 6) has demonstrated, there are often simultaneous processes of commensuration and incommensuration in encounters of religious others, contextually emphasizing or erasing religious boundaries in a continuing negotiation of difference. Both of these processes are at times required to make building up an ethics across borders thinkable and actionable. These findings go beyond a projection of religious identity as nothing but a barrier or boundary to interaction that can be heightened and mobilized for political ends. Rather, religious identity is fundamentally related to notions of self and other, constantly negotiated in interpersonal interactions as well as in societal debates in the public sphere.

Despite analyses claiming a continued hardening of religious boundaries, as one might expect with the increasing influence of Islamic conservatism, the case studies in these chapters have shown that deliberation about the significance of religious difference is ongoing. The salience of religious boundaries is not simply heightened in the current political climate; boundaries are instead continuously negotiated on multiple levels. Though an increasing emphasis on religious boundaries can go along with the mobilization of religious identity for political ends, in the case of interreligious dialogue, it can also be required to forge an ethics across borders. At SMA, Lokon, and MAN, the processes of commensuration and incommensuration that are taking place in the context of ethical deliberation about religious difference are ongoing in various ways. For example, at Lokon School, the administration engages deeply in a form of commensuration through a multicultural approach, though it is ultimately implemented through a situated Catholic universalism.

Just as it is important to understand the contextual significance of religious difference and its ethical negotiation, it is also important to consider processes of deliberation taking place on various levels. This book has interrogated an assumption of interpersonal and public ethical culture as mere analogues, focusing particularly on the question of religious and national belonging. The significance of religious boundaries does not necessarily remain across various levels (interpersonal, institutional, public) as individuals negotiate embodied and discursive forms of religious belonging and difference in everyday encounters and navigate different modes of subjectivity.

LINKING INTERPERSONAL AND PUBLIC ETHICAL DELIBERATION

Youth in Manado and across Indonesia are encountering imaginaries of belonging, acquiring an understanding of how they fit in their neighborhoods and in the nation. These frameworks are not exclusively channeled by educational institutions, but schools are critical arenas of deliberation. While trying to fulfill multiple roles and working toward various aspirations, youth draw on ideas of coexistence and belonging that depend on varying modes of subjectivity, a process that requires ethnographic sensitivity in order to uncover how these individual and interpersonal ambiguities can potentially have a bearing on the broader structures contributing to them. This is where the institutional level offers important insights for illuminating the connections between the deliberations taking place in the public sphere and the everyday, localized, interpersonal interactions.

This book has offered a framework for rethinking how interpersonal ethical deliberation connects to the emergence of a public ethical culture. Debates about plurality and citizenship in Manado's public sphere (chapter 7) have evinced tension between two frames of belonging, as some groups sought to promote Manado as a place of diversity in harmony, while others prioritized maintaining its status as a Christian-majority region. The case studies of particular schools have demonstrated how aspects of these debates were differentially channeled through them. This tension manifests in the public high school SMA, as its administration promotes the celebration of religion and diversity discursively while securing a Protestant majoritarianism enacted through the use of space, sound, dress, and food, and expressed through identities and positionality framed in relation to Christians as a local majority and national minority. At the private Catholic school Lokon, questions about diversity and cohesion are reframed as national issues, where students are encouraged to become Christian leaders of the nation, yet local and historical circumstances contribute to the possibility of the school's existence and motivate this desire to put North Sulawesi more centrally in the national imaginary. Debates in the public sphere impact the strategy of teachers at MAN to give Muslim students the solid religious foundation required to remain strong in their faith as a minority in their local environment, as well as to properly enact tolerance toward religious others.

The analysis of the Catholic school Lokon (chapter 4) most directly addresses the links between small-scale deliberation and public ethical culture in critiquing the evaluation of post–New Order development projects as decidedly neoliberal in their approach toward producing pious, self-governing subjects (Rudnyckyj 2010). I demonstrate how the school's approach manifests not only an attempt at self-transformation, but also a commitment and contribution to a multiconfessional Indonesia as a certain kind of moral community. Ethnographic attention shows how this goal is again deliberated by youth (and teachers) as they run into obstacles implementing the school's multicultural vision, which generally tends to advocate for an erasure of difference through the lens of Catholic universalism.

The strength of this approach lies in the consideration of deliberation at multiple levels, applying an interactive and processual conception of education. Through this analysis, it becomes clear how deliberation and the forms of agency it entails can impact social structures at a number of different levels, starting small but ultimately proving significant in the potential to impact public ethical culture. This understanding is linked to an intentional focus on the role of institutions in the deliberation taking place on these multiple levels, as well as a theoretical perspective of education as a process.

ETHICS, DELIBERATION, AND INSTITUTIONS

This book has taken schools as important arenas of deliberation and as institutions that can shed light on the connections between interpersonal and societal-level ethical deliberations on religious difference. These linkages demonstrate why institutions should figure more centrally into ongoing theoretical conversations on ethics. The anthropology of ethics has highlighted the level of individual subjectivity, bringing insight into the ambiguities and uncertainties experienced by individuals (Schielke 2009), and the significance of ordinary and everyday interpersonal interactions (Das 2010; Lambek 2010; Mattingly 2014b). It has also at times downplayed the entanglements of ethics and politics. While some works have offered linkages to "grand schemes" (Schielke and Debevec 2012) or to broad moral systems (Robbins 2004), they have done so without mechanisms to explore how these broad ethical systems relate to the individual subjective experience. A notable exception is David Kloos's (2018) analysis of ethical striving in Aceh, Indonesia, which links the reflections taking place about how to properly implement Islamic values in everyday life to shifts in religious and state authority in the post-tsunami context. In doing so, he points to the necessity of being cognizant of the entanglements of ethics and politics, going beyond caricatures of religious and political identity and demonstrating how ethical discourses are able to resonate on multiple levels.

A theoretical approach to ethics that is concerned with the emergence of ethical frameworks only through everyday interactions potentially overlooks the streams of ethical traditions socialized by the institutions that sustain them. It is in this context that I intervene, arguing for the importance of investigating institutions as a mechanism toward discerning the relationship between multiple levels of social analysis. By taking schools as the point of departure—but not the exclusive site of my analysis—I have shed light on the process of ethical deliberation taking place within and beyond them, influenced by public ethical streams yet always located in particular school environments. This approach has sought to build up an understanding of how public debates and a constant reworking of public ethical currents can ultimately become channeled through (or sidelined by) schools and, in turn, put into action in varied ways by youth. Youth navigate ambiguous and sometimes seemingly contradictory imperatives, figuring out how best to act and to move forward while necessarily working within and among multiple ethical frameworks. While this navigation certainly takes place as ethical discourse becomes grounded in individual subjectivities, it also takes place through deliberation, where political realities impinge on this social and interpersonal process.

In framing political questions about the place of religion within the national imaginary as fundamentally ethical questions about inclusion and exclusion of the Other, I have elucidated the links between politics and ethics, and the ways in which they are entangled in deliberation about national belonging and the treatment of religious difference. For example, as Muslim students at MAN discuss whether only Muslims must avoid vices like hedonism or whether all people should be held to these standards, they are weighing how their religious teachings can be applied in a plural society. Catholics, Protestants, and students of other religious backgrounds come together at

Lokon to support a multicultural vision for Indonesia where Christian elites can impact the future of the country, but face obstacles in implementing everyday ethnic inclusion on the school campus. A Protestant student at the public school SMA asks how to respond in a Christian way to Muslims in Java protesting the building of a church, and a teacher replies with essentialized portraits of Christians as promoting love and Muslims as categorically against *orang kafir* (unbelievers, infidels). These instances of deliberation link both to interpersonal situations and localized settings, but also draw on politically tinged evaluations and figurations of others, as well as individuals' religiously mediated personhood, pointing to a mutual entanglement of ethics and politics that a focus on institutions can help to bridge.

Some instances of deliberation recounted were impassioned, like the teacher's speech that dovetailed with a majoritarian Protestant frame of belonging in Manado and voiced grievances related to the national situation of Christians. Others appeared banal, like the Muslim students wondering about the application of Islamic ethics in a plural society, whose question was ultimately brushed aside and never authoritatively answered. At times, deliberation was prompted by a clear administrative directive, like the multicultural education approach of Lokon. Others transpired primarily from interactions among students, like the Muslim girls at the public high school SMA negotiating together a way to participate in the school's dance team while maintaining modesty and propriety in line with Islamic principles.

In other words, the call for increased attention to institutions should not be interpreted as a call to describe institutional landscapes as flat and homogeneous, but rather a mechanism toward linking levels of analysis for which varied topographies, outlined through ethnographic detail, provide important evidence about the channeling of public ethical streams. In each of the three schools studied, debates about diversity are framed by the policies and everyday realities at the school. As the schools implement a national curriculum for both civic and religious education, it takes on specific meaning in Manado, where public discourses establish the importance of religious harmony for local identity without a clear blueprint for how to maintain it. The local context also shapes messages about religious diversity while moving toward a public sphere shaped by the tension between aspirational and majoritarian conceptions of belonging.

Using institutions as a point of departure further underscores how the frameworks for approaching religious difference in operation are not simply the result of a top-down internalization based on political doctrine or national ideology. The significant variation in the implementation of the national curriculum in these three main schools has made this reality abundantly clear. But even as each school pushes particular notions of belonging through discourse and practice at the institutional level, this still only provides a partial picture of the process of education as it unfolds. It is necessary to consider not only how the broad ethical streams in society influence the implementation of the curriculum and school policies in particular school contexts, but how they are deliberated and reshaped by this process.

For an anthropology of ethics that has concerned itself primarily with subjectivities, the individual has often taken primacy. This level of analysis is important, as ethical discourse becomes grounded in individual subjectivities. However, ethical reflection does not take place exclusively at the individual subjective level. Indeed, ethical subjects "can only be understood as emerging and sustained through historically instituted institutions, practices, and relations" (Laidlaw 2014, 179). Bringing in the institutional level can help to remedy this oversight, facilitating a mapping of ethical streams of influence that can potentially be scaled up. Rather than simply considering politics as a macro-level influence, this ethnographic approach toward schools as sites of deliberation has pointed to co-imbrication and mutual influence of ethics and politics and also has important insights for the anthropology of education.

EDUCATIONAL AND ETHICAL PROCESSES

The process of ethical reflection, spurred by the inevitability of ethical pluralism, is described by James Laidlaw as "reflective freedom" (2014, 177), and understood as central to ethical subject formation. It is also a fundamentally pedagogical process, with the potential to enrich a discussion about how ethical frameworks are socialized through institutions and traditions as well as everyday interactions taking place within these contexts. I have also indicated that bringing this perspective to the study of education can offer an insightful reframing of pedagogical processes. Rejecting static or top-down models of education, I have considered this pedagogical perspective on ethical reflection alongside a theoretical understanding of education as "deliberation" (Varenne 2007), wherein moments of learning through deliberation are important because of their potential to impact future actions. This theoretical approach to education, in its insistence that deliberation is a social activity, can also encourage studies of ethics that consider the dynamics and the consequences of interpersonal and public ethical deliberation, rather than exclusively documenting the individual subjective level.

While studies of ethics in relation to education might focus more heavily on the disciplinary aspects of pedagogy, I have instead put the focus on deliberation. This is not to deny the importance of ethical discipline in educational projects, as it becomes clear in each of the schools that teachers and administrators are highly focused on the goal of providing a religious (and ethical) foundation for their students by instituting religious discipline and practice. However, in focusing primarily on deliberation, I have situated it as an important aspect that is necessarily interrelated to regimes of ethical discipline (Hirschkind 2006). Recognizing this relationship helps to avoid assumptions about the modes of deliberation that may be engaged, particularly a view of deliberation that rests too heavily on its liberal, democratic interpretations.

The case studies presented throughout the book demonstrate that ethical deliberation (as a social activity) does not take place only through rational discourse. Discourse and argumentation are certainly important, as teachers continue to repeat the motto of aspirational coexistence, *"Torang Samua Basudara,"* or as students at Lokon remind each other not to be racist. When they do so, they also often cite particular ethical principles, drawing on religious teachings, ideas of citizenship, and other anchoring beliefs. Yet, the experience of and the response to the Other is also embodied. At the public high school SMA, as worship time begins, the public courtyard of the school is suddenly transformed into a Protestant space, an act that is not spoken, but that effectively shifts how individuals in that space are perceived to belong. Questions about who belongs are answered not only with words but with visceral reactions that also influence this process of deliberation. This can occur through social interactions involving food, for example, the provision of halal food for Muslim guests perceived as a gesture toward coexistence. Approaches toward diversity are not only explicitly talked about, they are enacted. Different ethical frameworks coexist, imbricate, and come to heads through discourse, but also through embodied practices, pointing to the importance of ethnographic observation and analysis of the forms of ethical reflection and deliberation.

In closing, I return to the madrasah classroom where Ibu Aisyah challenged her students to think about how to respect and value diversity as Indonesian citizens and as Muslims. As youth in Manado consider what this means in their own lives and their own relationships, they find themselves deliberating and navigating among varied ethical frameworks. This does not automatically mean that these moral registers will manifest for them as conflictual or contradictory. Ethical pluralism is central to the human experience, and is not necessarily experienced subjectively as a clash of values.

An examination of deliberation about ethical values underscores that living in light of ethical frameworks or an ethical tradition is not about a simple internalization of such values. It depends, rather, on the process of ongoing deliberation about which values to aspire toward, and how best to implement them. Youth in Manado are exposed to seemingly contradictory discourses about how to be pious, tolerant individuals and how to respect diversity. In other words, to speak of internalization here would be meaningless. Rather, ethical reflection must be examined as part of a pedagogical process in all of its contingency and uncertainty.

The centrality of deliberation about the ethics of belonging is certainly not unique to Manado or to Indonesia. On the contrary, in the historical moment in which this book was written, amid a continuing resurgence in populist movements and the evolution of a global pandemic that has exposed social fault lines in all societies, different visions of belonging are continuously being deliberated. This book has emphasized the ways in which educational institutions play a role in this process of deliberation, underscoring the ethical positioning that is inherent in questions about belonging, as well as the political and institutional realities that shape instances of deliberation.

NOTES

CHAPTER 1: INTRODUCTION

1. In Indonesia, a madrasah typically refers to an Islamic day school that covers lessons in both religious and secular subjects.
2. "Ibu" is the title of address for a woman in Indonesian, and "Pak" is the title of address for a man. All names used in the manuscript are pseudonyms, except references to public figures.
3. The Manadonese term *sudara* (like the Indonesian term *saudara*) is not gendered.
4. In this book, I use the term "Christian" to refer collectively to both Protestants and Catholics, or to talk about a broader Christian ethic or identity that is neither exclusively Protestant nor Catholic. My usage differs from the most common Indonesian usage of the terms, where "Christian" (*Kristen*) typically refers exclusively to Protestants, "Catholic" (*Katolik*) is used to refer to Catholics, and Protestantism and Catholicism are officially considered separate religions according to the Ministry of Religious Affairs. However, Indonesian Protestants and Catholics in North Sulawesi do often group themselves together when comparing themselves to Muslims, which is why in this case I discuss the attempt to promote a "Christian" atmosphere in a broad sense, as it works against what is perceived as the encroaching influence of Islam.
5. The Indonesian government recognizes Islam, Catholicism, Protestantism, Hinduism, Buddhism, and Confucianism as official religions. See chapter 2 for an outline of debates regarding the relationship between religion and state in Indonesia and a more detailed discussion of state policies toward religion.
6. Pancasila, meaning "five principles" (belief in a supreme God, just and civilized humanitarianism, national unity, consensual democracy, and social justice), is the foundation of the Indonesian nation. It is discussed in more detail in chapter 2.
7. This portion of the research was conducted under the scope of a project on Indonesian pluralities that brought together researchers from Boston University's Institute on Culture, Religion and World Affairs (CURA) and Universitas Gadjah Mada's Center for Religious and Cross-Cultural Studies (CRCS) and culminated in the publication of an edited volume (Hefner and Bagir 2021). The chapter on coexistence in Manado (Larson 2021) provides a broader social mapping of ethico-religious communities, analyses of incidents that brought up debates regarding pluralities, and the public reasoning and justification advanced in these debates.

CHAPTER 2: RELIGION, NATION, AND POLITICS OF DIFFERENCE THROUGH THE LENS OF EDUCATION

1 "Menolak segala kecenderungan dan usaha yang hendak memecah-belah keutuhan dan kebersamaan bangsa Indonesia di dalam NKRI dengan cara memasukkan gagasan 'Piagam Djakarta' dan bentuk-bentuk sejenisnya dalam bentuk apa pun ke dalam UUD 1945." The text of the recommendations from the Kongres Minahasa Raya (2000) was accessed from the personal archives of Bodewyn Grey Talumewo (n.d.), Minahasan historian.
2 The name of the Muslim students' club Rohis is an abbreviation of Rohani Islam (Islamic Spirituality), and the name of the Protestant students' club Rohkris is an abbreviation of Rohani Kristen (Christian Spirituality).
3 The abbreviation P4 (*P-empat*) is short for "Pedoman Penghayatan dan Pengalaman Pancasila."
4 The Campus Normalization Law, enacted in 1978, required university campuses to remain free from political activity. The repressive requirements of the law abolished student councils and banned student publications, among other measures of control (Aspinall 2005, 120).
5 I do not address the 2004 Competence-Based Curriculum, as it was quickly replaced by the 2006 School-Based Curriculum.
6 For example, within the text, there is a discussion of Q 10:40–41 and the importance of being tolerant toward nonbelievers. There is also a discussion of Q 5:32 and condemning actions that might harm others, especially violent actions.
7 Within the chapter, the following Bible verses are listed as references to support the teachings about diversity: 1 Peter 3:15, Galatians 3:28, Genesis 1:28, and Genesis 11:1–9.

CHAPTER 3: PUBLIC HIGH SCHOOL

1 In Manado, Valentine's Day is celebrated as a Christian holiday about God's love and the reflection of that love among his followers, as well as having popular connotations about romantic love.
2 *Dakwah* refers to outreach, either toward a deepening of piety among fellow Muslims or proselytization.
3 Referring to practices like veiling or closely following halal prescriptions as *fanatik* is not done exclusively by Christians, but also by traditionalist Muslims who might reject such practices, particularly those that are perceived as influenced by Salafism (Chao 2014, 247–248).
4 This lesson took place during the gubernatorial race in Jakarta, when Ahok was running for reelection, but before he became embroiled in accusations of blasphemy against Islam.

CHAPTER 4: PRIVATE CATHOLIC HIGH SCHOOL

Chapter 4 was originally published as "Developing Faith and Character to Develop the Nation: Perspectives from an Elite Indonesian Catholic School" in *The Mission of Development: Religion and Techno-Politics in Asia*, edited by Catherine Scheer, Philip Fountain, and R. Michael Feener. Leiden: Brill. Reprinted here with permission.

1. Batavia (on the island of Java) was the capital of the Dutch East Indies; it corresponds to present-day Jakarta.
2. The Morning Star flag is used by supporters of the Papuan independence movement. Raising the Morning Star flag is illegal in Indonesia, and those who do it can be charged with treason.

CHAPTER 5: PUBLIC MADRASAH

1. *"Astaga!"* is an expression of shock that can be roughly translated as "Oh my!" in this context, and is a shortened version of *"Astagfirullah"* (I seek forgiveness in Allah).
2. This discrepancy in overall hours per week spent at school is also partially due to the public school SMA's implementation of the national School-Based Curriculum (KTSP), which results in fewer classroom hours overall.
3. Derived from Arabic, *aurat* is a term that refers to parts of the body that should remain covered according to Islamic teachings.

CHAPTER 6: INTERRELIGIOUS EXCHANGE

1. Al-Kafirun is a chapter in the Qur'an that contains the verse (Q 109:6) interpreted as "To you be your religion, and to me my religion." The verse is commonly cited by Muslims in Manado as providing important guidance for living in a plural society. It is interesting to note that Burhani (2011, 330) has argued that this verse also underlies the national Islamic organization Muhammadiyah's approach to interfaith relations, with varying theological and sociological consequences.

CHAPTER 7: GOING PUBLIC

Portions of this chapter were originally published as "Scaling Plural Coexistence in Manado: What Does It Take to Remain Brothers?" in *Indonesian Pluralities: Islam, Citizenship, and Democracy*, edited by Robert W. Hefner and

Zainal Abidin Bagir. Notre Dame, IN: University of Notre Dame Press. Reprinted here with permission.

1. These representatives are from each of the official religions in Indonesia except Confucianism.
2. *Waraney* is a Minahasan term referring to a warrior or "someone elected in the Minahasan cultural order to guard or protect" (Tambayong 2007, 359, my translation).
3. *Walisongo* are figures, sometimes referred to as saints, who are recognized as having played a role in the spread of Islam in Java in the fourteenth century
4. It is interesting to compare and contrast the Minahasan case with the strong link between Minangkabau *adat* and Islamic identity. Jeffrey Hadler discusses *adat* as a "dynamic system" (2008, 179) that has at times conflated shari'a with *adat*, but has continuously evolved to incorporate new practices and understandings while maintaining both *adat* and Islamic practices.
5. Kyai Modjo and approximately sixty of his male followers were exiled to Kampung Jawa Tondano (in Minahasa) by the Dutch colonial government in the 1830s. They settled there and married local Minahasan women (Babcock 1981).
6. *"I Yayat U Santi!"* literally means "Raise and point up your sword!" and is often shouted by *waraney* during the *kabasaran* sword dance. According to GMIM pastor, professor, and Minahasan cultural observer W. A. Roeroe, the *kabasaran* dance and the cry *"I Yayat U Santi!"* are not limited to the narrow context of war but should also be understood as calling people to come together with determination to face challenges and continue moving forward without retreating (Roeroe 2003).

WORKS CITED

Abu-Lughod, Lila. 2005. *Dramas of Nationhood: The Politics of Television in Egypt.* Chicago: University of Chicago Press.

Adely, Fida. 2012. *Gendered Paradoxes: Educating Jordanian Women in Nation, Faith, and Progress.* Chicago: University of Chicago Press.

Adely, Fida, and James Seale-Collazo. 2013. "Introduction to Special Issue: Ethnographies of Religious Education." *Anthropology and Education Quarterly* 44 (4): 340–344.

Allison, Anne. 1991. "Japanese Mothers and Obentos: The Lunch-Box as Ideological State Apparatus." *Anthropological Quarterly* 64 (4): 195–208.

Anderson, Benedict. 2006 [1983]. *Imagined Communities: Reflections on the Origin and Spread of Nationalism.* New York: Verso.

Anderson, Bobby. 2013. "The Failure of Education in Papua's Highlands." *Inside Indonesia* 113 (July–September). http://www.insideindonesia.org/the-failure-of-education-in-papua-s-highlands.

Aragon, Lorraine V. 2000. *Fields of the Lord: Animism, Christian Minorities, and State Development in Indonesia.* Honolulu: University of Hawai'i Press.

Asad, Talal. 1993. *Genealogies of Religion: Discipline and Reasons of Power in Christianity and Islam.* Baltimore, MD: Johns Hopkins University Press.

———. 2003. *Formations of the Secular: Christianity, Islam, Modernity.* Stanford, CA: Stanford University Press.

Aspinall, Edward. 2005. *Opposing Suharto: Compromise, Resistance, and Regime Change in Indonesia.* Stanford, CA: Stanford University Press.

Azra, Azyumardi, Dina Afrianty, and Robert W. Hefner. 2007. "Pesantren and Madrasa: Muslim Schools and National Ideals in Indonesia." In *Schooling Islam: The Culture and Politics of Modern Muslim Education*, edited by Robert W. Hefner and Muhammad Qasim Zaman, pp. 172–198. Princeton, NJ: Princeton University Press.

Babcock, Tim. 1981. "Muslim Minahasans with Roots in Java: The People of Kampung Jawa Tondano." *Indonesia* 32:75–92.

Badan Pusat Statistik Sulawesi Utara (Statistics Indonesia—North Sulawesi). 2021. "Provinsi Sulawesi Utara Dalam Angka 2021" (North Sulawesi province in figures 2021). Accessed June 6, 2021. https://sulut.bps.go.id/publication/2021/02/26/ef5603fcc2c336b42cc0e4a5/provinsi-sulawesi-utara-dalam-angka-2021.html.

Bagir, Zainal Abidin. 2011. *Pluralisme Kewargaan: Arah Baru Politik Keragaman Di Indonesia* (Civic pluralism: New directions of the politics of diversity in Indonesia). Yogyakarta: Center for Religious and Cross-Cultural Studies, Gadjah Mada University.

Bakker, Laurens. 2016. "Organized Violence and the State: Evolving Vigilantism in Indonesia." *Bijdragen Tot de Taal-, Land- En Volkenkunde* 172 (2/3): 249–277.

Bamualim, Chaider S. 2011. "Islamic Militancy and Resentment against Hadhramis in Post-Suharto Indonesia: A Case Study of Habib Rizieq Syihab and His Islamic Defenders Front." *Comparative Studies of South Asia, Africa and the Middle East* 31 (2): 267–281.

Berger, Peter L. 2014. *The Many Altars of Modernity: Toward a Paradigm for Religion in a Pluralist Age*. Boston: De Gruyter.

Berkey, Jonathan P. 1992. *The Transmission of Knowledge in Medieval Cairo: A Social History of Islamic Education*. Princeton, NJ: Princeton University Press.

Bertrand, Jacques. 2004. *Nationalism and Ethnic Conflict in Indonesia*. Cambridge: Cambridge University Press.

Bhargava, Rajeev. 1998. "What Is Secularism For?" In *Secularism and Its Critics*, edited by Rajeev Bhargava, pp. 486–542. Oxford: Oxford University Press.

Boellstorff, Tom. 2005. *The Gay Archipelago: Sexuality and Nation in Indonesia*. Princeton, NJ: Princeton University Press.

Bornstein, Erica. 2003. *The Spirit of Development: Protestant NGOs, Morality, and Economics in Zimbabwe*. London: Routledge.

Boroma, Suhendro, and Ismit Alkartiri. 2003. *Soft Opening Monumen Bukit Kasih Toar Lumimuut: Tahun Kasih 2003 No Violence* (Soft opening for the Bukit Kasih monument, Toar-Lumimuut: The Year of Love 2003 No Violence).

Bourdieu, Pierre. 1977. *Outline of a Theory of Practice*. Translated by Richard Nice. Cambridge: Cambridge University Press.

Boutieri, Charis. 2013. "Inheritance, Heritage, and the Disinherited: Ambiguities of Religious Pedagogy in the Moroccan Public School." *Anthropology and Education Quarterly* 44 (4): 363–380.

Bowen, John R. 2010. *Can Islam Be French? Pluralism and Pragmatism in a Secularist State*. Princeton, NJ: Princeton University Press.

———. 2013. "Contours of Sharia in Indonesia." In *Democracy and Islam in Indonesia*, edited by Mirjam Künkler and Alfred Stepan, pp. 149–167. New York: Columbia University Press.

Bräuchler, Birgit. 2009. "Cultural Solutions to Religious Conflicts? The Revival of Tradition in the Moluccas, Eastern Indonesia." *Asian Journal of Social Science* 37 (6): 872–891.

Brenner, Suzanne. 1996. "Reconstructing Self and Society: Javanese Muslim Women and 'the Veil.'" *American Ethnologist* 23 (4): 673–697.

Brown, Wendy. 2006. *Regulating Aversion: Tolerance in the Age of Identity and Empire*. Princeton, NJ: Princeton University Press.
Bucholtz, Mary. 2011. *White Kids: Language, Race, and Styles of Youth Identity*. Cambridge: Cambridge University Press.
Burchell, David. 1995. "The Attributes of Citizens: Virtue, Manners and the Activity of Citizenship." *Economy and Society* 24 (4): 540–558.
Burhani, Ahmad Najib. 2011. "*Lakum dīnukum wa-liya dīnī*: The Muhammadiyah's Stance towards Interfaith Relations." *Islam and Christian-Muslim Relations* 22 (3): 329–342.
Bush, Robin. 2008. "Regional Sharia Regulations in Indonesia: Anomaly or Symptom?" In *Expressing Islam: Religious Life and Politics in Indonesia*, edited by Greg Fealy and Sally White, pp. 174–191. Singapore: Institute of Southeast Asian Studies.
Calhoun, Craig. 1992. "Introduction." In *Habermas and the Public Sphere*, edited by Craig Calhoun, pp. 1–50. Cambridge, MA: MIT Press.
Calhoun, Craig, Mark Juergensmeyer, and Jonathan VanAntwerpen. 2011. "Introduction." In *Rethinking Secularism*, edited by Craig Calhoun, Mark Juergensmeyer, and Jonathan VanAntwerpen, pp. 3–30. Oxford: Oxford University Press.
Casanova, José. 1994. *Public Religions in the Modern World*. Chicago: University of Chicago Press.
———. 2006. "Secularization Revisited: A Reply to Talal Asad." In *Powers of the Secular Modern: Talal Asad and His Interlocutors*, edited by David Scott and Charles Hirschkind, pp. 12–30. Stanford, CA: Stanford University Press.
Chao, En-Chieh. 2014. "'Not Fanatical': The Evolution of Sociable Piety and the Dialogic Subject in Multi-religious Indonesia." *Asia Pacific Journal of Anthropology* 15 (3): 242–264.
Coe, Cati. 2005. *Dilemmas of Culture in African Schools: Youth, Nationalism, and the Transformation of Knowledge*. Chicago: University of Chicago Press.
Cremin, Lawrence. 1976. *Public Education*. New York: Basic Books.
Crouch, Melissa. 2014. *Law and Religion in Indonesia: Conflict and the Courts in West Java*. Milton Park: Routledge.
Das, Veena. 2010. "Engaging the Life of the Other: Love and Everyday Life." In *Ordinary Ethics: Anthropology, Language, and Action*, edited by Michael Lambek, pp. 376–399. New York: Fordham University Press.
de Jonge, Christiaan, Arnold Parengkuan, and Karel A. Steenbrink. 2008. "How Christianity Obtained a Central Position in Minahasa Culture and Society." In *A History of Christianity in Indonesia*, edited by Jan S. Aritonang and Karel A. Steenbrink, pp. 419–454. Leiden: Brill.
Deeb, Lara, and Mona Harb. 2013. *Leisurely Islam: Negotiating Geography and Morality in Shi'ite South Beirut*. Princeton, NJ: Princeton University Press.

Dewey, John. 1916. *Democracy and Education: An Introduction to the Philosophy of Education.* New York: Macmillan.

Dill, Jeffrey S. 2007. "Durkheim and Dewey and the Challenge of Contemporary Moral Education." *Journal of Moral Education* 36 (2): 221–237.

Doumato, Eleanor, and Gregory Starrett, eds. 2007. *Teaching Islam: Textbooks and Religion in the Middle East.* Boulder, CO: Lynne Rienner Publishers.

Duncan, Christopher R. 2005. "Unwelcome Guests: Relations between Internally Displaced Persons and Their Hosts in North Sulawesi, Indonesia." *Journal of Refugee Studies* 18 (1): 25–46.

———. 2013. *Violence and Vengeance: Religious Conflict and Its Aftermath in Eastern Indonesia.* Ithaca, NY: Cornell University Press.

Eckert, Penelope. 1989. *Jocks and Burnouts: Social Categories and Identity in the High School.* New York: Teachers College Press.

Eickelman, Dale F. 1985. *Knowledge and Power in Morocco: The Education of a Twentieth-Century Notable.* Princeton, NJ: Princeton University Press.

Eisenberg, Andrew J. 2020. "Resonant Voices and Spatial Politics: An Acoustemology of Citizenship in a Muslim Neighborhood of the Kenyan Coast." In *Worship Sound Spaces*, edited by Christine Guillebaud and Catherine Lavandier, pp. 140–157. London: Routledge.

Ewing, Katherine P. 1990. "The Illusion of Wholeness: Culture, Self, and the Experience of Inconsistency." *Ethos* 18 (3): 251–278.

Fader, Ayala. 2009. *Mitzvah Girls: Bringing Up the Next Generation of Hasidic Jews in Brooklyn.* Princeton, NJ: Princeton University Press.

Fearnley-Sander, Mary, and Ella Yulaelawati. 2008. "Citizenship Discourse in the Context of Decentralisation: The Case of Indonesia." In *Citizenship Curriculum in Asia and the Pacific*, edited by David L. Grossman, Wing On Lee, and Kerry J. Kennedy, pp. 111–126. Hong Kong: Comparative Education Research Centre.

Ferguson, James. 1990. *The Anti-Politics Machine: "Development," Depoliticization, and Bureaucratic Power in Lesotho.* Cambridge: Cambridge University Press.

Fortna, Benjamin C. 2003. *Imperial Classroom: Islam, the State, and Education in the Late Ottoman Empire.* Oxford: Oxford University Press.

Foucault, Michel. 1997. *Ethics: Subjectivity and Truth.* Edited by Paul Rabinow and Robert Hurley. New York: New Press.

Fountain, Philip, Robin Bush, and R. Michael Feener. 2015. "Religion and the Politics of Development." In *Religion and the Politics of Development*, edited by Philip Fountain, Robin Bush, and R. Michael Feener, pp. 11–34. New York: Palgrave Macmillan.

Fox, Jonathan. 2008. *A World Survey of Religion and the State.* Cambridge: Cambridge University Press.

Fraser, Nancy. 1992. "Rethinking the Public Sphere: A Contribution to the Critique of Actually Existing Democracy." In *Habermas and the Public Sphere*, edited by Craig Calhoun, pp. 109–142. Cambridge, MA: MIT Press.

Furnivall, J. S. 2010 [1939]. *Netherlands India: A Study of Plural Economy.* Cambridge: Cambridge University Press.
Gade, Anna M. 2004. *Perfection Makes Practice: Learning, Emotion, and the Recited Qur'an in Indonesia.* Honolulu: University of Hawai'i Press.
Gal, Susan. 2002. "A Semiotics of the Public/Private Distinction." *differences: A Journal of Feminist Cultural Studies* 13 (1): 77–95.
Gaylord, Wendy. 2007. "Reformasi, Civic Education, and Indonesian Secondary School Teachers." In *How Diverse Societies Form Democratic Citizens*, edited by Doyle Stevick and Bradley A. U. Levinson, pp. 45–67. Lanham: Rowman and Littlefield Publishers.
Gulson, Kalervon, and Colin Symes. 2007. "Knowing One's Place: Educational Theory, Policy, and the Spatial Turn." In *Spatial Theories of Education: Policy and Geography Matters*, edited by Kalervon Gulson and Colin Symes, pp. 1–16. New York: Routledge.
Habermas, Jürgen. 1989. *The Structural Transformation of the Public Sphere: An Inquiry into a Category of Bourgeois Society.* Translated by Thomas Burger. Cambridge, MA: MIT Press.
Hadiz, Vedi R. 2018. "Imagine All the People? Mobilising Islamic Populism for Right-Wing Politics in Indonesia." *Journal of Contemporary Asia* 48 (4): 566–583.
Hadler, Jeffrey. 2008. *Muslims and Matriarchs: Cultural Resilience in Indonesia through Jihad and Colonialism.* Ithaca, NY: Cornell University Press.
Hansen, Thomas Blom. 1999. *The Saffron Wave: Democracy and Hindu Nationalism in Modern India.* Princeton, NJ: Princeton: Princeton University Press.
Hefner, Claire-Marie. 2016. "Models of Achievement: Muslim Girls and Religious Authority in a Modernist Islamic Boarding School in Indonesia." *Asian Studies Review* 40 (4): 564–582.
———. 2019. "On Fun and Freedom: Young Women's Moral Learning in Indonesian Islamic Boarding Schools." *Journal of the Royal Anthropological Institute* 25 (3): 487–505.
Hefner, Robert W. 2000. *Civil Islam: Muslims and Democratization in Indonesia.* Princeton, NJ: Princeton University Press.
———. 2007. "Introduction: The Culture, Politics, and Future of Muslim Education." In *Schooling Islam: The Culture and Politics of Modern Muslim Education*, edited by Robert W. Hefner and Muhammad Qasim Zaman, pp. 1–39. Princeton, NJ: Princeton University Press.
———. 2009. "Islamic Schools, Social Movements, and Democracy in Indonesia." In *Making Modern Muslims: The Politics of Islamic Education in Southeast Asia*, edited by Robert W. Hefner, pp. 55–105. Honolulu: University of Hawai'i Press.
———. 2012. "Islam, Economic Globalization, and the Blended Ethics of Self." *Bustan: The Middle East Book Review* 3 (2): 91–108.

———. 2014. "Modern Muslims and the Challenge of Plurality." *Society* 51 (2): 131–139.

———. 2017. "Christians, Conflict, and Citizenship in Muslim-Majority Indonesia." *Review of Faith and International Affairs* 15 (1): 91–101.

———. 2019. "Whatever Happened to Civil Islam? Islam and Democratisation in Indonesia, 20 Years On." *Asian Studies Review* 43 (3): 375–396.

———. 2021. "The Politics and Ethics of Social Recognition and Citizenship in a Muslim-Majority Democracy." In *Indonesian Pluralities: Islam, Citizenship, and Democracy*, edited by Robert W. Hefner and Zainal Abidin Bagir, pp. 1–36. Notre Dame, IN: University of Notre Dame Press.

Hefner, Robert W., and Zainal Abidin Bagir, eds. 2021. *Indonesian Pluralities: Islam, Citizenship, and Democracy*. Notre Dame, IN: University of Notre Dame Press.

Henley, David. 1996. *Nationalism and Regionalism in a Colonial Context: Minahasa in the Dutch East Indies*. Leiden: KITLV Press.

Henley, David, and Jamie S. Davidson. 2008. "In the Name of Adat: Regional Perspectives on Reform, Tradition, and Democracy in Indonesia." *Modern Asian Studies* 42 (4): 815–852.

Heuken, Adolf S. J. 2008. "Catholic Converts in the Moluccas, Minahasa and Sangihe-Talaud, 1512–1680." In *A History of Christianity in Indonesia*, edited by Jan S. Aritonang and Karel A. Steenbrink, pp. 23–72. Leiden: Brill.

Hew, Wai Weng. 2018. "Piety, Politics, and the Popularity of Felix Siauw." *New Mandala*, January 2. https://www.newmandala.org/piety-politics-popularity-felix-siauw/.

Hirschkind, Charles. 2001. "Civic Virtue and Religious Reason: An Islamic Counterpublic." *Cultural Anthropology* 16 (1): 3–34.

———. 2006. *The Ethical Soundscape: Cassette Sermons and Islamic Counterpublics*. New York: Columbia University Press.

Hoesterey, James B. 2012. "Prophetic Cosmopolitanism: Islam, Pop Psychology, and Civic Virtue in Indonesia." *City and Society* 24 (1): 38–61.

Hoon, Chang-Yau. 2014. "God and Discipline: Religious Education and Character Building in a Christian School in Jakarta." *South East Asia Research* 22 (4): 505–524.

Jacobsen, Michael. 2004. "Factionalism and Secession in North Sulawesi Province, Indonesia." *Asian Journal of Political Science* 12 (1): 65–94.

Jaffe-Walter, Reva. 2016. *Coercive Concern: Nationalism, Liberalism and the Schooling of Muslim Youth*. Stanford, CA: Stanford University Press.

Jaffrey, Sana, and Ihsan Ali-Fauzi. 2016. "Street Power and Electoral Politics in Indonesia." *New Mandala*, April 5. http://www.newmandala.org/street-power-and-electoral-politics-in-indonesia/.

Jerryson, Michael K. 2011. *Buddhist Fury: Religion and Violence in Southern Thailand*. Oxford: Oxford University Press.

Jones, Sidney. 2013. "Indonesian Government Approaches to Radical Islam Since 1998." In *Democracy and Islam in Indonesia*, edited by Mirjam Künkler and Alfred Stepan, pp. 109–125. New York: Columbia University Press.

Kaplan, Sam. 2006. *The Pedagogical State: Education and the Politics of National Culture in Post-1890 Turkey*. Stanford, CA: Stanford University Press.

Karrebæk, Martha Sif. 2012. "'What's in Your Lunch Box Today?': Health, Respectability, and Ethnicity in the Primary Classroom." *Journal of Linguistic Anthropology* 22 (1): 1–22.

Keane, Webb. 2016. *Ethical Life: Its Natural and Social Histories*. Princeton, NJ: Princeton University Press.

Kemendikbud (Kementerian Pendidikan dan Kebudayaan). 1983a. *Pendidikan Moral Pancasila SMTA Kelas 1* (Pancasila moral education SMTA class 1). 4th ed. Jakarta: PN Balai Pustaka.

———. 1983b. *Pendidikan Moral Pancasila SMTA Kelas 3* (Pancasila moral education SMTA class 3). 4th ed. Jakarta: PN Balai Pustaka.

———. 2013. "Kurikulum 2013: Kompetensi Dasar Sekolah Menengah Atas (SMA)/Madrasah Aliyah (MA)" (2013 Curriculum: Basic competencies for senior high school and madrasah). Jakarta: Kementerian Pendidikan dan Kebudayaan.

———. 2014a. *Pendidikan Agama Islam Dan Budi Pekerti SMA/MA/SMK/MAK Kelas XI* (Islamic religious education and Budi Pekerti SMA/MA/SMK/MAK class XI). Jakarta: Kementerian Pendidikan dan Kebudayaan.

———. 2014b. *Pendidikan Agama Katolik Dan Budi Pekerti SMA/SMK Kelas XI* (Catholic religious education and Budi Pekerti SMA/SMK class XI). Jakarta: Kementerian Pendidikan dan Kebudayaan.

———. 2014c. *Pendidikan Agama Kristen Dan Budi Pekerti: Bertumbuh Menjadi Dewasa SMA/SMK Kelas X* (Christian religious education and Budi Pekerti: Growing up to become an adult SMA/SMK class X). Jakarta: Kementerian Pendidikan dan Kebudayaan.

———. 2014d. *Pendidikan Pancasila Dan Kewarganegaraan SMA/MA/SMK/MAK Kelas X Semester 2* (Pancasila and citizenship education SMA/MA/SMK/MAK class X semester 2). Jakarta: Kementerian Pendidikan dan Kebudayaan.

———. 2014e. *Pendidikan Pancasila Dan Kewarganegaraan SMA/MA/SMK/MAK Kelas XI Semester 1* (Pancasila and citizenship education SMA/MA/SMK/MAK class XI). Jakarta: Kementerian Pendidikan dan Kebudayaan.

Kingsley, Jeremy J., and Kari Telle. 2016. "Introduction: Performing the State." *Bijdragen Tot de Taal-, Land- En Volkenkunde* 172 (2/3): 171–178.

Kjaran, Jon Ingvar. 2017. *Constructing Sexualities and Gendered Bodies in School Spaces*. New York: Palgrave Macmillan.

Kleinman, Arthur. 1988. *Rethinking Psychiatry: From Cultural Category to Personal Experience*. New York: Free Press.

Kloos, David. 2018. *Becoming Better Muslims: Religious Authority and Ethical Improvement in Aceh, Indonesia*. Princeton, NJ: Princeton University Press, 2018.

Kosel, Sven. 2010. "Christianity, Minahasa Ethnicity, and Politics in North Sulawesi: 'Jerusalem's Veranda' or Stronghold of Pancasila?" In *Christianity in Indonesia: Perspectives of Power*, edited by Susanne Schröter, pp. 291–322. New Brunswick, NJ: Transaction Publishers.

Künkler, Mirjam, and Alfred Stepan. 2013. "Indonesian Democratization in Theoretical Perspective." In *Democracy and Islam in Indonesia*, edited by Mirjan Künkler and Alfred Stepan, pp. 3–23. New York: Columbia University Press.

Kuru, Ahmet T. 2009. *Secularism and State Policies toward Religion: The United States, France, and Turkey*. New York: Cambridge University Press.

Kwok, Yenni. 2014. "Public Schools in Indonesia Feel Islamic Pressure." *New York Times*, June 15. https://www.nytimes.com/2014/06/16/world/asia/public-schools-in-indonesia-feel-islamic-pressure.html.

Kymlicka, Will. 1995. *Multicultural Citizenship: A Liberal Theory of Minority Rights*. Oxford: Oxford University Press.

Laffan, Michael Francis. 2003. *Islamic Nationhood and Colonial Indonesia: The Umma below the Winds*. New York: Routledge Curzon.

Laidlaw, James. 2014. *The Subject of Virtue: An Anthropology of Ethics and Freedom*. New York: Cambridge University Press.

Laidlaw, James, and Jonathan Mair. 2019. "Imperfect Accomplishment: The Fo Guang Shan Short-Term Monastic Retreat and Ethical Pedagogy in Humanistic Buddhism." *Cultural Anthropology* 34 (3): 328–358.

Lambek, Michael. 2010. "Towards the Ethics of the Act." In *Ordinary Ethics: Anthropology, Language, and Action*, edited by Michael Lambek, pp. 39–63. New York: Fordham University Press.

Larson, Erica M. 2021. "Scaling Plural Coexistence in Manado: What Does It Take to Remain Brothers?" In *Indonesian Pluralities: Islam, Citizenship, and Democracy*, edited by Robert W. Hefner and Zainal Abidin Bagir, pp. 37–73. Notre Dame, IN: University of Notre Dame Press.

———. 2022. "Learning to Navigate the Ethics of Boundaries: Schools, Youth, and Inter-Religious Relationships in Manado, Indonesia." *Journal of the Royal Anthropological Institute* 28 (2): 432–450.

Leigh, Barbara. 1999. "Learning and Knowing Boundaries: Schooling in New Order Indonesia." *Sojourn: Journal of Social Issues in Southeast Asia* 14 (1): 34–56.

Levinson, Bradley A. 1999. "Resituating the Place of Educational Discourse in Anthropology." *American Anthropologist* 101 (3): 594–604.

Li, Tania. 2000. "Articulating Indigenous Identity in Indonesia: Resource Politics and the Tribal Slot." *Comparative Studies in Society and History* 42 (1): 149–179.

———. 2007. *The Will to Improve: Governmentality, Development, and the Practice of Politics*. Durham, NC: Duke University Press.

Lindsey, Timothy. 2012. *Islam, Law and the State in Southeast Asia*. Vol. 1. London: I. B. Tauris.

Lintong, Jonely C. 2015. "Sejarah Berdirinya Universitas Kristen Indonesia Tomohon" (History of the establishment of the Christian University of Tomohon). In *Semangat yang tak pernah Padam: Peringatan 50 tahun Universitas Kristen Indonesia Tomohon* (The spirit that never dies down: Commemorating 50 years of the Christian University of Tomohon), edited by Denni H. R. Pinontoan, pp. 2–23. Tomohon: UKIT Press.

Liwe, Amelia Joan. 2010. "From Crisis to Footnote: The Ambiguous Permesta Revolt in Post-Colonial Indonesia." PhD diss., University of Wisconsin–Madison.

Mahmood, Saba. 2005. *Politics of Piety: The Islamic Revival and the Feminist Subject*. Princeton, NJ: Princeton University Press.

———. 2016. *Religious Difference in a Secular Age: A Minority Report*. Princeton, NJ: Princeton University Press.

Mair, Jonathan, and Nicholas Evans. 2015. "Ethics across Borders: Incommensurability and Affinity." *HAU: Journal of Ethnographic Theory* 5 (2): 201–225.

Marsden, Magnus. 2005. *Living Islam: Muslim Religious Experience in Pakistan's North-West Frontier*. Cambridge: Cambridge University Press.

Mattingly, Cheryl. 2014a. "Moral Deliberation and the Agentive Self in Laidlaw's Ethics." *HAU: Journal of Ethnographic Theory* 4 (1): 473–486.

———. 2014b. *Moral Laboratories: Family Peril and the Struggle for a Good Life*. Oakland: University of California Press.

McGregor, Katharine E. 2002. "Commemoration of 1 October, 'Hari Kesaktian Pancasila': A Post Mortem Analysis?" *Asian Studies Review* 26 (1): 39–72.

Menchik, Jeremy. 2015. *Islam and Democracy in Indonesia: Tolerance without Liberalism*. New York: Cambridge University Press.

———. 2019. "Moderate Muslims and Democratic Breakdown in Indonesia." *Asian Studies Review* 43 (3): 415–433.

Morfit, Michael. 1981. "Pancasila: The Indonesian State Ideology According to the New Order Government." *Asian Survey* 21 (8): 838–851.

Mujiburrahman. 2006. *Feeling Threatened: Muslim-Christian Relations in Indonesia's New Order*. Amsterdam: Amsterdam University Press.

Munro, Jenny. 2018. *Dreams Made Small: The Education of Papuan Highlanders in Indonesia*. New York: Berghahn Books.

Nilan, Pam. 2003. "Teachers' Work and Schooling in Bali." *International Review of Education* 49 (6): 563–584.

Nishimura, Shigeo. 1995. "The Development of Pancasila Moral Education in Indonesia." *Southeast Asian Studies* 33 (3): 303–316.

O'Neill, Kevin Lewis. 2009. *City of God: Christian Citizenship in Postwar Guatemala.* Berkeley: University of California Press.

Panggabean, Samsu Rizal. 2017. "Dua Kota Dua Cerita: Mengapa Kekerasan Terjadi Di Ambon Tapi Tidak Di Manado?" (Two cities two stories: Why did violence happen in Ambon but not in Manado?). In *Ketika Agama Bawa Damai, Bukan Perang: Belajar Dari "Imam Dan Pastor"* (When religion brings peace, not war: Learning from "imam and priest"), edited by Ihsan Ali-Fauzi, pp. 117–156. Jakarta: PUSAD Paramadina.

Parker, Lyn. 2002. "The Subjectification of Citizenship: Student Interpretations of School Teachings in Bali." *Asian Studies Review* 26 (1): 3–37.

Patandianan, Marly Valenti, and Nono S. A. Sumampouw. 2016. "From Colonial Site to Contemporary Political Tension: Colonial Urban Planning Legacy upon the Formation of Socio-Political Identity in Manado, North Sulawesi." In *Proceedings of the Tenth International Symposium on City Planning and Environmental Management in Asian Countries* (Makassar, Indonesia, January 9–11), pp. 65–70.

Pemberton, John. 1994. *On the Subject of "Java."* Ithaca, NY: Cornell University Press.

Picard, Michel. 2011. "Introduction: 'Agama', 'Adat' and Pancasila." In *The Politics of Religion in Indonesia: Syncretism, Orthodoxy, and Religious Contention in Java and Bali*, edited by Michel Picard and Remy Madinier, pp. 1–20. London: Routledge.

Pierson, Paul. 2000. "Increasing Returns, Path Dependence, and the Study of Politics." *American Political Science Review* 94 (2): 251–267.

Pinontoan, Denni H. R. 2018. "Politik Identitas Dalam Masyarakat Multikultural Minahasa" (Identity politics in multicultural Minahasan society). In *Praktik Pengelolaan Keragaman Di Indonesia: Konstruksi Identitas Dan Eksklusi Sosial* (Practices of diversity management in Indonesia: Identity construction and social exclusion), edited by Mohammad Iqbal Ahnaf, Trisno Sutanto, Subandri Simbolon, and Azis Anwar Fachrudin, pp. 103–132. Yogyakarta: Center for Religious and Cross-Cultural Studies, Gadjah Mada University.

Pomalingo, Samsi. 2004. "Dialog Antarumat Beragama: Studi Kasus Tentang BKSAUA Di Manado, Sulawesi Utara" (Interreligious dialogue: Case study on BKSAUA in Manado, North Sulawesi). Master's thesis, Gadjah Mada University.

Ratag, Mezak A., and Ronald Korompis. 2009. *Kurikulum Berbasis Kehidupan: Pandangan Tentang Pendidikan Menurut Ronald Korompis* (Curriculum based on life: Perspectives on education according to Ronald Korompis). Tomohon: Yayasan Pendidikan Lokon.

Renwarin, Paul Richard. 2006. "Matuari and Tona'as: The Cultural Dynamics of the Tombulu in Minahasa." PhD diss., University of Leiden.

———. 2015. "Ber-Ekumene Di Kampus Theologica" (Ecumenism on the theological campus). In *Semangat Yang Tak Pernah Padam: Peringatan 50 Tahun Universitas Kristen Indonesia Tomohon* (The spirit that never dies down: Commemorating 50 years of the Christian University of Tomohon), edited by Denni H. R. Pinontoan, pp. 45–53. Tomohon: UKIT Press.

Republika. 2016a. "Maraknya LGBT Ini Kata Menteri Anies Baswedan" (The rise of LGBT according to Minister Anies Baswedan). *Republika*, January 25. http://nasional.republika.co.id/berita/nasional/umum/16/01/25/01gxly361-maraknya-lgbt-ini-kata-menteri-anies-baswedan.

———. 2016b. "Ideologi Pancasila Harus Diterapkan Dalam Setiap Kurikulum" (Pancasila ideology must be implemented in each curriculum). *Republika*, March 2. http://www.republika.co.id/berita/nasional/umum/16/03/01/o3d7xj294-ideologi-pancasila-harus-diterapkan-dalam-setiap-kurikulum.

———. 2016c. "KPK: Agama Tidak Benarkan Korupsi" (KPK: Religion doesn't condone corruption). *Republika*, March 1. https://www.republika.co.id/berita/o3d5ub313/kpk-agama-tidak-benarkan-korupsi.

Ricklefs, M. C. 2012. *Islamisation and Its Opponents in Java: A Political, Social, Cultural and Religious History, c. 1930 to the Present.* Honolulu: University of Hawai'i Press.

Robbins, Joel. 2004. *Becoming Sinners: Christianity and Moral Torment in a Papua New Guinea Society.* Berkeley: University of California Press.

———. 2016. "What Is the Matter with Transcendence? On the Place of Religion in the New Anthropology of Ethics." *Journal of the Royal Anthropological Institute* 22 (4): 767–781.

Roeroe, W. A. 2003. *I Yayat U Santi: Injil dan Kebudayaan Di Tanah Minahasa* (I Yayat U Santi: The Bible and culture on Minahasan land). Tomohon: UKIT Press.

Rosaldo, Renato. 2003. "Introduction: The Borders of Belonging." In *Cultural Citizenship in Island Southeast Asia*, edited by Renato Rosaldo, pp. 1–15. Berkeley: University of California Press.

Rudnyckyj, Daromir. 2010. *Spiritual Economies: Islam, Globalization, and the Afterlife of Development.* Ithaca, NY: Cornell University Press.

Rusli, Almunauwar Bin. 2020. "Muallaf's Dilemma in Minahasa: A Case Study of Faith and Political Choice." *Topik* 43 (1): 23–32.

Salim, Delmus Puneri, Srifani Simbuka, and Muzwir Luntajo. 2016. "Politics and Religious Freedom in Indonesia: The Case of West Sumatra and North Sulawesi." *Jurnal Studi Pemerintahan (Journal of Government and Politics)* 7 (4): 594–618.

Salim, Hairus, Najib Kailani, and Nikmal Azekiyah. 2011. *Politik Ruang Publik Sekolah: Negosiasi Dan Resistensi Di SMUN Di Yogyakarta* (Politics in public schools: Negotiation and resistance in public schools in Yogyakarta). Yogyakarta: Center for Religious and Cross-Cultural Studies, Gadjah Mada University.

Schielke, Samuli. 2009. "Being Good in Ramadan: Ambivalence, Fragmentation, and the Moral Self in the Lives of Young Egyptians." *Journal of the Royal Anthropological Institute* 15:S24–S40.

———. 2015. *Egypt in the Future Tense: Hope, Frustration, and Ambivalence before and after 2011.* Bloomington: Indiana University Press.

Schielke, Samuli, and Lisa Debevec, eds. 2012. *Ordinary Lives and Grand Schemes: An Anthropology of Everyday Religion.* New York: Berghahn Books.

Schröter, Susanne. 2010. "Christianity in Indonesia: An Overview." In *Christianity in Indonesia: Perspectives of Power*, edited by Susanne Schröter, pp. 9–30. New Brunswick, NJ: Transaction Publishers.

Seligman, Adam B., and Robert P. Weller. 2012. *Rethinking Pluralism: Ritual, Experience, and Ambiguity.* New York: Oxford University Press.

Setara Institute for Democracy and Peace. 2017. "Indeks Kota Toleran Tahun 2017" (Tolerant city index—Year 2017). November 16. https://setara-institute.org/indeks-kota-toleran-tahun-2017/.

Shiraishi, Saya. 1997. *Young Heroes: The Indonesian Family in Politics.* Ithaca, NY: Cornell University Press.

Shweder, Richard A., Manamohan Mahapatra, and Joan G. Miller. 1987. "Culture and Moral Development." In *The Emergence of Morality in Young Children*, edited by Jerome Kagan and Sharon Lamb, pp. 1–83. Chicago: University of Chicago Press.

Shweder, Richard A., and Nancy C. Much. 1991. "Determinations of Meaning: Discourse and Moral Socialization." In *Thinking through Cultures*, edited by Richard Shweder, pp. 186–240. Cambridge, MA: Harvard University Press.

Sidel, John T. 2006. *Riots, Pogroms, Jihad: Religious Violence in Indonesia.* Ithaca, NY: Cornell University Press.

Simon, Gregory M. 2014. *Caged In on the Outside: Moral Subjectivity, Selfhood, and Islam in Minangkabau, Indonesia.* Honolulu: University of Hawai'i Press.

Slama, Martin, and James B. Hoesterey. 2021. "Ambivalence, Discontent, and Divides in Southeast Asia's Islamic Digital Realms: An Introduction." *CyberOrient* 15 (1): 5–32.

Smith-Hefner, Nancy J. 2007. "Javanese Women and the Veil in Post-Soeharto Indonesia." *Journal of Asian Studies* 66 (2): 389–420.

Song, Seung-Won. 2008. "Back to Basics in Indonesia? Reassessing the Pancasila and Pancasila State and Society, 1945–2007." PhD diss., Ohio University.

Spyer, Patricia. 1996. "Diversity with a Difference: Adat and the New Order in Aru (Eastern Indonesia)." *Cultural Anthropology* 11 (1): 25–50.

Stambach, Amy. 2000. *Lessons from Mount Kilimanjaro: Schooling, Community, and Gender in East Africa.* New York: Routledge.

———. 2006. "Revising a Four-Square Model of a Complicated Whole: On the Cultural Politics of Religion and Education." *Social Analysis* 50 (3): 1–18.

---. 2010. *Faith in Schools: Religion, Education, and American Evangelicals in East Africa*. Stanford, CA: Stanford University Press.
Starrett, Gregory. 1998. *Putting Islam to Work: Education, Politics, and Religious Transformation in Egypt*. Berkeley: University of California Press.
Steenbrink, Karel A. 2003. *Catholics in Indonesia, 1808–1942*. Vol. 2, *The Spectacular Growth of a Self-Confident Minority, 1903–1942: A Documented History*. Leiden: KITLV Press.
Stepan, Alfred. 2011. "The Multiple Secularisms of Modern Democratic and Non-Democratic Regimes." In *Rethinking Secularism*, edited by Craig Calhoun, Mark Juergensmeyer, and Jonathan VanAntwerpen, pp. 114–144. Oxford: Oxford University Press.
Suhadi, Mohamad Yusuf, Marthen Tahun, Budi Asyhari, and Sudarto. 2014. *Politik Pendidikan Agama, Kurikulum 2013 Dan Ruang Publik Sekolah* (The politics of religious education, the 2013 Curriculum, and the public sphere of the school). Edited by Zainal Abidin Bagir and Linah K. Pary. Yogyakarta: Center for Religious and Cross-Cultural Studies, Gadjah Mada University.
Sumampouw, Nono S. A. 2015. *Menjadi Minahasa: Torang Samua Basudara, Sabla Aer, Dan Pembentukan Identitas Sosial* (Becoming Minahasa: We are all brothers, *Sabla Aer*, and social identity formation). Yogyakarta: Gadjah Mada University Press.
Swazey, Kelli. 2013. "A Place for Harmonious Difference: Christianity and the Mediation of Minahasan Identity in the North Sulawesi Public." PhD diss., University of Hawai'i.
Syafruddin, Didin. 2011. "In Search of a Citizenship Education Model for a Democratic Multireligious Indonesia: Case Studies of Two Public Senior High Schools in Jakarta." PhD diss., McGill University.
Talumewo, Bodewyn Grey. n.d. Personal archives.
Tambayong, Yapi. 2007. *Kamus Bahasa dan Budaya Manado* (Dictionary of Manadonese language and culture). Jakarta: PT Gramedia Pustaka Utama.
Taylor, Charles. 2002. "Modern Social Imaginaries." *Public Culture* 14 (1): 91–124.
---. 2007. *A Secular Age*. Cambridge, MA: Belknap Press of Harvard University Press.
Taylor, Charles, and Amy Gutmann. 1994. *Multiculturalism: Examining the Politics of Recognition*. Princeton, NJ: Princeton University Press.
Thufail, Fadjar. 2012. "When Peace Prevails on Kasih Hill: The Protestant Church and the Politics of Adat in Minahasa." *Asian Ethnicity* 13 (4): 359–371.
Tribun Manado. 2016. "50 Tahun HUT Pernikahan Korompis Luncurkan Buku Mendidik Dari Hati. Tribun Manado" (50th wedding anniversary, Korompis launches the book "Educating from the Heart"). *Tribun Manado*, February 13. https://manado.tribunnews.com/2016/02/13/50-tahun-hut-pernikahan-korompis-luncurkan-buku-mendidik-dari-hati.

Triyanto. 2013. "Civic Education as a Tool for Moral Education by Integrating the Five Basic Principles (Pancasila)." *Asian Journal of Humanities and Social Studies* 1 (4): 218–220.

van Bruinessen, Martin. 2013. "Introduction: Contemporary Developments in Indonesian Islam and the 'Conservative Turn' of the Early Twenty-First Century." In *Contemporary Developments in Indonesian Islam: Explaining the "Conservative Turn,"* edited by Martin van Bruinessen, pp. 1–20. Singapore: Institute of Southeast Asian Studies.

van den End, Thomas, and Jan Aritonang. 2008. "1800–2005: A National Overview." In *A History of Christianity in Indonesia*, edited by Jan Aritonang and Karel Steenbrink, pp. 137–228. Leiden: Brill.

van Klinken, Gerry. 2003. *Minorities, Modernity, and the Emerging Nation: Christians in Indonesia: A Biographical Approach*. Leiden: KITLV Press.

Varenne, Hervé. 2007. "Difficult Collective Deliberations: Anthropological Notes toward a Theory of Education." *Teachers College Record* 109 (7): 1559–1588.

———. 2008. "Culture, Education, Anthropology." *Anthropology and Education Quarterly* 39 (4): 356–368.

Warburton, Eve, and Edward Aspinall. 2019. "Explaining Indonesia's Democratic Regression: Structure, Agency and Popular Opinion." *Contemporary Southeast Asia* 41 (2): 255–285.

Warner, Michael. 1992. "The Mass Public and the Mass Subject." In *Habermas and the Public Sphere*, edited by Craig Calhoun, pp. 377–401. Cambridge, MA: MIT Press.

Weatherbee, Donald E. 1985a. "Indonesia in 1984: Pancasila, Politics, and Power." *Asian Survey* 25 (2): 187–197.

———. 1985b. "Indonesia: The Pancasila State." *Southeast Asian Affairs* 12:133–151.

Weber, Eugen. 1976. *Peasants into Frenchmen: The Modernization of Rural France, 1870–1914*. Stanford, CA: Stanford University Press.

Weichart, Gabriele. 2004. "Minahasa Identity: A Culinary Practice." *Antropologi Indonesia* 74:55–74.

Willis, Paul E. 1977. *Learning to Labour: How Working Class Kids Get Working Class Jobs*. Farnborough: Saxon House.

Wilson, Chris. 2008. *Ethno-Religious Violence in Indonesia: From Soil to God*. New York: Routledge.

Wilson, Lee, and Eryanto Nugroho. 2012. "For the Good of the People?" *Inside Indonesia* 109 (July–September). https://www.insideindonesia.org/for-the-good-of-the-people-2.

Zemmrich, Eckhard. 2020. "Making Sense of Shifts in Perspectives: Perceiving and Framing Examples of Interreligious Learning in Indonesia." *Islam and Christian Muslim Relations* 31 (2): 151–172.

Zigon, Jarrett. 2008. *Morality: An Anthropological Perspective*. Oxford: Berg.

INDEX

Page numbers in boldface refer to illustrations

2013 Curriculum, 53, 55–62, 69, 128, 129, 133, 134, 142

accommodation, 42, 68, 70, 89, 93, 129, 131, 153, 179, 191; of Muslims, 82–85, 165; of Protestant majority, 78; of religious difference/diversity, 2, 63, 67, 72–77, 80, 82, 94, 112, 171, 172
adat, 14, 29, 179, 180, 185–192, 194–199, 200, 201, 216n4
affective, 14, 15, 21, 23, 139
Ahok, 9, 38–39, 92, 196, 202, 214n4 (chapter 3)
Aliansi Makapetor, 194, 195, 200
Al-Kafirun, 78, 177, 215n1 (chapter 6)
aspirational coexistence, 13, 14, 29, 72, 73, 90, 91, 96, 123, 163, 167, 172, 179, 183, 185, 191, 192, 194, 198, 201–202, 203, 210

belonging: national, 1, 14, 15, 17, 27, 31, 40, 98, 112, 179, 198, 205, 207; religious, 1, 2, 6, 10, 27, 28, 44, 64, 66–67, 72–74, 78, 85, 89–90, 93–94, 112, 115, 153, 154, 157, 161, 162, 166, 179, 205. *See also* ethics of belonging
Bhinneka Tunggal Ika, 2, 42
Bible, 62, 107, 114, 151, 168, 214n7
BKSAUA, 183–185, 191, 194, 195
Bolaang-Mongondow, 11, 68, 102, 128, 130, 156, 181
Brigade Manguni, 186, 189

Catholic: Church, 105, 108, 114; education, 28, 57, 60, 62, 96, 98–100, 102, 106, 108, 110, 112–115, **120**, 154, 169, 206; majority, 30, 96; seminary, 155, 157, 159, 165, 166, 170; students, 66, 67, 70, 117, 173; teachings, 62, 99, 114, 154, 174
Catholicism, 34, 60, 108, 113, 115, 165
Catholics, 4, 10, 35, 80, 102, 105, 207, 213n4
character: building, 62, 63, 96, 105, 108, 109, 123–124, 130, 133, 136, 144–145, 150; education, 27, 53, 55–56, 58, 69, 95, 131, 132–133, 135
Christian: identity, 62, 92, 98, 180, 187–188, 197; majority, 6, 9, 36, 79, 89, 92, 93, 180, 181, 196, 205, 205; minority, 14, 79, 90, 92, 93, 204, 205; and the nation, 36, 39, 44, 71, 90, 95–96, 98, 123, 192, 198, 202–204, 208; teachings, 62, 71, 90–91, 187; values, 61, 98, 108, 109, 111, 123. *See also* Protestant
Christianity, 4, 5, 18, 36, 39, 91, 97, 98, 101, 102, 108, 111, 124, 149, 150, 164, 172, 180, 186, 197, 198
church, 11, 61, 62, 79, 90, 91, 94, 102, 105, 114, 115, 176, 177–178, 188, 189, 193, 196, 208
citizens, 1, 2, 13, 15, 16, 22, 30, 43, 44–46, 48, 51, 52, 55, 58–60, 62, 91, 109–110, 112, 121, 127–128, 133, 140, 153–154, 202, 203, 210
citizenship, 8, 9, 14, 15, 27, 29, 53, 55, 58, 79, 96, 98, 112, 118, 120, 122–123, 197, 203, 205, 210
civic education, 1, 25, 26, 45, 49, 51, 53–60, 61, 69, 91, 140, 141, 202
civic values, 97, 109, 110, 111, 112, 123, 127, 133
coexistence: plural 3–4, 7, 8, 13, 31, 71, 189; religious 3, 5–8, 13, 15, 20, 27, 30, 36, 41, 78, 84, 127, 154, 156–157, 167, 171, 173,

231

179, 183, 196–198. *See also* aspirational coexistence; *under* majoritarian
commensuration, 28, 156, 160, 163, 165, 171, 173–175, 177, 182, 204. *See also* incommensuration
competency: spiritual and social, 56–57, 63, 134–135
conflict, 5–8, 13, 38, 41, 54–55, 59, 61–62, 90, 94, 123–124, 126, 141, 160, 172, 183–186, 188– 191, 194, 195; post-conflict, 11, 190, 191
corruption, 53, 55, 109–111, 116, 120, 142
curriculum: development, 26, 41, 46, 48–49, 53; national, 6, 16, 22, 23, 27, 44, 45, 52–53, 67, 208, 209

decentralization, 5, 8, 13, 37, 50, 51, 52, 97–98, 107, 122, 123, 181, 186
deliberation: as discursive, 93–94, 153; as embodied, 93–94, 153, 210; as rational, 19, 21, 23, 67, 210. *See also under* education
democracy: and education, 52–57, 64, 108; Indonesian, 5, 7, 8, 9, 15, 27, 31, 35, 37, 54, 96, 103, 121, 122, 203, 213n6; liberal, 33, 54; and Pancasila, 35, 50–52, 53, 63, 213n6; pro-democracy movement, 49, 64; and religion, 7, 15, 51–52
democratization, 13, 36, 52, 97, 98, 107, 122, 123, 181, 186. See also *reformasi*
development: national, 28, 41–46, 47, 59, 97–100, 109–110, 126, 202, 206; of Papua, 116–120; and religion, 96–98, 109, 121–124
discipline, 16–17, 18, 20, 42, 57, 105, 116, 123, 127, 134, 137, 147, 153, 154, 210
diversity: respect for, 1, 28, 58–62, 79, 93, 99, 106, 108, 134, 154, 160, 210–211; state management of, 8, 32, 41–43, 51, 63; in the curriculum, 57–62, 113–114, 128, 140–141

education: as deliberation, 2–3, 7, 16–20, 22–23, 67, 153, 178, 210; and modernization, 17, 31, 40, 121; as a multicentered process, 3, 8, 16, 17–18, 19, 41, 64; as reproduction, 2–3, 19. *See also under* Islamic
Eid al-Adha, 131, 133–134
embodiment, 10, 27–28, 66–67, 72–75, 83, 85, 86, 89–90, 93–94, 153–154, 157, 166, 205, 210. *See also under* deliberation
ethical: affordances, 20–21; discipline, 16–17, 20, 127, 153–154, 210; dispositions, 2, 18, 20, 23–24; frameworks, 2–3, 15, 17, 21–24, 27, 40, 50, 86, 93, 97, 154, 156, 180, 207, 209–210, 211; normativities, 72, 74, 179; pluralism, 22–24, 209, 211; reflection, 3, 21–22, 73, 156, 207, 209–211; self-making, 20, 21, 23, 153–154, 203; socialization, 2–3, 6, 8, 21, 23–24, 146
ethics: across borders, 156, 174, 177, 204; and ambiguity, 24; of belonging, 1, 2, 15, 156, 182, 201, 211; and institutions, 23; and politics, 2, 15, 182, 207, 208, 209
ethnic: group(s), 5, 11, 37, 47, 68, 102, 117, 118, 130, 160, 180, 181, 182, 191; identity, 5, 36, 122, 180–181, 185–187, 189, 190–192
ethnicity, 10–11, 14, 42, 47, 57, 59, 68, 91, 95, 117
exclusion, 2, 15, 36, 63, 74, 80, 197, 207
exclusivism, 5, 33, 61, 98, 122, 190, 191, 192, 197, 198, 203
extracurricular activities/clubs, 25, 44, 63, 69, 70, 71–72, 74, 80, 88, 89, 93, 103, 125, 130, 132, 135, 144

fanatic, 83, 86, 164, 168, 214n3 (chapter 3). *See also* radical
FKUB, 91, 183, **184**, 185, 194, 195, 201

GMIM, 11, 37, 68, 69, 80, 102, 157, 168, 183, 185, 187, 188, 191, 216n6
Gorontalo, 11, 68, 130, 181, 193
grades, 56–57, 136–137, 140

hadith, 61, 136, 139, 140
halal, 67, 81–85, **85**, 129, 131, 152, 165, 166–167, 169–171

identity politics, 50, 63, 64, 187, 190–192, 197, 199, 203, 204
inclusion, 2, 14, 15, 33, 74–75, 80, 81, 99, 116–117, 120, 123, 180, 182, 188, 190, 191, 193, 207–208
incommensuration, 28, 156, 159, 163, 171, 173–175, 177, 182, 204. *See also* commensuration
intolerance, 8–9, 31, 50, 59, 62, 122, 160, 168, 178, 203
interreligious: dialogue, 6, 26, 28, 59, 114, 140, 155, 157, 168, 189, 173, 175, 177–178, 204; harmony, 59–61, 72, 141, 144; interaction, 11, 26, 152, 161–163, 172, 173; organizations, 29, 179, 180, 182–185, 192–199; relations, 3, 50, 89, 91, 153; tolerance, 56, 62, 143, 168
Islamic: conservatism, 7, 9, 202, 203–204; education, 18, 44, 60–61, 69, 70, 76, 83, 87, 89, 128–130, 135, 144–146; ethics, 20, 28, 96, 134, 137, 142, 144, 150, 153, 203, 208; identity, 133, 135, 216n4; organizations, 15, 45, 83, 93, 130, 201; radicalism, 54, 185; state, 34–38, 46, 51, 97; teachings, 9, 28, 61, 77, 93, 127–128, 130, 140–141, 148, 150, 151, 165, 215n1 (chapter 6)

JAJAK, 5, 185, 193
Jakarta Charter, 35, 37–38
Java, 8, 46, 50, 54, 55, 62, 74, 84, 86, 90, 93, 100, 102, 107, 145, 157, 173, 208, 215n1 (chapter 4), 216n3; Javanese, 11, 14, 56, 130, 181, 191
Jesus, **12**, 62, 65, 81, 105, 107, 110, 168
jilbab, 74, 85–89, 155, 165

kafir, 90, 92, 208
kerukunan beragama. *See* religious harmony
Kongres Minahasa Raya, 37–39, 186, 214n1 (chapter 2)
Kotamobagu, 125, 126, 135, 181
KTSP, 52–53, 69, 215n2 (chapter 5)

Laskar Jihad, 38, 186, 189
love, 5, 62, 71, 90–91, 107, 113, 114, 164, 193, 208, 214n1 (chapter 3)

majoritarian, 30, 154, 180, 194, 203, 208; coexistence, 13, 29, 67, 72, 74, 75, 84–85, 89, 91, 94, 163–165, 168, 201–202; majoritarianism, 67, 196, 205
Maluku, 5, 11, 38, 101, 186, 191
Manadonese: identity, 181–182; Muslims, 85, 89, 168; people, 5, 13, 68, 94, 167, 193
Minahasa: background on, 10–11; history of missionization in, 100–103; and Indonesian nationalism, 36–39; status of, 28, 101–103, 123
Minahasan: homeland, 114, 187, 189–190, 192; identity, 5, 11, 14, 180–182, 187–191, 193, 197
Minahasans, 6, 11, 14, 37, 38, 100–101, 106, 107, 123, 181, 186, 191, 198, 200
moral: action, 28, 127, 132–133, 140, 143, 146, 149, 150, 153; breakdown, 23; codes, 28, 41, 140, 143; community, 109, 121, 123, 206; development 21, 58; education, 26, 27, 43, 45–46, 48–50, 121–122, 146; foundation, 54, 55, 56, 62, 72, 145; frameworks, 21, 98, 179; registers, 21, 24, 211; values 18, 54, 56, 57, 96, 99
morality, 17, 50, 58, 82, 89, 97, 109, 111, 121, 127, 132, 135, 188
mosque, 11, 70, 76, 77, 78, 79, 129, 130, 131, **132**, 135, 136–137, 139, 145, 161, 177; Al-Khairiyah, 193–196
MUI, 9, 82, 195
multicultural: citizenship, 15; education, 95, 98–99, 106–107, 116, 120, 154, 204, 206, 208; multiculturalism, 10, 60, 75, 82, 96, 108, 116, 124
Muslim: guests, 84, 152, 169, 171, 210; neighborhood, 11, 79; students, 1, 33, 65, 68, 69, 70–71, 74, 75–78, 81, 82–84, 87–90, 94, 118, 129, 152, 158,

234 : INDEX

160, 163–165, 167, 206, 207, 208; youth, 28, 88, 151, 200
Muslims: accommodation/toleration of, 82, 84, 140, 164, 189; as fanatic/radical, 83, 85–86, 89, 164, middle-class, 9, 11; as a majority, 7, 30, 74, 81, 86, 90, 92, 93, 129, 149, 156, 181, 183; as a minority, 78, 127, 132, 140, 142; non-Muslims, 83, 86, 140–142, 149; as outsiders, 5, 75, 89, 190, 194, 198, 202

Nahdlatul Ulama, 130, 200
nation building, 15, 40, 42, 124
national unity, 1–2, 7–8, 30, 35, 38, 42–43, 46–47, 55, 60, 62, 91, 92, 94, 126, 213n6
nationalism, 14, 34–36, 39, 49, 96, 122
nationalist: consciousness, 15, 34; goals, 14, 18, 97; movement, 35, 36; principles/values, 96, 112, 114, 118, 198, 201, 202
New Order, 27, 31, 37, 41–46, 49, 51, 55, 57, 58, 59, 63, 64, 110, 121–122; post–New Order, 186, 206
North Maluku, 5, 8, 188, 191
North Sulawesi: background on, 3–6; map of, 4; role in the nation, 28, 36, 37–39, 96–97, 100, 197, 203, 206

Pancasila, 8, 34–35, 39, 58, 63, 64, 71, 110, 114, 126, 140, 141, 190, 192, 197, 200, 213n6, 214n3 (chapter 2); redefining, 31, 50–55; under Suharto, 41–43, 45–49
Papuan students, 99, 106, 107, 116–120, 154
peace, 4, 5–6, 13, 47, 59, 62, 80, 89, 113, 141, 144, 160, 173, 175, 178, 185, 190, 193, 198, 202
pedagogical: methods/strategies, 16, 18; process 17, 23, 209, 211
Pelsis, 71, 75, 92
Permesta, 37
pesantren, 128–129, 130, 144, 145–146, 147–148, 162
piety, 8, 16, 32, 44, 50, 51, 78, 86, 87, 89, 96, 122, 125, 127, 132, 135, 139, 214n2 (chapter 3)

plural society, 3, 7, 13, 24, 28, 40, 52, 60, 61, 140–144, 153, 174, 192, 203, 207, 208, 215n1 (chapter 6)
PMP, 45–49, 55, 57, 58, 63
politics of difference, 27, 32, 38, 40
positioning: majority/minority, 29, 67, 89–93, 94
proselytize, 45, 58, 61, 62, 113, 161, 164, 214n2 (chapter 3)
Protestant: majority, 1, 3, 29, 30, 67–68, 72, 78, 89–90, 92, 94, 102, 106, 127; students, 65, 66, 67–71, 75, 77, 87, 89, 92, 94, 115
Protestantism, 11, 34, 60, 108, 115, 213n5
Protestants, 4, 35, 77, 79, 80, 89, 92, 102, 183, 207, 213n4
public: debate, 8, 27, 33, 191, 197; ethical culture, 3, 7, 14, 17, 21, 23, 24, 27, 29, 31, 33–34, 63, 64, 197, 205, 206; reasoning, 21, 179, 189, 198, 213n7
public sphere: definition of, 20; place of religion in, 31, 39–40, 50, 201; vs. private, 20, 32

Qur'an, 129, 132, 136, 152, 168, 176; recitation of 74, 93, 125, 126, 127, 130, 137–139, 140, 151, 153; verse(s) in, 61, 78, 141, 143–144, 177, 215n1 (chapter 6)

race, 42, 75, 91, 92, 106, 116–120; racism 114, 116, 119, 210
radical, 8, 19, 83, 84, 88–89, 164, 185, 186, 200–201. *See also* fanatic
reflective freedom, 3, 22–23, 209. *See also* ethical reflection
reformasi, 35, 49, 55, 108, 122, 124
religion-state relationship: 30–33, 39–40, 52, 63
religious: boundaries, 10, 28, 157, 159–163, 171–173, 176, 204–205; conversion, 11, 98, 161, 162, 175; freedom, 13, 32, 33, 36, 39, 58, 183, 188, 192, 197, 198; greetings, 28, 72, 74, 78–81; harmony, 3–6, 8, 13, 14, 29, 47, 59, 61, 73, 75, 83, 91, 94, 123, 127, 164, 179, 181, 183, 185, 189–190, 192–196, 198, 208; identity, 3, 5, 11, 24,

36, 50, 62, 84, 113, 122, 144, 159, 161, 176, 180, 181, 182, 188, 191, 198, 204; leaders, 5, 48, 145, 155, 157–158, 159, 172, 176, 177, 185, 193, 195, 199, 201; pluralism, 2, 50–51, 112, 174; theme park, 29, 192–197, 202; values, 28, 54, 60, 96, 97, 98, 108, 109, 113, 135, 140, 144, 152, 162. *See also under* belonging

retreat (event), 25, 65–66, **66**, 69, 87, 92, 105, 119

Rohis, 44, 71, 76, 78, 87, 94, 200, 214n2 (chapter 2)

SARA, 42, 91, 195

scale, 8, 14, 20–21, 27, 67, 72, 107, 119, 180, 197, 198, 202, 206; scale-up, 7, 64, 180, 209

schools: as sites of deliberation, 2–3, 7, 8, 10, 16, 18, 21–23, 25–26, 27, 29, 31, 33, 40, 58, 63–64, 66–67, 73, 75, 78, 88, 90, 93–94, 98, 109, 113, 123–124, 127, 153–154, 179–180, 197, 201–210

secession, 9, 37–39

secular, 17, 30, 32–35, 39, 52, 73, 86, 97, 108, 146, 213n1; state, 18, 31, 40, 48, 64,

secularism, 9, 27, 31, 32–34, 40, 51, 63, 96

silaturahim, 125, 141

solidarity: with co-religionists, 188; with religious others, 152, 171; with the United States, 38 soundscape, 78–81, 90

subjectivity, 2, 3, 15, 20–22, 23, 24, 72, 99, 157, 181, 193, 206, 207, 209; modes of, 10, 205

Sumpah Pemuda, 95, 131

textbook, 1, 26, 31, 53, 63–64, 69, 77, 114, 131, 142; 2013 Curriculum, 57–62; PMP, 46–49

tolerance, 6, 28, 29, 32, 47, 55, 56, 58, 59, 60–63, 73, 83, 84, 90–91, 106, 112–114, 127–128, 141, 143, 144, 152, 159, 160, 162, 164, 168–169, 171, 183–184, 192, 198, 204, 206; vs. coexistence, 15

tolerant, 4, 22, 61, 85, 89, 140, 153–154, 162, 164, 168, 169, 203, 211, 214n6

Tomohon, 10, 15, 79, 103, 105, 107–108, 129, 155, 157, 169, 172

Torang Samua Basudara, 4, 126, 182, 191, 195, 210

uniforms, 28, 67, 68, 72, 74, 86–88

universalism, 174; Catholic, 96, 99, 116, 204, 206

Upacara Bendera, **104**

Vatican II, 62, 113–114

veil. See *jilbab*

violence, 6, 8, 38, 41, 50, 53, 116, 122, 160, 164, 186, 188, 190, 214n6; prevention of, 61–62, 191; state, 33. *See also* conflict

Wahid, Abdurrahman, 38

worship: differences in, 46, 172, 175; freedom of, 51, 58–59, 90; houses of, 5, 42, 46, 178, 183–184, 193–194; sessions, 15, 65, 69, 70–71, 77–78, 106, 123, 151, 152, 165; space for, 28, 74–77, 81, 89, 182, 197

ABOUT THE AUTHOR

Erica M. Larson is a research fellow at the Asia Research Institute, National University of Singapore. She received a PhD in anthropology from Boston University and has published in the *Journal of the Royal Anthropological Institute*. Her research examines questions related to religious pluralism, education, and ethics in contemporary Indonesia.